Computing Legacies

Computing Legacies

Digital Cultures of Simulation

Peter Krapp

The MIT Press
Cambridge, Massachusetts
London, England

The MIT Press would like to thank the anonymous peer reviewers who provided comments on drafts of this book. The generous work of academic experts is essential for establishing the authority and quality of our publications. We acknowledge with gratitude the contributions of these otherwise uncredited readers.

This book was set in Stone Serif and Stone Sans by Westchester Publishing Services. Printed and bound in the United States of America.

Library of Congress Cataloging-in-Publication Data

Names: Krapp, Peter, author.
Title: Computing legacies : digital cultures of simulation / Peter Krapp.
Description: Cambridge, Massachusetts : The MIT Press, [2024] | Includes
    bibliographical references and index.
Identifiers: LCCN 2024000982 (print) | LCCN 2024000983 (ebook) |
    ISBN 9780262549837 (paperback) | ISBN 9780262380881 (epub) |
    ISBN 9780262380898 (pdf)
Subjects: LCSH: Computer simulation—Social aspects. | Digital media—
    Social aspects. | Computers and civilization.
Classification: LCC QA76.9.C66 K73 2024 (print) | LCC QA76.9.C66 (ebook) |
    DDC 003/.34019—dc23/eng/20240220
LC record available at https://lccn.loc.gov/2024000982
LC ebook record available at https://lccn.loc.gov/2024000983

10 9 8 7 6 5 4 3 2 1

Contents

Contents

Introduction

"The digital heritage," UNESCO points out, "embraces cultural, educational, scientific and administrative resources."[1] As simple as it may seem, such a statement has programmatic implications, and the aim of this book is to unfold a series of them. The following chapters discuss cultural, educational, scientific, and administrative cases where our computing legacies revolve around techniques of simulation. Cultural organizations (libraries, museums, archives, universities) play important roles in preserving not just knowledge but access to it, understanding of it, and context for it. The UNESCO charter on digital heritage emphasizes access but also warns about privacy, calls for a balance between the rights of creators and the interests of the public, outlines measures guarding against loss, and foregrounds continuity in digital heritage. These values are hardly controversial, though they may prove incompatible in practice.[2] Trying to respond to that broad scope, this take on digital heritage therefore sets out to look at how simulation plays a pivotal role in computer museums, university administration, computer music, and online games. Music has been radically transformed by computing, in ways that go to the core of what we think music is and does. Computing has fostered a wide range of play that in turn raises questions that challenge our notions of playing games. Museums of computing already grapple with wicked problems before one considers computer-mediated communication as part of their brief; as UNESCO warns, "the instability of the Internet is an additional risk for knowledge."[3] Higher education has embraced digital culture in unforeseen ways, not just for the delivery of courses or online collaboration but also in its administrative structures. In scenarios like these, digital culture hinges on the use of simulation as a cultural technique.

Stewardship is not the only angle here, yet in engaging notions of digital heritage, it is worth noting that our institutions of cultural memory have been severely disrupted, undermining the abilities of libraries, archives, museums, and universities to parse, collect, and interpret said heritage. One factor is the severe defunding of institutions of cultural memory in the twentieth and twenty-first centuries; another is the apparent ease of copying and duplication in digital domains, creating the illusion both of a cornucopia of new information and of redundant storage, when in fact a lot of important information falls through the proverbial cracks.[4] And digital heritage is not just whatever concerns science and technology museums, nor is it what the cloud may store (until the cloud fails).[5] As institutions of cultural memory struggle with the rapidly disappearing recent past, historiographical methods (or media archaeology as one alternative) appear to be in competition with classificatory methods from library science, and those in turn seem to compete (for resources as well as for attention) with the quantitative methods of data science and the social sciences. But the focus here will not be what to do about tweets, blog posts, or SMS messages, nor the metadata and advertising databases that encompass location and social graphs in various networks.[6] The story here is not simply the history of computing, either; in turn, the history of computing is neither the history of devices nor the history of human–computer interaction, nor the history of computer science. Instead, in considering the institutions of continuity invoked by UNESCO, I take as pivotal in digital heritage the notion of simulation, and not as metaphor but as decisive practice.

A media history of simulation promises to excavate three salient aspects: it profiles simulation as cultural technique, tracing hypothetical literacy from ancient thought experiments to computing. It discusses simulation as a theory of the digital media age—gaming and virtual worlds help debunk common sense realism as anti-speculative. And it interrogates simulation as cultural critique, despite totalizations suggesting that we already live in a simulation. The chapters of this book illustrate a cultural condition in which simulation is conceptualized not just as a particular object or technology, but as a cultural technique—a set of practices by which modeling, emulation, and serious play are constitutive in how we comprehend and relate to our mediated situation. The question of our digital heritage foregrounds the role that simulations play in the preservation of cultural memory. In this pursuit, the emphasis is less on viewpoints, histories, and perspectives of underrepresented individuals or groups than on the way digital culture is presented and preserved, whereby our recent past itself is all too often under-represented and misconstrued. My research design here, in other words, is not a descriptive or sociological one, but instead excavates conceptual conditions of possibility of digital culture, large parts of which are in peril of elision due to the vicissitudes of our presentist era. This is not a study of subcultural formations that purport to develop alternatives to our major institutions of cultural memory, nor is it an engagement with demographic niches or academic microclimates; the point is that the mainstreaming of digital computing, networks, and increasingly large-scale simulations raises the stakes for everyone. Rather than draw on the conventions of cultural studies, this study is influenced by a conceptual approach that in anglophone media studies is labeled "German Media Theory," despite the fact that its adherents are often neither German nor focused on theoretical discourse alone. I also rely on Bowker and Star, who exhorted researchers to reconsider the development and deployment of standards and archives as "active creators of categories as well as simulators of existing categories" that deserve attention as "spaces that are otherwise lost forever."[7] The history of simulation is interdisciplinary, drawing on informatics, the history of science, and media archaeology; in this constellation, I put an emphasis on intellectual diversity instead of a predetermined sociocultural critique.

After this introduction establishes some of the contextual signposts that situate the overall project in its interdisciplinary constellation, I will discuss what it means to consider simulation a cultural technique. As chapter 1 establishes the conceptual claims of this framework, it also reflects on the quintessentially historical role emulation plays in digital culture. The next chapter extends that approach in turning to how museums of computing grapple with the challenges of presenting and preserving the hardware and software of computing. Rather than compare the varied practices of archives, libraries, and other collections devoted to digital culture, here the focus will be on museums, because it is worth noting just when and how they devote themselves to the history of computing, including the revolutionary changes wrought by networking. Emulating the look and feel of legacy devices is also the topic of the third chapter, which discusses the sounds of retro-computing. Here we see that simulating history raises thorny questions about how to faithfully represent the past while keeping it accessible. The fourth chapter turns to the dimensions opened up by networked interactions, particularly in online gaming. The ways in which massively multiplayer games illustrate simulation as a cultural technique range from their use in communication and training, in testing the epistemic status of models, or in simulating (counterfactual or faithful) historical events. Finally, the fifth chapter turns to the use of simulation in serious games by discussing a piece of interactive software that sought to model the administrative processes of higher education. Let me unpack by way of an introduction a little more of what each chapter sets out to do; a conclusion will then seek to pull it all together again.

It is an axiom of computing that a universal Turing machine ought to be able to run any program for any other computer that is likewise a universal Turing machine; in other words, computers can impersonate each other.[8] This idea not only lays certain theoretical foundations for computing, it also holds a promise for digital heritage, as new machines can emulate older ones. Thus, simulation has important implications for archives, museums, and the preservation of digital culture. This raises interesting issues in computer history. For example, John Walker, perhaps best remembered for his contributions to AutoDesk, created an online museum to celebrate Charles Babbage's Analytical Engine.[9] In addition to documentation, his site offers a Java emulator of Babbage's blueprints, and Walker placed a sufficient premium on the emulation's authenticity that he felt the need to compose a lengthy essay on his approach. This may strike some as odd, since in fact Babbage's Analytical Engine was never in fact built, so even the most detailed and painstaking emulator could not be authentic in a historical sense. Nonetheless, Walker's point that "in order to be useful an emulator must be authentic—it must faithfully replicate the behavior of the machine it is emulating" stands.[10] The chapter on simulation as a cultural technique analyzes in detail the motivations behind such efforts, and the museum chapter will follow suit in discussing whether the fulsome promises of simulation for musealizing preservation can in fact be fulfilled.

In simulation, we see a compound legacy of cybernetics and scenario planning as inherited by digital media from midcentury control systems research, integrating operations research, game theory, and techniques modeling feedback in complex systems. As Turkle pointed out in 2009, "Twenty years ago, designers and scientists talked about simulations as though they faced a choice about using them. These days there is no pretense of choice."[11] What held for the study of science and technology then has only become more urgent for a rapidly expanding range of disciplines. Simulations revolutionized the sciences in nearly every possible field of study; but when scholars in media history look at simulation, they need not consider it the exclusive domain of natural and technical sciences. A profile of simulation as a cultural technique can explore controversial claims made on behalf of simulations and investigate to what extent virtual worlds and serious games may corroborate them. As the conclusion will spell out in more detail, each chapter of this project elucidates an inflection point where quantitative data become qualitative evaluations: modeling epidemics for scientific study or for entertainment, the way museums try to cope with technical aspects of our computing heritage, data mining and espionage in virtual worlds, the pivotal but constrained role for digital culture of simulating sounds (where numerical calculations turn into music), and serious gamification in higher education.

"Simulations have a particularly epistemic quality, they bring a very particular knowledge into the world."[12] This is what discussing simulation as a cultural technique seeks to elucidate. Cultivation used to invoke a relation between nature and technology that would characterize cultural techniques as mere agricultural melioration; but while this older sense of the phrase has not fully disappeared, in recent decades it was joined by a conceptual dimension that foregrounds how activities like speaking, writing, reading, imaging, and calculating are distinct from hunting, gathering, cooking, or building shelter.[13] The distinguishing aspect is an epistemic dimension— these are techniques that do symbolic work. Moreover, we acquire such techniques independently of the goals we pursue with their help, and they both need and generate media. Thus the history of cultural techniques is dependent on media as their conditions of possibility, but by the same token media are manifestations of cultural techniques. In short, "cultural techniques are practices committed to the framing of cultures and collectives and conveyed by means of the media and educational institutes."[14] We shape our tools, and thereafter they shape us.

The growing reach of simulation as a cultural technique necessitates that we "examine how electronic media is changing the ways the concept of the museum 'object' is understood both by curators and visitors."[15] This implies investigating how museum curators and historians engage with simulation techniques in museum spaces to explore not only our recollection of past computing but also what might have been if certain aspects of the history of networked computing had developed differently. A 2014 *Museums in the Digital Age* report states that the latest in museum trends includes "content diversification, immersive experiences, and sustainable and open spaces."[16] This implies online interactions as an extension of museum presence. To that end, the museum chapter surveys different approaches to internet history, from archival forms to exploring the tense relationship between testimonials and grand historical narratives in the unraveling of the past development of networked computing. Attempts to tell the story of computing as culminating in the net we now use contrast sharply with various prior efforts to assemble computer networks as nonlinear, noncentralized means of producing nodes and hyperlinking.[17] Recent attempts to musealize the history of computing take off at a particular historical moment when the long-term ambitions for the potential of networked computation as a universalized knowledge system become increasingly overwhelmed by the commercial logic of contemporary privatized platform models. The insight that the musealization of computing took hold in the 1990s and is still accelerating is not merely subjective, but can be quantified in the number of computer museums and in the growing attendance at computing exhibits. Schools and universities are fostering that trend, as museums partner with them in didactic and pedagogical initiatives, "keeping the museum's philosophy up to date."[18] Museums are among the oldest cultural institutions, so one may be tempted to see growth as an indicator of increased prosperity accelerating an old trend. In that case, our orientation toward the past would be nothing new, and we are simply able to indulge in it more now.[19] But this is clearly an insufficient description; we can recognize in the current view of past computing a measure of the speed and force of the current rate of change in computing.

Objects from the history of computing become worthy of museum exhibits when the original phase of their nonimitative constitution is complete; if museums did not display something that is especially worthy of protection, conservation, research, communication, and enjoyment, then there would be no need for museums. This, however, means that even the most famous objects the public worships in various muses' temples are increasingly replaced by replicas to protect their irreplaceable originals; nowhere is this more evident than in museums of computing that increasingly display emulated software or hardware replicas. Mumford even complained that "the museum in America led inevitably to the baser sort of reproduction."[20] Museums of computing save remnants of computer culture from destructive processes, but in so doing computer museums are in fact funded and motivated by that very same destructive process. The changed presence of the past is complementary to the rate of change in the presence of the future. Not even the most prosaic calculating device is exempt from aestheticization, as long as there are not too many of its kind extant. Even the most avid collector cannot stay up to date unless they start their own museum to permanentize and institutionalize the act of acquiring and conserving, researching, and communication of the digital heritage; to stop acquisition confronts one with the historicization of one's own selective activity, decreasing the probability that the collection would still be recognized in the future for its lasting value. This historicization of computing is owed to the temporal structures of the digital industries; their evolutionary processes eliminate from current use anything that is incompatible with the latest paradigms, and after a suitable moment of oblivion such relics then return as collectibles. Their special cultural function is not only a compensatory historicist interest but incorporated into didactic narratives that likewise continue to morph and update.

A notable exception to this tendency is retro-computing, which pushes beyond software emulation and hardware simulation and keeps old computing actively usable, albeit for unexpected ends. One of the most striking examples of this kind of saving digital detritus from historical obsolescence is the remarkable career in electronic music of 8-bit and other retro chiptunes. At first glance, using early digital devices for music-making seems rather odd, but it does have a significant tradition. Beyond illustrating a technique that allows one to interpret procedures of one form of communication, namely music, in terms of another type of formal structure, namely programming, computing promised twentieth-century composers an even more important objective: "the development of compositional procedures which yield musical structures that specifically exploit the logic of digital computer processes."[21] This means not only using computing to impact musical elements like pitch, timbre, rhythm, the application of rules for tonal distribution and harmonic routines, melodic conventions, contrary motion, and so on, but also a generalized model for music-making that has roots in statistical analysis of style. Notably, early experiments would involve subjective tests (asking qualified musicians about stylistic integrity, structural cohesiveness, and general musical interest of computer music results) but also analytical tests in which the computer is asked to regard its own music as a sample and compute its probabilities.[22] While this remained an austerely academic exercise for a while, eventually it spilled over into entertainment. Chiptunes are now encountered in a range of popular genres, and for a while passed for a creative avant-garde cross-fertilizing numerous new music styles—ironically, since they were technically a kind of rear guard.

Every new technology of repetition seems to accelerate forgetting, and by the same token aids memory—and it also shows that new media generate not just hype, but also nostalgia. One example of the ubiquitous streams of audiovisual media sensurrounds is 8-bit music, the sound of retro-gaming. The role of music in games is a reliable indicator not only of technical and design progress but of aesthetic dimensions that are too often neglected in game studies. Feedback is clearly at work in how simulations reboot, respawn, and replay the sound of digital culture, as inversions and perversions of the media dialectics of attention and distraction. Such simulated sounds signify nostalgic returns to something that never was: they reflect a desire for access to hardware and software, for the right to repair and modify—in short, it is a manifestation of playful exploration. And audio, while usually relegated (both in terms of technical and financial resources expended, and in terms of what is typically front of mind for the gamer) to secondary importance, is crucial for a believable spatial and immersive simulation, so when it comes to the fore, this also inverts assumptions about simulation.

Contrary to the dubious consolations of simple time lines, culture is recursive and self-reflexive, and while there certainly are quantitative and qualitative changes over time, they do not unfold in teleological progression. Academics know this, and yet we risk predictions; even as techniques of simulation are increasingly what we rely on to offer extrapolations, scholarship in my field of digital culture has a rather mixed track record. In 2004, just as I started teaching regular courses in game studies, James Newman could still assert (in a text titled "Future Gaming: Online, Mobile, Retro") that "virtual reality and online gaming are, perhaps, the most obvious examples of false starts resulting from consumer resistance." By now, we realize that neither the online model nor the mobile model were false starts, and VR currently enjoys yet another hype cycle. Newman correctly predicted that "one possible videogame future is decidedly backward-looking"—namely the growing attraction of retro-gaming.[23] Cultural memory can keep current (or back) any purportedly obsolete, dated, or aging aspect, and it routinely does. Computing's pasts can reboot, respawn, and replay in various ways: we witness the reentry of what progress supposedly excludes, inversions and perversions of the media dialectics of attention and distraction, even nostalgic returns to what never was (like FakeBit), the uncanny return of the repressed, and the unexpected revival of cybernetics in serious simulations.

Instead of parsing the phrase *cultural technique* in terms of a purported tension between culture and technology, between the hard and the soft sciences, a realm of future-oriented sciences of exploration and a realm of past-oriented disciplines of interpretation, the core claim in using the phrase *cultural technique* is that such divisions are misleading. Digitization "gutted the carefully cultivated distinction among media as well as cultural, technical, and life sciences."[24] Studying cultural techniques sidesteps mutual rearguard actions in the academic trench skirmishes of the culture wars, opening up to a research design that enables a rigorously historical and conceptual account of the epistemic power of images and of programmatic inscription (beyond binaries of orality and literacy) to fully account for production, storage, and transmission of rich data. This still leaves uninterrogated a suspicion that simulation is essentially technical—yet in a fundamental sense, simulation is limited neither to the computer age nor to cybernetic concepts; indeed, as a cultural technique it has ancient roots. Furthermore, simulation also functions as a critique of the real world.[25] Turkle, for instance, suggested we take the cultural pervasiveness of simulation as a challenge to develop a new social criticism: "This new criticism would discriminate among simulations. It would take as its goal the development of simulations that help their users understand and challenge their model's built-in assumptions."[26] Thus, later chapters here will to turn to controversial claims made on behalf of simulations, and investigate to what extent virtual worlds and serious games can test, corroborate, or falsify them.[27] Critical thinking means asking questions that explore assumptions—and simulations rely on making exactly that pivotal step very explicit. In the end, simulations would be incomprehensible if they were just restricted to symbols or numbers—so they are still about storytelling, which is, of course, the humanities' domain. The humanities bring not just storytelling expertise to this, but interpretive competence.

When cybernetics called for a "discipline of simulation" in the late 1950s and early 1960s, at first it meant the implementation of models by dint of electromechanical analog computing. Simulations applied computing and cybernetic theory, for example, to understanding homeostatic physiological functions at the Dynamic Simulation Laboratory run by Rockland State Hospital in the 1950s, and social scientists used role-play simulations to model international conflict resolution.[28] But scholars soon foresaw that once digital computing became fast enough to support more complex operations, it would furnish "simulation for vividness" in models that would strike observers as more clear and convincing, "simulation for deduction and exploration" that would make questions tractable or help explore them in new dimensions, and by the same token also provide for "simulation as archive," whereby models store the collected knowledge of an entire discipline. This central assemblage of a growing number of interdisciplinary contacts would all support a model that "would then itself be both archive and computer."[29] Today we consider cybernetics a historical topic, but the idea that computing ought to function as archiving is consequential for the history of technology. Indeed, companies like PIQL currently promise that they will store "immutably" first instructions to build a computer to read the archive, then the OS, then the software, until finally "you can replay the past."[30] A playful use of computing is often simply brushed aside in the history of technology and the history of media as mere gaming. Indeed, computer games struggled to gain academic acceptance and sustained attention; but while not every simulation is a game, arguably every computer game relies on modes of simulation. Many serious simulations, both analog and digital, aim directly at interactive use that is ludic and exploratory. Two chapters here address such situations, one in a detailed analysis of the higher education simulator *Virtual U*, the other asking how espionage and counter-intelligence in massively multiplayer online games challenges notions of play in particular, and of collaborative computing online in general.

The use of virtual worlds and games for simulating history affords more or less accurate scenarios or help reenact historical events with their most relevant cultural dynamics.[31] Already in the eighteenth and nineteenth centuries, educators and strategists took tabletop and floor games seriously as heuristic and training tools, and painstaking battle reenactment, considering dimension and scale, agents and scenarios in great detail, operated between analysis and synthesis, abstraction and illustration, speculative experimentation and strategic historical veracity.[32] These and more recent "serious games" are simulations that allow us to test the epistemic status of models and the pragmatic quality of their material, while affording the scaling of projection and reduction or of the spatiotemporal representation of artifacts and processes. The limits of such modeling—of abstraction, reduction, formalization—foreground that these are not just models of or for something, but structures that have their own self-referentiality, which is to say mediality. Similarly, when cybernetic models exhibit their own dynamic instead of erasing their constitutive contribution to knowledge production, they resist becoming imperceptible or anesthetic, and appear as media. This has become especially notable in computer-mediated communications.

Obviously, a lot more military war gaming takes place than ever appears in print, but even in the realm of public policy the robust tradition of scenario planning and simulation has not always yielded very detailed academic literature. Espionage and counterintelligence activities have been radically transformed by networked computing and compartmentalized SIGINT focus areas in acoustic, electronic, and other signals intelligence. These technologies of surveillance do not so much capture events as they occur but rather divert the flow of information obtained by various highly specialized means of interception through computational arrays of storage, filtering, and selection that only prepare the ground for future recall and interpretation. Smart noise techniques may mask the transmission of sensitive messages by simulating their garbled appearance elsewhere; deception jamming broadcasts false and misleading information that simulates real data. As Dourish notes, "where once nuclear and military strategists might have worried over a missile gap, they might now look at the list of the world's most powerful supercomputers and worry instead about a simulation gap."[33] It is therefore particularly interesting to see what happens when more than one intelligence agency gets deeply involved in espionage and counterintelligence inside the virtual worlds of massively multiplayer online games. The specter of systematic multinational surveillance in massively multiplayer online games forces us to contemplate how "the discrimination between play and non-play, like the discrimination between fantasy and non-fantasy, is certainly a function of secondary process."[34]

Bateson demonstrated how this leads into paradoxical metacommunication, eroding misplaced faith in the magic circle:

> By placing into question the validity of a clear line of demarcation between game and non-game, we open up the analysis of game involvement beyond the formal parameters of the game. . . . By leaving behind an either/or perspective and focusing on the specificities of the individual engagement, we open up our inquiry to a richer understanding of the feedback loop between player and game that is not normatively pre-determined by simplistic binaries.[35]

In considering the vast electronic monitoring capacities of the modern state security apparatus and the information-generating capacities of colleges and universities, digital heritage is concerned not only with the difference that computing made and makes, but with computer-mediated communication. Collated by the Internet Engineering Taskforce, the Requests for Comments (RFCs) are organized working notes that, since 1969, document the development of the internet (as initiated by Steve Crocker, and later shepherded by Jon Postel for twenty-eight years). RFC1958 reflects: "A good analogy for the development of the internet is that of constantly renewing the individual streets and buildings of a city, rather than razing the city and rebuilding it."[36] Like the mythic argonauts' boat, the internet is constantly being rebuilt. Interestingly, the RFCs also offer a sprinkling of what passes for humor among engineers. Observing that "historically clients and servers strived to maintain the privacy of their keys," although "the secrecy of their private keys cannot always be maintained," RFC7169 (from April 1, 2014) by Sean Turner proposes a certificate extension for use in certain PKIX (X.509 Public Key) Certificates, namely the "No Secrecy Afforded" extension, or NSA for short. This RFC explains that in certain circumstances, "a client or a server might feel that they will be compelled in the future to share their keys," thus compelling them to give up on forward secrecy; in other cases the certificate can be used "to indicate that their keys have in fact been shared with a third party."[37] In a sly dig at Boolean algebra, the RFC goes on to suggest that "TRUE indicates that the key has been shared with a third party, and making the extension FALSE indicates that the key may have also been shared with a third party but the signer does not want to overtly indicate that the key has been shared"—and so it is clear that the extension in fact states that keys are not secure either way. As Wendy Chun wondered, given that the internet is one of the most compromised and compromising forms of communication, why has it been bought and sold as empowering and freeing—as a personalized medium? More recently she revisited the issue, admonishing that "to address the pressing issues posed by the many networks around us, we need to focus on modes and modalities of publicity, instead of simply and constantly defending a privacy based on outdated notions of domesticity."[38] Indeed, privacy remains an urgent discussion for media studies.

Inversely, a humorous RFC by Steve Crocker (RFC1776 from April 1, 1995) sets out to poke fun at the media theory of Marshall McLuhan in proposing that "The Address Is the Message" and suggesting that "it's not what you know but who you know, the IPng focused on choosing an addressing scheme that makes it possible to talk to everyone while dispensing with the irrelevant overhead of actually having to say anything." However, while Crocker jokes that security experts may hail this as a major breakthrough since it would render moot any questions of confidentiality and integrity, he correctly, if perhaps inadvertently, predicted that intelligence and law enforcement agencies would forget about key escrow and instead focus on metadata. Indeed, in 2014, former CIA and NSA director Michael Hayden said, "we kill people based on metadata."[39] A push beyond advertising has led to rampant exploitation of personally identifying information online, including but not limited to locations, IP addresses, and phone numbers as well as contacts. This directly impacts not only the availability and profitability of games, but also just as clearly impacts game quality.[40] The trade-offs in aiming for scale, for a new mass market, are that these models are increasingly optimizing not for extended play hours or maximum entertainment value (as the marketing for console games positioned its blockbuster titles in direct competition with cinema and television), but for secondary consumption, be it in ancillary in-game trade or in bundling and selling gamers' time (and information) to advertisers. If surveillance capitalism now drives much of the internet, this has consequences for our academic frame of reference for digital culture.

Game studies has yet to come to terms with the confessional moment of Snowden's autobiography: "It was the NES—the janky but genius 8-bit Nintendo Entertainment System—that was my real education."[41] A few reviews pointed out that "Snowden's new book *Permanent Record* is the autobiography of a gamer."[42] But is digital espionage still the great game? Once the national security data-mining dragnet reached the playing fields of elves and trolls, how does that influence the design, publication, play, and critical reception of games? In turn, the rise of online gaming has not only changed the way we think about role-playing, but also transformed the strategy genre; networked computing also spawned virtual worlds that are not strictly speaking games but venues for congregating, exploring, communicating, and commerce. While systematic exploration and exploitation of virtual worlds by intelligence and security branches of various governments has received some journalistic coverage, the salient issues of secrecy and surveillance in virtual worlds are rarely being addressed in academia. A lesson from the history of computers is that the freedom of players to do what they want, when they want at the interface is paid for by deprivation of freedom on the back end of the system.[43] Given the necessity of real-time interaction between humans and computers, the gamer is a figure "in the loop" whose time-critical behavior must be integrated into the micro-temporal structure of the system, discretized into tiny time segments. By the same token, games also monitor players by checking whether they conform with the interface and observe the rules of the game. Massively multiplayer online role-playing games (MMORPGs) make this infrastructural dynamic explicitly thematic and therefore might help unfold such analysis. In the paranoid exploitation of networks via data mining and surveillance capitalism (dominant organizational forms for networked communication in general), we can see how this disrupts the so-called magic circle of MMORPGs. Jameson already warned about the "representational shorthand for grasping a network of power and control even more difficult for our minds and imaginations to grasp: the whole new decentered global network," but now, as Zuboff warns, "unimpeded accumulation of power effectively hijacks the division of learning in society, instituting the dynamics of inclusion and exclusion upon which surveillance revenues depend."[44] Here the form of attention is the roving paranoid surveillance focusing on metadata, hoovering up the social graph so agencies can know who connects when to whom. Finally, the simulation of administrative control by computing relies on basic cybernetic principles for its organizational shape, thus the form of attention is a recursive automation in subroutines that put the player in the loop only for certain pivotal decisions—here the attentive spotlight is on certain decisive moments that have consequences for the interaction of complex systems, black-boxing many other factors that play a crucial part.[45] In this shape, serious games seek to emulate the otherwise unmanageable interplay of data sources they model.

And this brings me to the chapter dissecting the simulation of university administration. In an era that once again touts distance education, continuous education, and flexible employment as solutions to certain social and economic problems of our time, it is hardly surprising when, among the simulation games on offer, we also encounter a serious game that sets out to construe a comprehensive simulation of higher education. So when administrators and think tanks converged on the idea of a higher-education-administration game in the late 1990s, the result was indeed telling. The chapter on the Windows title *Virtual U* analyzes the college simulator from a number of vantage points, not least from the perspective of faculty members at the largest public research university in the world, at a time when it had to undergo massive changes after the 2008 financial crisis. As I end by discussing the simulation of higher education, we are reminded that the alma mater was never supposed to be a foundry, mint, or treadmill.[46] In *Virtual U*, three trends converge: management games increasingly in use in education, training simulations developed for enterprises (from nuclear plants to military tactics), and commercial interactive entertainment software of the type that includes successful titles like *SimEarth*, *SimHealth*, and *SimCity*. To discuss *Virtual U* means engaging the "serious games" concept as well as touching on the controversies around what has come to be called gamification.[47]

1 Simulation as Cultural Technique

It may be correct that "essentially all models are wrong but some are useful."[1] Yet Flusser argued, in an essay on "The Crisis of Our Models," that legacy models of scholarship neither furnish historical fidelity nor account for contemporary media technologies that revolutionized every field of knowledge generation and distribution.[2] Starting from "the suspicion that some new media of communication might offer possibilities for the elaboration of new types of models," Flusser and others of his generation pioneered what has come to be called media studies as they encountered television and video art, and computation and communication networks. To theoretical thinkers and those experimenting with new media, there was a manifest need for an intervention in the interstice between exclusionary academic practices, supplementing spatial models (writing, graphs, illustrations) with time-based modeling (films, videotapes, simulations). To postulate new models is to surmise that cultural technologies not only have to be accounted for, but also (and by the same token) come to the aid of interpretive modes that are the legacy of academic divisions of labor since the Enlightenment roots of the research university. Rather than contesting theories, we can explore models—scaled-down, modest, functional, pragmatic, dynamic ways to develop and test hypotheses.

One major trend of the past five decades is a confluence of massive computation at speed, with numerous variables giving rise to pattern detection as it moves from data to image to data, and input and control devices that have greatly expanded the affordances of the information age, as the networked computer is "becoming the 21st century's epistemology engine," inheriting the role of the camera obscura for philosophers like Descartes or Locke.[3] One can distinguish between a model of something, and a model for something, in saying provisionally that the former helps us render a question or problem so as to make it tractable and accessible, whereas the latter implies an exemplary, guiding, or normative role.[4] Yet both kinds of models are exercises of the imagination. A model can fulfill expectations and thus confirm theoretical hypotheses, or it can violate them and thus question the basis for its modeling—"as a tool of research, then, modeling succeeds intellectually when it results in failure."[5] It follows that modeling may be useful, appropriate, stimulating, but by definition never strictly true; its pragmatic payoff is in isomorphic abstractions that allow us to test for variations and variables in scenarios and case studies.[6] In short, models are tools for the understanding of phenomena; counting, measuring, and weighing give rise to the construction of instruments and machines; in turn, such machines can calculate, advancing the use of formulaic expression of theorems and axioms, rules and laws.[7] This leads to the point where complex models can serve to illustrate, depict, visualize, and test speculative or hypothetical constructs and ideas. Invoking these processes is, of course, not in the least to suggest that the humanities emulate the sciences, become quantitative sciences, or use computing to lend a scientific veneer to what they continue to pursue.[8] On the contrary: the study of media technologies suggests that it would radically impoverish our intellectual landscape to leave to the techno-sciences the interpretive and heuristic tasks that are the expertise of the humanities. So this chapter sets out to consider simulation as a cultural technique.

While most commentators today discuss simulation as primarily a digital computing capacity, it arguably has historical roots in the seventeenth-century invention of calculus, in eighteenth-century astronomy, and in nineteenth-century laboratory research into dynamic processes.[9] And just as cameras, telescopes, and microscopes transformed the sciences, computers introduced epistemic transformations. Once the 1940s facilitated the transition from mechanical simulators to electronic (first analog and later digital) computing, practically anyone motivated to harness modeling for their disciplines transitioned to a computational approach.[10] The overall trajectory of this narrative sees the rationality of quantification leading to computing infrastructure and thus to the shaping of our lived reality by algorithms into an increasingly artificial techno-scientific world.[11] A vexing question about simulation's inroads is whether it amounts to an empirical extension of our capacities through instrumental observation and detection.[12] Simulations permit studies on the behavior of models, crossing the formerly relatively secure boundaries between theory and experiment.[13] Simulation is a science of the artificial.[14] As technologies transform media history, from war gaming to early digital computing and from flight simulators and radar screens to the affordances of immersive graphic user interfaces and control devices, the modalities of human–computer interaction distinguish simulation after 1945 from broader connotations of modeling.[15] On this background, we can see networked computing in terms of industrial art, cultural artifacts, and gateways to alternate realities, without dismissing ludic aspects as misuse of serious equipment.

Discussing simulation as a cultural technique means confronting and emphasizing the epistemic implications of how the conceptual tools we shape thereafter shape our thoughts. Indeed, "cultural techniques reveal that there never was a document of culture that was not also one of technology."[16] Simulation is a great topic for media studies because when we study the connection of knowledge and media as historical epistemology, we look at the symbolic systems, machines, institutions, and practices that contribute to the formation, dissemination, and maintenance of knowledge. "The term cultural techniques refers to operations that coalesce into entities which are subsequently viewed as the agents or sources running these operations."[17] This may strike some as somewhat techno-deterministic, but it would be negligent to ignore the radical shift introduced by networked computing. Though some object that "recent developments like cultural techniques strip technical media, and technics more generally, of any autonomy or quasi-autonomy in relation to culture," media studies arguably cannot retreat into fan studies, sociology, or other consumer reports without ceding insightful access to what we talk about when we talk about media.[18]

> Any state of the art account of cultural techniques—more precisely, any account mindful of the technological state of the art—must be based on a historically informed understanding of electric and electronic media as part of the technical and mathematical operationalization of the real.[19]

Cultural techniques are "basic operations and differentiations that give rise to an array of conceptual and ontological entities which are said to constitute culture."[20] Outside the laboratory sciences, simulation is also used in modeling other media by dint of computing. Holograms, virtual spaces, simulated cameras, CGI animation, and more are the consequences that radically reconfigured our audiovisual environments.[21] Siegert even claims that after the universal discrete machine, technical media *only* exist as simulations.[22] All the more surprising, then, that "computer simulation has not yet been reviewed from the standpoint of media history," as Pias lamented a decade ago.[23] Simulation has, of course, proven powerful not only in speculative and experimental endeavors but in training as well. "Simulation is a technique—not a technology—to replace or amplify real experiences with guided experiences that evoke or replicate substantial aspects of the real world in a fully interactive manner."[24] This means that simulation opens up to other fields, as Krämer and Bredekamp summarily articulate:

> Numerical simulation ushers in a form of writing which makes possible new forms of scientific visualization that, in turn, are establishing themselves as a third form of scientific practice side by side with lab work and theorization. This use of computers has hence advanced to the level of a cultural technique.[25]

Computer pioneer Licklider considered simulation as important as the invention of writing.[26] A computer simulation realizes the behavior of a model system under certain boundary conditions for a given set of parameters; to have a convincing simulation you need to make sure that the model, its parameters and the boundary conditions are well defined.[27] Here one may distinguish between data-driven models, existence-driven models, and exploratory models.[28] Data-driven models help predict processes such as climate, weather, traffic, car accidents, or explosions. A comparison of the simulation results with observed data leads to a more accurate simulation by tuning the corresponding parameters: if the following initial conditions are satisfied, the following behavior will be observed. Existence-proof models are used to prove the hypothetical existence of phenomena in certain parameter ranges that have not yet been observed or explored. An example of this category is the hypothesis of self-reproducing machines, which we enjoy today as the "game of life."[29] The goal of exploratory models is to study problems for which a theory or meaningful mathematization is not (yet) available—often based on computer programs that represent something like thought experiments. They are driven by the aim to realize a certain fictitious system; exploratory computational models have much in common with traditional thought experiments, yet are impossible to achieve in a laboratory—the laboratory is in the mind.

The advent of computing and what it can do for academic research and experiments, as well as for human communication and entertainment, is characterized by cybernetic modeling of dynamic systems in such a way as to render their specific traits and interactions tractable for exploration.[30] The many disciplines transformed by simulation are less divided by their objects of inquiry than they are connected by their strategies of practice.[31] Rather than offer exact analytic solutions, however, they in fact invest in hypothetical and heuristic explorations.[32] Simulations function as "mediating instruments between theory and experiment" that disclose a space of "theories and empirical evidence, as well as stories and objects which could form the basis for modeling decisions."[33] Pivotal is the recognition that the simulation experience is much more about the *how* than the *what*. This is where cultural techniques conjoin the performative and the constative; "if the telling of stories plays a decisive role in the establishment of networks," Weber points out, "then the means or medium by which such telling is disseminated will constitute an essential factor in the shaping and maintaining of networks."[34] Furthermore, simulations revolve less around scientific laws or first principles than around rules, which is what makes them playable in a trial-and-error approach; they are at their best when rendering explorable the kind of phenomena and interactions that are hard, dangerous, or simply not feasible to access otherwise.

Simulation does not, at first, belong exclusively to digital culture, as it has deep historical roots in analog modeling. "At every stage of technique since Daedalus or Hero of Alexandria, the ability of the artificer to produce a working simulacrum of a living organism has always intrigued people," Wiener's seminal account of cybernetics pointed out.[35] In debating the nomenclature of computing, it was clear early on that analog and digital simulation coexist, as for instance a wind tunnel can simulate aeronautical conditions by analogy, and the digital rendering of underlying reality is a human artifact for the sake of description—hence, Bateson pointed out that "It seems to me that the analogical model might be continuous or discontinuous in its function."[36] However, the advantage of digital technology is exponential speed and complexity, the fact that entire sets of rules or guidelines can be programmed rather than laboriously consulted turn by turn. Indeed, "the study of cultural techniques would have to show how digitization became the materiality of ontologization of the twentieth century."[37] Arguably, simulation confirms that "the concept of cultural techniques highlights the operations or sequences of operations that historically and logically precede the media concepts generated by them."[38] Input devices and displays draw you in by dint of haptic and optical feedback to their variable actions; seductively repetitive tactile and audiovisual interactions are what distinguishes computer-mediated models. Indeed, "the system of technology itself has a feedback effect upon the society at large that may indeed bring qualitative changes in our experience of the world"—which suggests that "we are all caught up in cybernetic systems of complex interactions."[39] Interpretive feedback is always a dynamic process of self-correction: "it is cybernetic in nature as it involves a feedback of effects and information throughout a sequence of changing situational frames."[40] Feedback, as an evidently central concept for games as for game studies, harks back to a partly obscured yet still vital legacy in digital culture, namely that of cybernetics. As Hayles justifiably emphasizes, "for media studies, cybernetics remains a central orientation, represented by approaches that focus on flows within and between humans and intelligent machines."[41] Here, feedback is a way to achieve (self-)regulation in complex systems, whether in the shape of positive or negative feedback that reenters a system. Examples of negative feedback (maintaining a stability known as homeostasis) include the thermostat regulating the temperature in your home, or the pancreatic mechanism regulating blood sugar levels via insulin; examples of positive feedback (enhancing change and sometimes associated with vicious cycles) range from how platelets aid in blood clotting around a wound to the design of a stereo amplifier (or Jimi Hendrix exploiting feedback on his amplified guitar). As Bateson points out, "in environments, ecosystems, thermostats, steam engines, societies, computers and the like, chains of causation form circuits which are closed in the sense that causal interconnection can be traced around the circuit and back through whatever position was arbitrarily chosen as the starting point," but by the same token they are open "in the sense that the circuit is energized from some external source and loses energy," as well as "in the sense that events within the circuit may be influenced from the outside or may influence outside events."[42] The various analogies between biological and technical or social systems may not always convince you as legitimate transfers, but admittedly they give rise to thought-provoking models that can become tractable as simulations.

As "fundamental constituents" of any civilizational form or process of organization, media are ordering devices.[43] Since the early days of cybernetics, the amount of information in a system—biological, social, or technical—is considered a measure of its degree of organization.[44] In their organizational forms, we can also see inflections of the basic organizational principles that are conditions of possibility for models, simulations, and games:

> Our computers retain traces of earlier technologies, from telephones and mechanical analogs to directorscopes and tracking radars. As users, too, we inherit the legacies of machine operators from earlier ages. When we articulate a mouse to direct a machine, do we not resemble Sperry's pointer-matching servomechanisms? When we interpret glowing images and filter out signals from noise, do we not resemble a pip-matching radar operator? The user, computer operator, or even net surfer of today is no recent invention but a historical, technological descendent, an aggregate that includes pilot, machinist, human computer, telephone operator, radar tracker, fire control officer, and antiaircraft gunner.[45]

Joining information with feedback, creating a framework in which humans and machines can be understood in similar terms, and creating artifacts that make these ideas materially tangible, digital culture pivots on the constitutive role of feedback, regulation, noise, and other cybernetic concepts. Hayles diagnosed that "contemporary media studies would scarcely be conceivable without the contributions of cybernetics."[46] And indeed, it has been argued that "computer games, or more precisely the circuit of game and player in the act of playing, is literally (for the duration of the game at least) cybernetic."[47]

What if thought experiments were not only a way to articulate the pivotal but often obscured connections between fiction and simulation, between philosophy and science, between storytelling and critical argument, but also a way to reconcile the supposedly hard-science culture of computer simulation and the so-called artistic and humanistic tradition of posing critical questions? What if these two cultures in fact were one and the same, derived from the same stories and insights? Another way to formulate that guiding supposition is to ask whether computers in fact do or do not give rise to a culture of the thought experiment that transcends and actualizes the status of the merely theoretical, fictional, or imaginary.[48] One of the most elaborate examples might be the recently rediscovered Rainer Werner Fassbinder film *World on a Wire* (1973), a low-budget yet highly inventive adaptation of the dystopian American novel *Simulacron-3* (1964) by Daniel Galouye, about a corporation manufacturing a supercomputer that generates and supports a virtual world that is robust enough that the artificial intelligence entities in it believe themselves to be real. The film's setting in the Institute for Cybernetics and Futurology is portrayed as a labyrinth of reflections, steeped in art-historical allusions but entirely in the service of artificial life and simulated reality. Similar territory is pursued by Greg Egan's influential novel *Permutation City* (1994). Is consciousness merely information processed in certain ways, regardless of what machine or organ is used to perform that task? Or is this invalidated by reminding ourselves that a hurricane model does not make anything wet, a fusion plant simulator does not produce energy, a metabolic model does not consume actual nutrients—so a model of the human brain does not amount to giving rise to actual thought?[49] What if cellular automata could, given enough time and processing power, evolve into a structure complex enough to permit flight from this planet and its constraints into a realm that is unlimited by everything that holds humanity down? What if every thought experiment, even as it pushes at the material constraints of our existence on earth, was by the same token partly practicing that step off-world, out of place, out of time? Suppose you could overcome gravity and the grave? What if global warming, infectious diseases, overpopulation, and other urgent questions confronting humanity today could be addressed at the planetary level? This kind of thought experiment may seem like the province of science fiction (what if there was another planet that could sustain human life?)—but in this age of the rapid emergence of many dire emergencies, that supposition has become the pivot of our engagement with planetary problems. Whereas our default mode of troubleshooting environmental, pedagogical, political, or aesthetic crises had been ad hoc, partial, local—but increasingly now, our problems are of a planetary scale, and require attention to possible solutions at a larger scale. A global response would require a model at a much larger scale—what if a large-scale solution to large-scale problems could be modeled, tested, improved, and deployed? What if all the various emergency responses demanding full attention were to be connected on a scale that integrated them into a global geometry of attention, or a planetary model? What if one modeled that kind of whole-earth response?

Computers are faster than humans at chaining together complex branching cascades of what-if, what-if, what-if. Even if some may wonder whether computing is not also part of the problem, increasingly we assume that computing must be part of the solution, too. But let us slow down and look back on a longer history of simulation and thought experiments. There are numerous well-known examples both in science and in philosophy of thought experiments—whether we think of Maxwell's demon, Schrödinger's cat, the Turing test, or Searle's Chinese room. Outlining the trajectory of a brief history of the thought experiment, we may find that the gesture is somewhere between falling and throwing (yourself). In the history of science, serious thought experiments date back to the day Thales of Miletos (in Asia Minor or what is now the west coast of Turkey), speculating about the stars above, fell into a well. Considered by Aristotle one of the Seven Sages of Greece, and by Bertrand Russell as the first philosopher, Thales wanted to explain natural phenomena without reference to mythology. However, this pre-Socratic stargazer is said to have been observed falling into the well by a maid who laughed at his distracted tumble. So at the anecdotal origin, we also have to deal with a lack of recognition for the thought experiment. Nonetheless, Thales's rejection of mythology and insistence on testing hypotheses based on general principles is at the root of the scientific process, of rational thinking.

Albert Einstein improved on the experimental setup when he observed a Berlin roofer tumbling down. Just like Thales, if the roofer had not survived and been observed, our intellectual history would be much poorer, since he shares with Einstein the bystander the fact that during free fall he felt no gravity. This insight was gained without risk to Einstein's life and limb. When the need to calculate ballistic trajectories and the fluid dynamics of weather and of explosions spurs on the development of computing toward the end of World War II, thought experiments start to be conducted more regularly "in silico." But this practice could draw on a long tradition in political consulting, military history, and games. From antiquity to the eighteenth century, people knew chess, for instance, as a model of pre-gunpowder combat. The nineteenth century saw the Prussian *Kriegspiel* adopted by other military commands as a way to prepare officers for informed decisions. And by the turn of the twentieth century, feedback from the front was regularly injected into training before experience grew stale.

Simulation is particularly useful in closed systems; one example is the airplane. It is costly to train people on the real thing—they can get hurt, and expensive planes can be destroyed, so it is better to train pilots on airplane simulators.[50] One might say that action games today still mostly depend on the setup of a flight simulator providing instant feedback on twitchy controls, in the rhetorical order of the metaphor: this rolling log, this bucking bronco is a plane. This trajectory of throwing yourself into the sky in order not to fall continues from the wooden Link Simulator to the next generation of Microsoft Flight Sim games.[51] Mastering its controls in a first-person perspective affords the users a speed or other rush, transgressive thrills that please the id. In the mode of role-play, the critical element is not so much time and speedy reaction as it is the making of decisions, in the rhetorical order of metonymy: you go this way or that way, you are dwarf or orc, you have long hair or short, as you perform the constitutive tasks of the ego in a second-person perspective. And the third-person perspective of strategy games affords oversight, laying down rules like the superego and seeing how they play out—tax rates, religious prohibitions, laws, surveying the tabletop or board or floor game in the rhetorical mode of synecdoche, whereby a tank or a plane stands for armies, a tree stands for the forests cut down to make room for pasture in South America, and the critical element is neither a series of individual performative substitutions nor reaction speed, but the coordination of large-scale systems.

For the complex systems in epidemiology or economics, simulation can still be a good introduction to dynamic system behaviors, a way to explore options and test the validity of assumptions. When Alice falls down the rabbit hole, grabbing a jar of marmalade on the way down, the thought experiment is still a preglobal one: what if you fell right through the center of the planet? Would you accelerate and pop out the other side? Where would that be? When Lewis Carroll wrote in the 1860s, people could still suppose the earth is hollow, and indeed hollow earth theories remained popular until explorers fought their way to the North and South Poles. A century later, Buckminster Fuller seized the nascent planetary consciousness and suggested that we are all hurtling through outer space, that we are falling through nothingness on Spaceship Earth. His planning games, meticulously arranged on large maps that could cover the floor of a gym or conference hall, soon gave rise to computer-based planning exercises that shifted the metaphor further: Operating System Earth—how would you run the planet? It took a minimal observer's distance from the earth to arrive at this new planetary consciousness: not by coincidence did the Apollo shot of the "blue marble" become the omnipresent logo of the green movement, the most trafficked photo in the history of mankind. Today, there are numerous institutions researching simulation and its uses for government, military, and business: the Technical Support Working Group, the Modeling Virtual Environments and Simulation program at the Naval

Postgraduate School, the Air Force Agency for Modeling and Simulation, the Navy Modeling and Simulation Office, the National Simulation Center. Even when computer simulations use fundamental theory to generate models, they have to beware of any confirmation bias and strive to use simulations as tests of the underlying theory.[52] As more of our most pressing problems are global in scope, an interesting extension of the trajectory of simulation is the "Living Earth Simulator" or "Large Knowledge Collider" proposed by Swiss sociologist Dirk Helbing.[53] To predict infectious disease outbreaks, combat climate change, or foresee financial crises, Helbing wants to connect the knowledge of domain experts across all scientific fields with a large-scale, real-time data mining capacity. His grant proposal to the European Union asked for funding of a billion euros. Resembling to some critics the Seldon Plan (named after Isaac Asimov's character Hari Seldon in the seminal science fiction *Foundation* series), the "Large Knowledge Collider" would simulate all systems that are critical to managing our planet. In short, ideas about simulation are often put into service as the mythology for a virtual world.[54]

Regrettably, the popular imagination misrepresents simulation as totalizing. Journalist Neil deGrasse Tyson and philosopher Nick Bostrom tend to express this phantasm provocatively in a probabilistic manner, surmising that there is a 20 to 50 percent chance we are already living in a simulated virtual world. This may lend an apparent scientific veneer to the supposition, but so far that is all it is: a guess that does not permit falsification or verification. Not content with those odds, Elon Musk went out on a limb to assert that "the chance we are not living in a computer simulation is one in billions." At Code, a tech conference in California in June 2016, the SpaceX and Tesla CEO added that if we are not in a *Matrix*-style world, then the world is about to end. Small wonder that some people would rather opt to believe in the simulation, even if it is cold comfort. This forced choice— "either we will make simulations that we cannot tell apart from the real world or civilization will cease to exist"—is so reductionist as to almost obscure the fact that it is merely rhetoric.[55] But we need to parse the two pivotal assumptions Musk made to arrive at his formulation: on the one hand, to assume that the rate of improvement from *Pong*'s two rectangles and a dot to photorealistic 3D graphics must be extrapolated without limitations to erase the possibility of distinctions between reality and simulation, and on the other hand that, as Bostrom's philosophical provocation from 2003 had it, no civilization has yet arrived at this inflection point without it carrying the seeds of destruction. It will surprise nobody that in our contemporary media cycles, such utterances by "thought leaders" generate headlines; it was a little odd nonetheless when Bank of America Merrill Lynch ran with the hypothesis in September 2016, advising its investment clients that since "we are already approaching photorealistic 3D simulations that millions of people can simultaneously participate in," it is conceivable that we already live "in the Matrix." Did they comprehend those movies before making that reductive claim? Granted, the point of their advertisement was to estimate global markets for alternative reality, virtual reality, and computer game technologies by the year 2022, which are certainly burgeoning.

There are education, training, and research communities dedicated to exploring simulations, many of them using role-play.[56] While simulations model selected features of a particular reality, games go beyond that and take players into fantasy, but this does not necessarily invalidate serious gaming as a heuristic for research and teaching. Indeed, it has a very robust history in military and industrial training exercises and in political scenario planning.[57] Simulation games allow participants to explore and analyze actual as well as potential problems in their respective domains, both by interacting and in debrief afterwards.[58] While evolving technical infrastructures have brought a lot of simulations into the realm of computing and online, there are also training games and experimental live-action simulations that explore particular challenges in environmental protection, nursing, airline crisis management, business strategy, construction management, social psychology, and many other areas, with varying degrees of verisimilitude.[59] Political scientists have been simulating terrorism to stimulate training as well as academic research.[60] It is only logical that telematic hyper-control also yielded simulations of surveillance: "The simulation of surveillance is a control strategy that informs most of the latest diagnostic and actuarial technologies we associate with the information age—computer profiling and matching, expert decision-systems and cybernetic intelligence, electronic polling, genetic mapping and recombinant procedures, coding practices of all sorts, virtual reality."[61] We need to return to these ideas in chapter 4; suffice it to say that computer simulations are increasingly deployed in highly complex models of processes that are dangerous or otherwise risky to explore more directly, and in a range of scientific disciplines simulations have become the main instrument of experimentation and validation, whether for reasons of expense or safety, or because the scenarios explored have not yet occurred in the reality the models are based on.

Whether seen from military training or from research in international relations, it is likewise evident that the role of simulations has grown in this domain; examples include strategic and counterterrorist simulation exercises at the National Defense University and the Army War College, going back to SIPER (Simulated International Processes), GLOBUS (Generating Long-Term Options by Using Simulation), or SIMPEST (Simulation of Military, Political, Economic, and Strategic Interactions).[62] Der Derian even went so far as to suggest that simulations created a new space in international relations, where "things happen and the consequences have no origins except the artificial cyberspace of the simulations"; the USS *Vincennes* mistakenly shot down an Iranian civilian airliner on July 3, 1988, because they had trained only with military airplanes appearing on their simulated systems, and forgot the distinction between combatant flights and civilian flights on their perfectly functional naval radar system.[63] As Allen surveyed the secret world of the creators, players, and policy makers using simulations to explore and rehearse their options, at times the simulations are prescient and offer unheeded warnings, but just as often they can seem like flights of fancy.[64] This has led some critics of simulation methods to grouse that the distinction between simulation and fiction might become impossible to draw.

If simulation mostly now refers to modeling dynamic systems with the aid of computing (or more generally the mediatic constitution of artificial worlds and virtual realities), there is, of course, a much longer philosophical tradition grounded in the semantics of the term's Latin origins. As fascinating as these are, they led to "terminological difficulties" and a "pejorative air," whereby to simulate means "to assume or have the mere form of" something.[65] In this manner, simulation appeared antimimetic—undermining any distinction between original and copy.[66] Thus, twentieth-century philosophers embraced simulation as (renewed) anti-Platonism.[67] Cultural commentators even based on this a description of media society as a cultural Möbius strip of pseudo-events that become imitations of themselves.[68] Yet simulation as cultural technique actually intends to faithfully reproduce selected characteristics of something that remains a referent, and this "process of representing the dynamic behavior of one system in the behavior of another system" is therefore not anti-referential at all.[69] Nonetheless, some readers in the humanities may have come to associate the terminology of simulation with Baudrillard, whose use is metaphorical rather than referring to simulation as a technique; here we will not engage with that rhetorical use of simulation, save to make one point. Baudrillard argued we went from a classical age of counterfeit (interfering in the simple distinction between reality and appearance) to an industrial age of communication media (interfering in the simple distinction between production and reproduction) and hence on to an age of simulation based on the manipulation of code to model and test, to encrypt and decrypt. To Baudrillard this announced the transition "from a capitalist-productivist society to a neo-capitalist cybernetic order," whereby simulations test reality rather than the other way around, giving rise to "social control by anticipation, simulation, and programming."[70] Whether one goes along with the hyperbole of such extrapolations, Baudrillard is not fundamentally wrong to diagnose the rise of models, games, tests, tree diagrams, flow charts, and other digital operational forms that produce a new mediality beyond simple distinctions between reality and reproduction, image and copy. "After the metaphysic of being and appearance, after that of energy and determination, comes that of indeterminacy and code," he surmised, characterized by "cybernetic control, generation from model, differential modulation, feedback"—this description of how code is a new operational configuration is not inaccurate.[71]

But if media studies is the introduction of the question of technology into the humanities, it proposes a shift from narrative traditions to "networks of technologies and institutions that allow a given culture to select, store, and process relevant data."[72] Invoking these processes is, of course, not in the least to suggest that the humanities emulate the sciences, turn to quantitative methods, or use computing to lend a scientific veneer to what they continue to pursue. On the contrary: what the study of cultural technologies in general, and media studies in particular, powerfully suggests is that it would radically impoverish our intellectual landscape to leave to the techno-sciences the salient interpretive and heuristic tasks that are the expertise of the humanities. As Kittler sought to draw a distinction between fiction and simulation, he ended up coming down rather forcefully on simulation's side.[73] Into the eighteenth century the reference for speculative world-building was nature. Modern imagination sought the unexpected by looking inward to subjectivity for inspiration; today, we build computational worlds. Fiction is immune to negation—we do not find a lot of meaning in statements like "Faust did not make a deal with the devil" or "Anna Karenina did not commit suicide." But if we usually only affirm what is and negate what is not, to simulate means to affirm what is not and to negate what is. Here cultural techniques merge the performative and the constative; if the telling of stories plays a decisive role in the simulation of complex situations, then the means of disseminating such tales constitute an essential factor in the shaping and maintaining of simulations. This means turning to the conditions of possibility of sharing our world-building, considering a history of cultural artifacts as gateways to alternate realities. Such models help train us in "hypothetical literacy." Gaming has a long history from before eighteenth- and nineteenth-century tabletop and floor games to calculating trajectories and explosions, from flight simulators to radar screens, and on to our immersive graphic user interfaces and control devices.

With reference to Foucault's "optimization of systems of difference" in the modeling of confinement, discipline, and risk management in response to the contagions of leprosy, pestilence, and smallpox, Pias tells the story of how the Transportation Analysis and Simulation System developed at the National Infrastructure Simulation and Analysis Center in 1995, initially devised to simulate traffic in Portland, Oregon, was expanded after 9/11 to incorporate epidemiological scenarios—TranSims became EpiSims.[74] Therefore, "it is no accident that meanwhile professional epidemiologists have become interested in virtual game communities like that of the worldwide World of Warcraft," as Pias concludes.[75] Indeed, epidemiologists started a decade and a half before COVID-19 to use massively multiplayer online games to model epidemic contagion.[76] The task of strategy games has the flow of data as its driver, optimizing command and control, but their trade-off is that they are slow. Simulations offer safe training driven by feedback principles, optimizing survival, but the trade-off is that those systems need to abstract and omit variables. Equation-based modeling takes that logic into the computer age, driven by complex calculations, optimizing the predictive value of the model, but the trade-off is that the computer models become a black box. Agent-based modeling sought to improve on this setup in a distributed model, driven by artificial intelligence, optimizing individual behavior, but the trade-off is that they are very decentralized. "The Living Earth Simulator" or "Large Knowledge Collider" takes global modeling as its task, driven by data-mining technology to optimize collective behavior. Of course, the trade-off of such a totalizing model is that it seeks to model entire interacting global networks from the vantage point of a drive to master the totality of an inscrutably complex world picture.

Consider how simulations model a pandemic and what that allows us to say about digital culture. During the year 2020, early in the COVID-19 pandemic, an eight-year-old simulation game suddenly became increasingly popular, rising to one of the top games in the Apple app store, surpassing *Minecraft*. *Plague Incorporated* was developed by a UK studio in 2012 and a few years later was also published as a board game; *Pandemic 2.5* was a similar title that likewise lets you play with viruses or bacterial diseases or parasites that are infecting the planet, illustrating how popular that mobile game category had become. Soon *Plague Incorporated* was banned from the iOS app store in China (and also from Steam, another big game distributor), either in an attempt to mitigate negative press around the spread of COVID-19 or because of a recent update in the game that allows you to spread not just a virus but also fake news, which certainly would have caught the attention of the censors. About 130 million players downloaded *Plague Inc.* before, in an updated version, it also let you save the world instead of infecting everyone. Now, on the one hand, the sudden surge in popularity has to do with the fact that many people had more time on their hands because of pandemic mitigation; on the other hand, the same could not be said about movies like *Virus* by Kinji Fukasaku (1980), one of the most expensive Japanese science fiction films of all time. Interactive simulations make coping with a pandemic just that much more palpable and tractable.[77] Of course, games are not always scientific models, but they do draw on how science uses modeling; while every game is a simulation, not every simulation is a game. Colleagues at UC Berkeley published a "mask simulation" early in the COVID-19 pandemic to demonstrate the effect of wearing a face mask and how they can curb the spread of the coronavirus. An epidemiologist in Germany developed a COVID-19 simulator at COVID. sim.eu, treating certain aspects of the spread and mitigation measures as variables, thus letting the user explore various concepts of social distancing or lockdowns to enhance or prevent herd immunity. It shows what kind of infection peaks to expect, it lets you extrapolate from assumptions and evaluate hypotheticals, longer or shorter periods, stricter or less-strict social distancing, and assumptions on how many people would in fact observe those rules. Such simulations would be incomprehensible, they would not be good communication, they would not be good testing, if they were just restricted to symbols or numbers. So they use a kaleidoscopic range of info-graphics, displays, and other ways to convey very complex data. This gives rise to new forms of interactive storytelling, of inviting people to explore a complicated data set, a complicated situation, a virtual world. Advances in computer graphics that such simulations rely on make issues tractable not just to specialists but also to a more general audience. There are networks of technologies and institutions that allow us as a culture to selectively store and process data and manipulate the data on a screen. A whole his-tory of cultural artifacts and gateways to alternate realities allows us to play with hypotheticals. Simulation is not just for climate models—out of these developments rose new entertainment genres, including games and virtual (or augmented) reality.[78]

Related to pandemic simulations, whether in serious laboratory work or in entertainment software, is the concept of contact-tracking apps and their potential role in fighting the virus or mitigating the spread of the virus. The apps proposed to map the spread of the virus in real time on media networks, rather than in simulated scenarios. These apps, however, were viewed very differently depending on which country or which area in the world you look at. People in European countries have different expecta-tions and values than people in various Asian countries or in the United States—not just different technical models that are competing for our atten-tion here, but also different values in terms of the protection of privacy or policies about data retention. That has far-reaching consequences for our trust in institutions, whether they are public institutions like governments or health organizations, or private institutions like technology companies that might offer such tracking apps. And it has consequences for our mobile communication infrastructure in general, and this is something that people in game studies are concerned about because a lot of mobile games already rely on ways to track and trace the activity and location of mobile devices. Tracking may be used for ludic ends, but clearly also for advertising and data brokering. Tracking apps are more meaningful if more people use them—they fail if too few people opt in. If two different countries that share a border have different pandemic contact-tracking apps, you lose data the moment people cross borders or into a different network. Apple and Google proposed a tracking app that logs device locations automatically via Bluetooth, and in the event of a positive COVID-19 diagnosis would notify those whose devices had been near the newly diagnosed person's device. In this model, devices would download the keys of every newly diagnosed person each day; trolls could prank people with false positives or flood the app with an overwhelming number of keys. Around the globe, discussions around tracking apps raised serious questions: what authority would be invoked to suggest action with nudges, to issue or enforce quarantines, or for punitive measures? How long would this data set be kept and who would have access? The majority of apps in the Android and Apple stores already contain a number of advertising trackers, aggregating location data, IP numbers, and daily usage. Tracking information is sold to data brokers, along with information from cookies, mobile device identifiers, phone numbers, and email addresses. The proper use of the data collected is not easily controlled by device owners who opted in: Britain's National Health Service raised concerns about a tracking database. Moreover, even in wealthy societies, not everyone has a smartphone; a third of older people do not, yet they are in higher risk categories. Two billion people who do own smartphones use neither the Apple iOS nor the Google Android systems; another 1.5 billion people use mobile phones that do not have the Bluetooth chips that detect proximity between devices. These were not the only problems with modeling the pandemic via the mobile network. The "Trace Together" app in Singapore was soon dropped in favor of a full lockdown. The "Stop Corona" app from the Austrian Red Cross was leaking information in the Microsoft cloud. South Korean tracking combined mobile data with facial recognition and credit card information to be effective; the result was a level of pervasive surveillance that many disliked. App development led by the consortium PEPP-PT grappled with strict European privacy regulations, delaying the app code-named DP-3T. The German app "Corona Datenspende" from Thryve gathered vital signs, including pulse, temperature, and sleep patterns, but proved insufficient for a reliable COVID-19 diagnosis. To be effective in spotting virus hotspots, apps would need to be in use by many more people than are likely to download an intrusive app. Self-reporting of a diagnosis needs to be confirmed by health care providers; in the United States, many tests provided incomplete results. Correlating data sets could reveal the identities of COVID-19–positive users, and faulty signals between phones could cause confusion.

Lest we jump to the conclusion that this kind of real-time network modeling only happened with hindsight, there had been a range of pandemic simulations in the years before COVID-19. Many nations had experience with such simulations, but it failed to get them to a state of readiness. In 1995, Sandia National Labs ran an Epidemiological Simulation System to model immunological responses to communicative diseases.[79] There was a 2012 study on pandemics by RAND, and in 2015 Bill Gates warned in a TED Talk about a coming pandemic. There was a 2017 exercise by Homeland Security for the Obama White House on preparing for a contagious respiratory disease. The National Security Council heard a presentation in 2018 about the centenary of the flu epidemic. In October 2019 in New York City there was a tabletop simulation exercise conducted by Johns Hopkins's Center for Health Security about a possible threat to the US by a pandemic. The threat just was not fully communicated to the stakeholders to make decisions based on the scenarios that had been explored. It is not enough to watch films like *Dawn of the Planet of the Apes* from 2014 to see that viruses are a threat to humans—that is escapism. Policy makers need more serious modes of engagement without being alarmist, and simulations do that very well. Simulations allow you to take some responsibility for how these factors come together. Hence the CDC in 2020 became interested in *Plague Inc.* as a nontraditional route to raise public awareness of epidemiology and disease transmission, because a game creates a compelling world that might engage the public on serious topics—more so than a press release. Doing so requires a type of media literacy (a hypothetical literacy) that simulations foster. Trying to understand what a coronavirus is or does was modeled very differently in two very influential studies. One was run by Imperial College London and another by a second university consortium; for a while the government of the United Kingdom was torn between the two models. They access the same facts but make different assumptions—one, for example, assumed that half of the population would follow guidance on social distancing, but if only a quarter of your population follows political or health officials in such guidance, that changes things.

Simulations allow us to make more obvious what humanities scholars and students do all the time, which is to question assumptions and to play around with hypotheticals that make not just stories, books, films, or non-fiction accounts, but also board games, role-play, and planning simulations the object of interpretation. Studying the increasingly influential role of simulations in a growing number of research fields led many experts to worry about the extent to which disciplines must trust their simulation techniques. Consider these claims made on behalf of a simulation of processes that proved decisive in the history of technology, in international politics, and in proto-computing: "We drastically speed up the Bombe machine, a complex and computationally intensive electromechanical system used to decrypt the Enigma machine during WWII, by recreating it on the DE1-SoC."[80] One must applaud the work done by these Cornell students and their interest in the Enigma and the Bombe as crucial episodes in the history of media technology. Unfortunately, their simulation is not historically accurate. In their video they assume positions and settings of the rotors and notches, including the message setting, then their simulation figures out the plugboard settings, since this is changed daily and is the largest contributor to the key length. Their written description confirms this misunderstanding: "The Bombe machine, which can be thought of as consisting of multiple Enigma machines, is mainly used to figure out plugboard connections and consists of linked drum banks each processing one letter-encryption pair." In fact, the Bombe was built to figure out the rotor and notch settings, and the message setting is determined from each message. The Bombe provides the setting of one pair of plugs. The rest of the plugs, despite their huge key length, are then manually determined on Enigma emulators. The big breakthrough that allowed for the design of the Bombe (essentially emulating cryptographic capacities of the Enigma) is figuring out how to separate the solution of the rotor settings from the plugboard settings—this reduced the 76-bit key of the Enigma machine to solving a 29-bit key. This is central to understanding the seminal contribution of Polish mathematician Marian Rejewski, a theoretical breakthrough emulated by the UK/US Bombes. Even if you had captured an Enigma machine and knew the wiring of the rotors and reflector, and even if you knew the German operating procedures using ten plugboard cables, the Enigma was forbiddingly complex. Crucially, Rejewski mathematically separated the solution of the rotors from the plugboard—enormously consequential given the key spaces involved, as an example may show. An Enigma has a 76-bit key, made up of the plugboard (47 bits) and the rotors (29 bits).[81] So if you built and ran 100,000 Enigma replicas, each with an operator working nonstop, and they each checked one key setting per second, it would take almost twice the age of the universe (currently believed to be 13.8 billion years) to break this particular key; then the key would change the next day. After Rejewski's groundbreaking distinction, those same 100,000 Enigma operators may break the settings in under two hours. Obviously, 100,000 operators checking a key per second is still impossible, but with the Bombe automating those efforts, it became practical to break the Enigma in real time.[82] In this example, a lot depends on how much knowledge operators have—if they do not know the wiring of the rotors, the key space for one rotor alone is larger than a plugboard's key space (fewer possible permutations for a plugboard no matter how many wires you use). The pivotal step that gives the modeling traction is not just the automation of the brute force attack but the distinction between contributing cryptologic mechanisms: it is what made simulating the Enigma's permutations by the Bombe plausible.

Since the rotor setting has the smaller key length, this can be determined by the Bombe, and the plugboard setting, left unsolved by the Bombe, becomes the remaining cryptogram. Wrens were able to collect multiple plugs from a Bombe stop.[83] One could only directly find the plug of whatever letter was plugged into the test register, but was it possible for the Wrens to move the test register plug to other points of the menu of the stopped Bombe, inject current, and observe the test register. Some Bombes had a consecutive plug knockout function; it took advantage of a security blunder where Germans would not allow a letter to be plugged to the letter next to it in the alphabet. If you learn that at a given Bombe stop, A plugs to B, that is a false stop, and you can eliminate it. One would need to produce a list of all plug settings, or at least all plugs that could be learned from the currently plugged menu, to check for these. The Navy Bombe auto-checked and printed the plugs (even in three-rotor mode), but not the British three-rotor Bombe—a separate Checking Machine (effectively a non-stepping Enigma) was used in a manual procedure.[84] In short, the sophisticated Cornell simulation of the recent past in analog computing is a misrepresentation of how the Bombe simulated the Enigma. Simulations can yield valuable insights yet also misguide us by dint of seductive interpretive surfaces.

As Edwards articulated, the epistemic knowledge generated by the cultural technique of simulation tends to be a future scenario, for example, in terms of climate change or in terms of mutually assured nuclear destruction.[85] Such scenarios enact a closed world, making it tractable for modeling.[86] This taming of unpredictability in a complex chain of what-if decision trees methodically reduces contingency, oriented not toward events but to their avoidance. By the same token, such simulations only provide solutions or options for the very crises they have made conceivable, comprehensible: for the exact knowledge they model. This modifies the social construction of past, present, and future: "the distance between experience and expectation that makes the present the ground for an open future is restructured" to the extent that we invert the relation between experience and expectation: simulations are embedded in multiple expectations and await experience.[87] For "knowledge based on simulations is hyperconstructible"; the hypothetical literacy that simulations require also thematizes their performative horizon.[88]

But if simulation can be seen as an effort to model and explore the near future, the same technique also lends itself to emulating computing's recent past: it can serve the maintenance and preservation of computational performance, namely in emulation. If simulations aim to head off detrimental options in hypothetical scenarios, emulation is the use of the same technique to keep legacy computing operable. In one case study of legacy computing at a top-twenty-five US mutual insurer, solutions introduced from 1955 on were stacked in such a way that by 1978, actuarial and business data from seven earlier computing environments were emulated on top of each other to provide continuity of operation.[89] The acquisition, collection, storage, and sharing of information from and about our digital heritage can seem uncomplicated—a CD-ROM, for example, appeared easy to use, a stable technological object not affected by water or sunlight and readily copied (unless copy protection makes that a legal issue). But its legibility depends on the proper drive, which may not work forever, using software that can depreciate, interfacing with other hardware that is no longer current. . . . The durability and readability of digital storage media varies greatly but is generally more limited than that of analog storage media. Optical and magnetic storage solutions offer between five and twenty years of reliability before they need to be copied or otherwise migrated, and the rapid innovation in digital technologies creates additional hurdles for preservation.[90] Moreover, stored data require interpretation, as not just any software can access any data in any format. Hence emulation is a way to vouchsafe lasting accessibility of digital objects in the context of their

particular software and hardware, from the appropriate application down to operating systems, hardware affordances, and clock rates. This is particularly relevant for multimedia, as audio and video and animation or moving images require medium-specific reproduction, and this applies even more so for computing artifacts; static images or text can be represented in analog format, but interactive software (operating systems, applications, databases, computer games, interactive simulations) cannot.[91] Whether digital objects are strictly speaking born digital or digitized, their continued accessibility and legibility depends on robust preservation strategies, including emulation or simulation.[92] While simulation tends to be understood as a reduction to specific properties in an abstract model, emulation aims for equivalent results—the same input is expected to yield the same output, regardless of the internal states of a system and its degree of abstraction from what it models. The distinction between simulation and emulation is hardly a strict one. Library and information science, computer science, archival work and museum curating converge on the need to maintain and preserve (some of the) interactive aspects of legacy software and hardware, not just for the history of computing in general but for particular uses that include (but are certainly not limited to) electronic music, interactive art, and computer games, as well as a range of other interactive multimedia artifacts.[93]

In terms of the look and feel of historical computing, dynamic environments pose peculiar challenges.[94] The higher the amount of interactivity and multimedia representations, the more complex the task of preserving or at least commemorating an authentic experience in its technical, economic, and pragmatic dimensions (not to mention legal aspects).[95] Long-term preservation of digital data can draw on migration or emulation; migration of dynamic data involves preserving the bitstream in a forward-secure backup, so that the data remain accessible even as the data carriers age, keeping up to speed with newer read and write peripherals and storage technologies.[96] More static data can also migrate from digital to analog storage, whether on paper or microfilm or other sustainable media, but this is impractical for dynamic and interactive digital objects. Emulation, by contrast, seeks to do justice to the interactive dimensions of digital objects, and is widely considered the only reliable way to re-create the original functionality, look, and feel.[97] This seeks to preserve the full context of the physical and logical form of digital objects, and is possibly less expensive than migration to other formats, though emulation requires more initial investments, which makes it inappropriate for short-term preservation.[98] Long-term preservation in turn means more than storage—while reliable storage is needed, data also need to remain accessible in new technical constellations: legible for newer software and addressable by newer peripherals. Reliable long-term storage of digital data on analog media like microfilm, for instance, is only a partial answer to the issues raised by interactive software, even if microfilm plotters can be connected to networked computers and configured in such a way that primary information and metadata can be redigitized.[99] As Dourish reminds us, "Thinking about emulation and about the need to read between the lines of representations forces us to adopt a vertical, rather than a horizontal, view—one that cuts through the layers and understandings the complete instantiation of mechanism that makes a system operate."[100] The storage, transmission, and processing of bitstreams requires a double notation, of source code and of machine binary. The source code describes the function of a program in a form that is somewhat accessible to humans via the annotated syntax programming languages; the machine binary describes the program as executable for a particular hardware and operating system. Any proprietary applications that generate their output in a data format not easily transliterated into other formats risk rapid obsolescence, which is one argument for open source software and open standards.

> The object of attention in an emulation, then, is not simply the sequence of instructions that need to be transformed into some different sequence that suits the host processor; rather, the emulation needs to reproduce and reenact the entire mechanism into which those instructions fit when they are taken not as representations of computational action but as components of the mechanism.[101]

The boundaries of what emulation can achieve often have to do with a lack of documentation of source code or with copy protected or proprietary technology. As the next chapter will discuss in more detail, neither museal conservation of legacy technology nor simulation of its look and feel on newer devices are exclusive solutions—they require each other as a reference and corrective.

Emulators are themselves dynamic digital objects that deserve some historic attention but are difficult to preserve—they either become obsolete or they need another emulator to keep running on new platforms. Emulation is therefore itself a historical topic in computing. The concept was formulated by IBM in the 1960s when they introduced new computers and a new operating system, OS/360, that were incompatible with their previous products of the IBM 7070, 7090, or 7094 generation. Larry Moss and Stuart Tucker proposed a combination of hardware and software modifications that would permit the transfer of older inputs onto the run time for the 360 architecture, thus simulating the older machines in the newer environment. As a result, a 360 computer could then behave, when needed, like a 7070 computer. They felt, however, that their combination of software, microcode, and hardware went beyond the concept of simulation, and proposed the term emulation instead. Tucker explained that "emulation is an interpretive technique using a combination of software and hardware" that runs in the manner of an interpretive routine simulator.[102] This interpretive technique arose from the constraints on storage, which meant that commands had to be implemented in additional hardware; at the time, a pure software emulation would have been too slow. But the acceleration of computer performance has eliminated such bottlenecks, and today emulation means the imitation of hardware by software. As long as Moore's law seems to be in effect, we assume future processors will be faster and more complex, and as a result, newer host systems need to work faster to achieve the original speed of the legacy system (although there is no linear correlation between processing cycles of original systems and adequate emulation speeds). This encompasses the emulator transcoding the CPU instructions (arithmetic and logical operations, registers and storage modes, input/output operations) as faithfully as possible to the functionality of the legacy processor; the emulator also needs to provide the structure of the original memory manager (ROM and RAM and memory controllers), the environment code (BIOS and firmware), and peripheral mapping. Tucker already recognized that for performance reasons it is best if the data bus is not itself emulated. Of course, "the more accurate the simulation the more software will run correctly," but this challenges datapath accuracy, cycle accuracy, instruction level accuracy, and dynamic recompiling at various levels of simulation for varying detail of simulation.[103] Most emulators aim for functional accuracy rather than painstaking internal reconstructions of resistor, condensator, or transistor behavior.

The main purpose of emulation is compatibility with older computing architectures; that orientation permits the extended use of legacy software, sandbox testing of new software for extant environments, compatibility with legacy peripherals, as well as the preservation of historically significant computing environments. Integrating emulators into the systematic preservation of hardware and software raises several pragmatic issues. The idea that a particular interactive setup is authentic can only be verified or falsified with reference to external context; it is not something that is somehow innate in the affordances of a digital environment.[104] Metadata can capture aspects of a particular look and feel, so the challenge is to embed them in human-readable formats along with the software and its emulator specifications in such a way that they will not be easily corrupted in storage, migration, and backup. The iterative process of making copies of digital storage is therefore sometimes called a transliteration, aiming for accessibility under the technical conditions of future systems. Retaining as much as one can of the function, form, appearance, and feel of a setup is the stated goal of preservation projects like CAMiLEON—"Creative Archiving at Michigan and Leeds: Emulating the Old on the New."[105] In 1986, the BBC Domesday project celebrated the nine hundredth anniversary of the Domesday book by recording a social snapshot of life in the UK on two virtually indestructible interactive videodiscs that could be accessed using a BBC microcomputer; but not much more than a decade later, the project was in peril of obsolescence. The CAMiLEON Project (1999–2003) emulated the obsolete BBC computer and videodisc player on which the original system ran. Thus software, mimicking a piece of hardware or software, lets other processes think the original equipment function is available in its original form, in this case rescuing the two interactive videodiscs from obsolescence. As it is impossible to retain working examples of every computer and every piece of software (and attempting to do so would be prohibitively expensive), emulation promises access to digital information in the future.

Emulation is a kind of software translation—presenting an environment to a binary data set that behaves just like its original target environment.[106] Yet whenever we take for granted that emulation affords a reasonably high degree of authenticity in representing or replicating digital culture, this assumption may need to be interrogated in qualitative and quantitative terms to illuminate critical differences and boundaries. Emulators like Virtual PC, QEMU, Bochs, or VMWare are certainly capable of running operating systems like MS Windows, MacOS, or GNU/Linux and of supporting a range of peripherals, but none of them are designed for digital preservation, and there is no guarantee that they will continue to perform in the near future.[107] The simulation or virtualization of older digital environments on newer ones is a burgeoning field, illustrated, for instance, by the JVM (Java

Virtual Machine) that can be implemented on a range of devices to execute programs developed for a variety of computers and operating systems. But for JVM to become a cross-platform solution to the questions raised by preservation, it would need to be supported as such—by a number of OEM manufacturers, developers, and content providers, not to mention customers and archives, libraries and museums. Other proposals for a universal virtual computer pursue a similar vision.[108]

The potential of emulators for long-term preservation depends on complex trade-offs; a truly accurate maintenance would retain even the hardware errors of the original system as authentic parts of the history of technology, but most emulators are more likely to introduce errors of their own than to reproduce glitches from the past. But if one loosely groups legacy devices into mainframes, arcade systems, home computer systems, PCs, consoles, and mobile devices, it is soon evident that not all of these groups have met with equal attention via emulation. While mainframes are emulated in SIMH or Hercules, arcade systems in MAME, home computers in VICE or MESS or ARAnyM, and PCs by dint of Virtual PC, SoftWindows, QEMU, VMWare, PearPC, DOSEMU, or Basilisk II, we see emulators for consoles that range from Stella or ZSNES and SNES9x to NeoCD, Gens32, Nebula, PCSX2, or Yabouse, while mobile devices can be emulated in GNUBoy (for the Nintendo GameBoy) or DeSmuME (for the Nintendo DS). There are essentially three categories of emulators: free hobby programs driven by retro-computing nostalgia (like MAME, the multiple arcade machine emulator), commercial virtual systems driven by operating systems progress (like Parallels), and academic emulators driven by the need for scientific and museal historiography (like Dioscuri). Retro-gaming trends also brought us Nintendo's Virtual Console, a download for the Wii that emulates games from the Nintendo, Sega, or C64 back catalog. By contrast, commercial emulators serve software development, as when Apple provides an iPhone simulator as part of its iOS Software Development Kit, permitting the engineering and testing of mobile apps on a computer using XCODE; the same is afforded by Google's Android Emulator and Microsoft's Windows Phone Simulator, but the rapidly rising number of mobile apps running on proprietary operating systems and bound by strict developer licenses prevent any effective collection, maintenance, and preservation of mobile app history. Games pose particular technical challenges in long-term digital preservation.[109] More than other dynamic digital objects, they rely on complex interactions using the multimedia capabilities of specific hardware in time-critical ways, and they are dependent on input devices and on the technical capabilities of graphic displays. Instead of executing the original game in its native operating system on original hardware, emulation seeks to render a faithful interactive environment of the original game's source code via an emulator (simulating the hardware, firmware, and support of the original setup) on a different host operating system and its different host hardware.

Emulation becomes difficult when multimedia productions such as games maximize the affordances of a particular device, which then has to be emulated in all its particulars. One instructive example in game studies is CRT emulation—pointing to the strong affinity between the Atari VCS and the CRT television as its authentic display, Bogost observed the texture, noise, color bleed, and afterimage typical of the original experience that has become obliterated by newer screens but can be carefully emulated.[110] Lest we jump to the conclusion that emulation is a matter of historic and academic importance that anyone in gaming ought to support, consider that as early as 1982, Coleco published an emulator that would permit Atari VCS cartridges to be playable on Coleco consoles—but they were sued for licensing fees and damages. Conversely, emulators like MAME (the multiple arcade machine emulator) can render legacy games designed for Commodore C64, Atari ST, or Amiga playable in open source transliteration. As early as 1997, Infocom offered ZMachine, emulating Zork and other interactive fiction on different architectures and operating systems.[111] In at least one case, emulation was accused of being so good as to provide an unfair advantage to a competitive player on a legacy game: when a "forensic analysis of controversial Donkey Kong world records claims those records were scored on an emulator and not on original hardware, essentially accusing the record holder of cheating."[112] The record had been controversial for years, illustrating the premium in gaming on performance; the forensic analysis also highlights subtle but evident differences between original hardware and the MAME emulator in terms of video orientation, screen transitions, and the presence of V-sync tearing a horizontal split in the image that occurs when your monitor's refresh rate and GPU's frame rate are not synchronized. Game emulators focused on older devices (one ought to add Sega, PlayStation 1, NES, or GameBoy, as well as Apple II, TI99/4A, and other console and computer game setups to those mentioned above) require simpler CPUs and memory management; nonetheless, a landmark report estimates that "over 70% of the efforts never resulted in a viable emulation," while some of the successful efforts were later abandoned.[113] In those legacy scenarios, the multimedia environment that is a computer game simulates complex constellations of space and collision detection, sound and moving images—data structured in a bitstream that can be stored, processed, or communicated; if proper error detection is used, the bitstream can be copied (almost) perfectly. Thus, digital interactive environments can be preserved independently of their original data carriers; whether games were first distributed on floppy disc, CD-ROM, DVD, flash drive, or as digital download, their bitstream can be migrated or copied intact to new formats that present it as functional to an environment ready to interpret it properly.[114] Digital rights management often prevents migration and copying, and errors may be introduced in migration, but generally the promise of networked computing is that intranet or internet distribution could keep older games playable for longer than the hardware and peripherals they were originally designed for. One project banking on networked services for emulation-based viewing was the European collaboration among national libraries called PLANETS (Preservation and Long-term Access through Networked Services) in the context of the Open Archival Information System (OAIS) Reference Model.[115]

The more archives and libraries (and to an extent museums and universities) go digital, the more a lot of legacy information is at risk.[116] This need not mean that only dynamic migration and emulation are viable while a museum approach is less sustainable; museums have explored various models to bridge that gap.[117] But admittedly, museums of computing tend to focus on the preservation of hardware and the media archaeological documentation of software. The older a device, the more costly it becomes in terms of time and effort to maintain its functionality, and many museums are therefore loath to expose their collectibles to every visitor, protecting them instead. Beyond historical education, museums harbor ambitions to preserve as much of the authentic experience as feasible under their circumstances, but undoubtedly the mere act of inclusion in a museum exhibit already shifts the reception of a computing device. Nonetheless, collaborative projects like KEEP (Keeping Emulation Environments Portable) see an important role for computing museums in providing a reliable reference for emulation; a groundbreaking report on preserving virtual worlds likewise recommended obtaining and comparing emulators along with original hardware and software for the robust preservation of interactive dynamic software environments.[118] Clearly, digital archiving, beyond any acquisition of information, also has methodological effects on the archive known as a museum.[119] As the next chapter, on museums of computing, will elucidate, this is where simulation comes to the fore—as a legitimate compromise between absolute interactive authenticity and passive musealization. Given the conundrums computer museums face, we need to explore whether, as some people have claimed, the internet may serve as (a simulation of) a museum of computing.

2   Is the Internet a Museum of Computing?

When does the computer get into the museum and how does the museum get into the computer? "Information technology constitutes the twist in the Möbius strip that takes us from arguments internal to a field (how is the past conceptualized in the case of a historical science) to its exterior (how is information about the past stored)," as Geof Bowker put it.[1] Of course, the internet is not a museum in any conventional sense—but then computers are not conventional media either, and a range of scholars have argued that the internet may be the most apt way to assemble, consult, commemorate, and musealize what we know about computing. Inversely, we may wonder to what extent computer history museums actually do justice to computer history, from analog and early digital machines to mainframes, and from minicomputers and microcomputers to the creation of decentralized networks, up to and including the history of the internet.[2] It is one thing to recognize that "what the educated public has come to think of as the Internet has evolved to encompass not just the hardware and software of the network itself but the mind-bogglingly diverse variety of human activities conducted over it"—but it is another thing to truly address the history at least of the hardware and software side, without getting bogged down yet by all that arises from networked computing.[3] How does our computational civilization cultivate awareness of its own historical conditions of possibility? What is the history of the internet a history of? While computing is so relentlessly hurtling into the future, how does the history of computing suddenly become museum-worthy? Rather disparate institutions contribute to the musealization of the internet, contingently and often not connected to each other, addressing distinct audiences.[4] Some critics see in this development the exhaustion of our institutional and individual capacity for coping with innovation in cultural memory—why should the internet

have (or even become) a museum? What time is left for a museum of the
internet when the internet at the same time has permeated almost every
business and administrative process, demanding growth in production per
time unit—including the production of museum artifacts? "Every attic is
an archive, every living room a museum. Never before has so much been
recorded, collected, and never before has remembering been so compulsive."[5] Consequently, observers are divided between those who like to see
the net hoover up all our digital traces, and those who wonder about "the
trash, cruft, detritus and intentionally opaque hoard of documents and
artifacts that constitute our digital middens."[6] What would be the arguments for historic preservation of the net? When do we get to process what
the internet was, what it has become today, and what it prompts us to do
next? Could there be a monument or memorial or museum of the internet,
whether by that we mean its infrastructure and backbone, or its full interactive culture that we protect and preserve for posterity?

Arguably, few technologies influence the twentieth and twenty-first centuries in as many ways as computing does, and few dispute the seminal
role of the internet, both of which ought to make museums of computing
(and thus museum exhibits of internet history) obvious and inevitable. It
hardly surprises us when someone like Tim Berners-Lee defends the web
as an "amazing resource" and argues that "it is vital enough that we must
all take greater action to enhance and defend it."[7] And indeed, it is hard
to "imagine how one might study the history of the developed world in
the late twentieth and early twenty-first centuries without recourse to the
archived web," as more and more of the primary sources of interest to
historians (news, correspondence, public records, etc.) are online, driving
more museums online.[8] But can computer history in general, and internet history in particular, lend itself to a taxonomic museological approach,
or are other approaches offering themselves that promise to grasp the full
stakes? And once museums go online, who gets to represent what (about
the internet) to whom (on the internet)? "As a model for developments
in the museum, the Internet brings with it issues in relation to power as
complex as those found in the traditional model of the museum," as Charlie Gere warns.[9] Methods of memorializing, commemorating, selecting and
excluding, emphasizing and revising are implicit and explicit constraints
on how museums represent computers and the internet, and how the internet represents computers and its own history (and prehistory).[10] There is

even an exhibition calling itself a "Museum of the Fossilized Internet" that aims to raise awareness for sustainable technology, and its curators offer virtual tours that seek to put the coal- and oil-powered internet of the past behind us.[11] If museums are already unreal "heterotopic" spaces in which the time of accumulation never stops building up a collection catering to any number of epochs, forms, and tastes, they seek to establish a perpetual hoard that they seek to protect from the ravages of time—of decay and shifting contexts, of bit-rot and oblivion.[12] This is certainly not to suggest that museums are somehow exempt from the second law of thermodynamics, or that they could do with computers and networks what the layperson cannot: keep them running without error.[13] But computer-mediated communications developed so rapidly and changed so many areas of human culture that museums devoted to computing in general and networked computing in particular are constantly challenged to keep exhibits didactically and historically meaningful.

No doubt the internet has technical and cultural dimensions worthy of being appreciated and protected against decay and disappearance; yet its history is rarely appreciated, rapidly decaying, and often deeply misunderstood and badly misrepresented—even by many of those who purport to save it.[14] Version control and persistence are explicitly not part of its architecture, a fact much deplored by net pioneers like Ted Nelson, who protested tirelessly that "it trivializes our original hypertext model with one-way, ever-breaking links and no management of version or contents."[15] Indeed, an exhibit on the webpage of the Museum of Media History devoted to Nelson's "Project Xanadu" documents the failures of incorporating version control into the net, and the mission of the Internet Archive's Wayback Machine is partly to remedy this lack.[16] Internet history cannot simply be the supply-side account of what is on offer at given points in its development, but needs to account for inflection points and reticular detours, mirroring how we traverse the internet itself. A simple history of the internet risks imposing a grand narrative that is necessarily incomplete and not inclusive, while facile pluralization into net histories risks dissolving into anecdotes, fan pages, or memoirs—neither option can vouch for a reliable analysis of salient aspects, from infrastructural developments to format wars and from hardware innovations to different use cases. There are any number of other "missing narratives" in internet history, and thus museums have also been part of the response.[17] Scholarship of net histories shows how much what we call the internet "is as much mythology as technology, a shared set of narratives that frame our expectations of the future."[18] Despite all this, we stake expectations on computers and the internet for filing, archiving, conservation, and memory—arguably, the computer has fundamentally redefined our concept of memory.[19] As Flusser argued, most epistemological questions can be traced back to the reification of cultural memory; perhaps, he speculated, the invention of electronic memory (as simulation of certain brain functions that exaggerates some aspects and neglects others) would show that these are perennial questions simply because they were put the wrong way.[20] Either way, as "things tumble with increasing rapidity into an irretrievable past," the distinction between history and memory challenges research, didactics, and museums.[21] If in the "non-spaced space or spaced-out space of the internet, everything is in a sense everywhere at all times, and everything is juxtaposed to everything else," it ought to be feasible to collect, open, tend to, and communicate the history of computing by dint of computers, and therefore the history of computer networks up to and beyond the internet, on the internet.[22] Yet such a project is suspended between a desire for an encyclopedic grasp of "internet history" and the surmise that such a reduction goes diametrically against the entropy of an ever-expanding reticular structure.[23] A museum is defined as a permanent institution in the service of society that acquires and conserves, researches and communicates the tangible and intangible heritage at stake for the purposes of education, study, and enjoyment.[24] "By putting 'the order of things' itself on display, museums are spaces for representing the space of representation as such."[25] This means we need to examine the formation of an "exhibitionary complex" as a set of cultural techniques.[26]

One of the consequences of the COVID-19 pandemic is a surge in online visitors to museums, and the expansion of museum offerings on the internet renewed interest in the notion of virtual museums.[27] Cultural historians jumped to the conclusion that "the concept of the imaginary museum, invented by Malraux at least as early as 1947, appears to preempt so much of our current discourse on virtualities and digitalities."[28] Though the nineteenth-century museum prefigured the mass media as purveyors of modes of representation, new technologies of reproduction led to new art forms and media artifacts that André Malraux praised as giving rise to his imaginary museum of 1947.[29] As COVID-19 prompted a surge of online visitors to museum websites, museums expanded their internet offerings. Arguably, the imaginary museum Malraux (who died in 1976) sketched out is not the virtual museum pursued online today.[30] His imaginary museum was neither a self-imposed restriction to reproductions, nor the abandonment of the museum as an institution, but rather a curatorial act as a work of art: it sought not to replace but to extend the exhibitionary impulse. Nonetheless, it is now claimed as a prescient precursor of digital exhibits, because it used media technology in the service of a museum without walls.[31] "To understand what is new about the ways in which museums organize and operate within global networks means looking at quite specific matters concerning, for example, the technical means of organizing those networks (the internet contrasted with earlier networks centered on rail and navigation, telegraphy and telecommunications), the forms of expertise they interconnect," as Tony Bennett has it.[32] Proponents of networked computing argue persuasively that access to cultural assets should be extended beyond exhibition spaces to capture economies of scale. While museum exhibits tend to display a small percentage of the actual holdings, web museums can potentially offer a lot more. But the topic becomes more complex once we consider the internet itself a cultural asset and seek to capture its history in a curated exhibit. If the museum genealogically is "an epistemological structure," then certainly so is the internet.[33] Wolfgang Ernst argues that "the inventoried collection is no longer the long-term database of a given past; nor is memory any longer assumed to be a stable condition of a future historiography but something to be maintained on an as-needed basis. The Internet itself constitutes the appropriate mode."[34] Even a cursory search will turn up virtual museums of computing—leveraging the net and its increasing capacity for high-resolution communications for the display of, and interaction with, representations of computer history, including the history of the net.[35] A Swiss museum of computing, Enter.CH in Solothurn, offers a virtual walkthrough of its old exhibits while it awaits the completion of a new building to house its physical exhibits.[36] The Stuttgart University computer museum posts documentaries on Twitch and YouTube.[37] Some virtual computer museums are online extensions of museums of computing, for example, the Virtual Museum Project of the Monash Museum of Computing History, which exhibits images of a Ferranti Sirius and a PDP-9 before pointing to computer networks (thereby legitimizing its online presence); some are purely virtual without physical collections.[38] Soon the internet as a whole appears to be a simulated museum of computing.

A decade ago, a presentation about internet history for a conference at the London Science Museum in June 2013 on "Making the History of Computing Relevant" opened with this ambivalent sentiment: "The online world and its origins is one of the most obviously relevant areas of computing history to the general public. It is also one of the hardest to effectively interpret and display."[39] The speaker, Marc Weber, works as internet history curator at the Computer History Museum in Mountain View, California.[40] Launched in 2009, their internet history program set out to tell stories—including its own story as the first comprehensive exhibit about the history of the online world. But it does not simply display routers and wires, servers and switches, satellites and radio towers, because while the infrastructure may be impressive, "the magic that eventually brings our screens to life is all on the inside, invisible. Also barely visible are the marks of the bitter, decades-long standards wars that form much of the history of networking."[41] Indeed, modems, LANs, and routers emerged from a wide variety of experimental prototypes.[42] But exhibiting a refrigerator-sized IMP from the original ARPAnet, a Cisco router, a dish antenna, or a Google server rack is not the best way to tell the story of the internet, and computers as display devices can conceal as much as they reveal.[43] The Computer History Museum's display of 3,200 objects (from a collection of over 75,000) begins with nineteenth-century telecommunications equipment before getting to packet switching networks for computing since the 1960s.[44] In a key didactic decision, visitors can follow two separate tracks—one about connecting computers, and one about connecting people—which also highlights how the web is distinct from, but reliant on, the net. A similar articulation is made by the Science Museum in London.[45] Foregrounding that the history of computing is not simply a lineage of devices, their "information age" gallery overturned the guiding principles of an earlier display of computing (since 1975) so as to represent technology-historical context alongside the computing artifacts themselves (since 2014).[46] It encompasses more than two centuries of networking, from Morse and telegraph wires to radio and television broadcasts and on to satellite, internet, and cellular communications.[47] Each of the six network displays is within sight of the other five, and while there are still exhibits of rare and invaluable devices, the story told is not only of musealizing communication history but of connections, shifting the emphasis to the network user.[48]

This raises questions about what a museum of computing wants to achieve, and how it can go about achieving this. What are the must-have exhibits, and how are they contextualized? When does the story begin, and how does it pull visitors in—without overwhelming or disappointing a range of anticipated viewers, from the most casual observer to the historian or engineer or collector? It may be worth surveying the offerings of a few museums to discuss, for the sake of readers who may have not visited these collections, how their exhibits accentuate histories of computing. Computer history was rather marginal until recently, and museums of computing are an even more recent phenomenon. The Charles Babbage Institute (CBI) and the History of Computing Committee of the American Federation of Information Processing Societies (AFIPS) were both founded in 1978.[49] The AFIPS committee produced a brochure called "Preserving Computer-Related Source Materials," distributed at the National Computer Conference in 1979; what was collected at first was mostly papers, with executable code and legacy hardware barely considered for "aesthetic or sentimental value."[50] Most computer museums only opened their doors in the 1990s: what does it mean that this impulse comes up in the decade before the end of the twentieth century? Is it a coincidence that this was also the decade when the internet was privatized and quickly became ubiquitous?[51] A decade before the end of the nineteenth century, Wilhelm Dilthey urged the collection of philosophical heritage in peril of obsolescence, confident that a spirit of the house would be tending and communicating such an archive.[52] While there is undoubtedly no "supreme reign of an objective spirit" in computer history, similar appeals are now made for the history of computing, with a comparable belatedness and confidence. Yet while stone, clay, parchment, or paper have significant longevity, and records inscribed that way can be consulted centuries later without a need for electricity or compatible devices, software depends on extant hardware (cards, tapes, disks, etc.), which decay far more rapidly.[53] While computers are now used to store and circulate what we wish to preserve and share, locally or in the cloud, their own archaeology and genealogy were neglected for decades. "The icons of a living culture do not begin as canonical works preserved in books and museums and taught in university classrooms. They begin as treasures of living memory."[54] A generation later, as living memories begin to fade, the impulse for collection and preservation awakens.[55] Many countries practice a thirty-year rule for the public release of nonsensitive government records, and governments have long been instrumental in the history of computing and the history of the internet, both as customers and as regulators.[56] But the first collections and exhibitions of computer history tended to be industry-driven or started as personal collections—not only the Computer History Museum in Mountain View (which started as an exhibit in a converted closet at DEC) as initiated by Ken Olsen and Gordon Bell.[57] An apt comparison here is the Living Computer Museum in Seattle, the world's best collection of fully operational vintage computers (from the private collection of Paul Allen).[58] DigiBarn is a collection started in 2001 in a barn in the Santa Cruz mountains, now almost exclusively online at digibarn.com and collaborating with the collection of System Source in suburban Maryland, which in turn has its roots in inventory that became obsolete before it was sold; both emphasize virtual tours over physical visits.[59] A similar small private collection started in 1990 at the American Computer & Robotics Museum in Bozeman, Montana.[60] Historian Gerard Alberts helped foment the formation of the Stichting Computer Erfgoed Nederland (SCEN, Foundation for Computer Heritage in the Netherlands), which connects a number of private collections of computer history.[61] Yves Bolognini collected 400 computers from before 1985 before donating them to the Museum for Communication in Bern.[62] The private collection of historical computers by software developer Boris Jakubaschk in Karlsruhe has been displayed at the ZKM and on his website, https://www.homecomputermuseum.de, since 1997. By definition, a private collection is not (yet) a museum, but an evolutionary step in the museum's prehistory—a *Wunderkammer*, initiated for curiosity's sake or for speculative or business or scholarly purposes. Some museum scholars have wondered whether "new media and the internet seem to imply new epistemological and aesthetic models, which have more in common with the private curiosity cabinets or *Wunderkammern* of the sixteenth to eighteenth centuries than they do with the late Victorian public museum."[63] That surmise about computer history museums needs to be explored further.

Even the largest computer history museum, the Heinz Nixdorf MuseumsForum (HNF) in Paderborn, Germany, emerged in the 1990s out of the private collection of a computer pioneer whose company was sold to

Siemens.[64] Nixdorf had collected over 1,500 objects by the time of his death in 1987, and though his foundation had envisioned a company-specific framework for their exhibition, eventually the scope was widened to five millennia of mathematics, writing, and communication.[65] In the former company headquarters, this collection is displayed diachronically from the abacus to the computer, with special galleries devoted to "cult objects" like the Apple I, CRAY 2, Enigma, Curta, or Zuse Z1, and to fifteen inventors in a hall of fame (with 152 more featured on "wall of fame" display). Eighty-five displays are interactive, including an abacus simulation, a Brunsviga 13RK mechanical calculator, and a Morse station, as the layout follows a didactic and historical progression from Mesopotamian calculations to robotics. Touch screens and display cabinets illustrate internet history under the header "The World at Your Fingertips."[66] Strangely, the HNF website claims that global networking of computers was instigated by the military as "a network that would operate even in the event of nuclear war," when in fact we have known since the early 1960s if not earlier that the electromagnetic pulse of a nuclear blast renders unshielded computers and networks inoperable (not to mention the power grid).[67] As at other computer history museums, the history of the internet is illustrated at the HNF by dint of evocative objects, including a teletext terminal, a Next Cube used by Tim Berners-Lee to develop his World Wide Web proposal, and the Trojan Room coffee machine that was the first to be monitored by webcam.[68]

Other German collections of computing history include those at the Deutsches Museum in Munich (exhibiting computers since 1988), and at the Deutsches Technikmuseum in Berlin (since 1990); a few of the most salient differences between their intentions, exhibitions, and collections are worth discussing before we return to the question of a museum of the internet in particular.[69] The computer exhibition in the Deutsches Museum in Munich, Germany, was originally designed by a pioneering professor of informatics, Friedrich Bauer, and involved around 700 objects and forty interactive exhibits.[70] The layout chosen for that exhibit was explicitly didactic, covering mathematical instruments, analog calculators, digitization, coding, automation, universal machines, and peripherals. This exhibit is now closed and is being redesigned; a separate exhibit addresses cryptology and was likewise recently overhauled. The Deutsches Technikmuseum in Berlin has an area devoted to computing, giving pride of place to Konrad Zuse, whose Z1 is exhibited centrally and contextualized as the beginning of an information age (a Z3 replica is also exhibited).[71] This museum also offers a separate exhibit with over 500 objects illustrating "the net," organized around the human–computer interface. Here one sees an Enigma to anchor a discussion of encryption and anonymity today, and the net exhibit explains packet switching in greater detail than other museums. It also displays switch hardware from the Frankfurt internet node, and offers an interactive display that lets visitors send and trace packets around an illuminated model.[72]

Museums of computing often lure their audience in with two popular aspects of digital culture—either with gaming or with the internet, as motivation for the intended audience to pay attention.[73] The faster our computers operate objectively, the more pressing the subjective impression that the interfaces and affordances of present computing and networking environments no longer resemble those of the most recent past, let alone the distant one. As Wolfgang Ernst points out, "the Internet constitutes a new type of transarchive already present in Ted Nelson's conception of hypertext and hypermedia: a dynamic archive, the essence of which is permanent updating."[74] While it may appear obvious what legacy systems are, this parlance is in fact messier than it seems.[75] It can denote working but dated code, obsolete systems, work that needs to be transcoded in order to interface with it, and thus carries the ambiguity of inheritance or discards. Without going into a treacherous logic of the supplement far beyond the equally slippery concept of the update or upgrade (to hardware or software), suffice it to point out that the internet ages before our eyes if we use a depreciated browser.[76] The history of the internet is surely not just about histories of the web, or the net, or computing, but about all of these in context. Consumers may bemoan planned obsolescence, and cultural critics may find upgrading paradoxical, but neither gesture provides a sustained frame of reference.[77] Now computer history rushes to remedy a belatedly recognized lack so as to counter the jejune presentism of superficial takes on digital culture.[78] But the past is only irreversibly past and recognizable as the past once the space of our experience and the horizon of our expectations are distinct from each other as they move us away from the irretrievably gone: "once movement away from the past became the criterion of progress, the function of accumulation was turned over to museums."[79] Media scholars have long argued that the hyper-dynamics of interactive computing brought on a notable acceleration: drawing on Marinetti and McLuhan, it was Virilio's thesis that we live through a "dromocratic" revolution.[80] This acceleration is characterized not only by exponential growth of data, but by the rapidly shrinking half-life of academic publications, and by the fact that what was announced as radically modern (and explicitly ahistorical) contemporary technology only a few decades ago is now consigned to conservation, historical protection, and the museum.[81] One wonders why we find the internet in the museum, and not just museums reaching out on the internet.

Museums need to be able to be outside the present without losing touch with the present. "Museums are repositories of temporality; they constitute an accumulated historical tradition."[82] Museal discourse hinges on the future perfect tense—this is where museum time conflicts with internet time.[83] In dynamic technical progress, computing accelerates the development of metrics and coordination that commenced with clocks and other mechanisms. Yet skeptics feel that high-tech civilization is more focused on the past than any other—which is why museums proliferate.[84] Every day a new museum opens somewhere in the world. In the US alone, there are over 33,000: in 2014, the Institute of Museum and Library Services, a federal cultural agency, released an updated Museum Universe Data File suggesting the count had doubled since the previous count of 17,500 from the year 2000.[85] Museums are community anchors and economic engines for tourism, they partner with schools, and they enjoy a robust reputation with the public. At the same time, we are used to failure and obsolescence in computing.[86] As Swade points out, "logical simulation as a virtual object in some respects survives the forensic test of historical utility and suggests in prospect a salvation for the conservator for whom deterioration spells failure."[87] Gordon Bell proposed a "Bell's Law for the Birth and Death of Computer Classes" as a general theory for the creation, evolution, and obsolescence of computers since 1951.[88] But is disappearance what drives a museum? And what about the apparently logical progression from vacuum tube computers to transistors to integrated circuits to microchips is truly more than hindsight? On the one hand, why would contemporary computing commemorate and venerate past iterations once they have fallen into disrepair and disuse? On the other hand, would a museum of the internet not be a premature epitaph? "Museums are the family sepulchers of the work of art," scoffed Adorno.[89] Avant-gardes have historically dismissed museums as cemeteries, as mere storage for dead culture, but now that much of our lives is enmeshed in networked computing, where are the cemeteries? Few social media companies and online providers have begun to think about what happens to someone's accounts and their extended online traces once they die. "In sepulchral museum culture, history itself seems to bow to the verdict of its own obsolescence."[90] What kind of regime is eager to erase the traces of the dead? Is a cemetery not a space away from the present and the future where we can reflect on our interpretation of the past? The genealogy of burial rites helps explain the story of cemeteries as ways of coping not just with individual death but with the vicissitudes of collective remembering. It is less important for museums and mausoleums whether their objects are dead or alive, as long as they exhibit the presence of a piece of the real.

Indulge for a moment the counterfactual notion of a museum of the internet that comes after the end of the internet (before we return to why the actually existing internet may be seen as simulating some functions of a museum of computing). The end is a powerful trope, which means that thoughts of the end are always already under serious auspices, whether we anticipate it as a threat or as salvation, as relief or as the root of all fear. But the end can come in many shapes and guises. It can mean completion or interruption, collapse or abandonment, winking out in exhaustion or stopping in sudden discontinuation. Because nothing that ends simply consists in having ended, it can be problematic to start at the end; any discussion of an end implies that what came to a conclusion had some recognizable trajectory or cohesion before. Sometimes this insight only comes as hindsight, belatedly and with regret. And so it is with the internet, which raised hype to unprecedented heights. This does not mean that one may say goodbye to the internet, let alone good riddance—and not every departure announces itself as final. At the end of the twentieth century, perceived as the end of a millennium, contemplating the end of something epochal came naturally; the internet's particular version of millennial finitude was the rush to prep for the Y2K "bug," which was largely prevented by reprogramming legacy code that had abbreviated dates. As "Y2K survivors" returned to a sweeping creative destruction of human institutions, from face-to-face education to museums, and from how we make and listen to music to the ways we play together, we forgot for a moment how computing rushed headlong into crisis by compressing years from four digits to two, abbreviating for the sake of efficiency the length of historical time.

We customarily distinguish between cyclical and linear concepts of time.[91] Calendars, rituals, festivals, sunrises, moon phases, tides, and seasons may return, but as soon as we use the past tense and future tense about structures that are not cyclical and have no recurring patterns, the grammar of our story changes. In cyclical time, an end is also a new beginning, but the ancient Egyptians already knew stories about cataclysmic events that prevent any cycle from rebooting. In either guise, time appears as a cultural variable—it allows finitude to appear as something we can narrate. But when we tell the story of the internet, do we wonder why it claims its own temporality? "Internet time" denotes instantaneous transmission without any expectation of posterity. Here internet culture deviates from pre-internet culture, conceived as aiming for lasting achievements. The aspiration in older media to legacy moments yields to the viral moment, the trending hashtag. Can the lasting cultural achievement of the internet be that nothing lasts, that we have no version control, no archive, no cultural memory, simply because everything is lost in a torrent of micro-updates? That surely seems like an excessively grumpy take, although we do encounter it in both popular and academic discourse on what the internet as such is, or was, or will have been.

The finitude of something perhaps more precious than those who take it for granted may realize is not simply a diagnosis but a warning. But is not the structure of the internet something that by definition is neither linear nor finite, but built for modular expansion and extension? How can there be an eschatology of a media assemblage that annihilates time to conquer distance? Beyond asserting the perceived recognition of something that can come to an end, it also usually implies a beginning from which that alleged continuity issued. The origins of the internet have been researched in depth, but that does not yet mean that we all recognize the internet as congruently deriving from oblique technical as well as conceptual roots and starting points—some point to the World Brain visions of H. G. Wells made concrete in Paul Otlet's pacificist-internationalist open reference network dating back to the First World War, some to designs by Vannevar Bush to solve technical issues of collaboration dating to the Second World War made concrete in Paul Baran's napkin sketches for RAND addressing network topology, some to the resulting ARPAnet connecting local networks to one another soon after the first delivery of an IMP router built by BBN to join otherwise incompatible computing installations at UCLA and the Stanford Research Institute in 1969. Every origin story shades the trajectory differently, reflecting the interest of those telling the story. Inversely, consciousness of an impending end, transposing it from the near future to the current state of mind, need not mean mourning or melancholia.[92] But to date, most discussions of the end of the net have been the realm of fiction, whether in airport novels or disaster movies, in science fiction or in other futurist extrapolations.[93] Like the mythical ship of Jason, the net is constantly rebuilt. We may draw a distinction between a lowercase "i" internet of users and an uppercase "I" Internet of networks and providers of connectivity.[94] The internet may promise all things to all people, but there are few nodes today that are not plastered with advertising, intruding on privacy, or breeding grounds for vicious trolling. As the history of the internet is musealized, do we talk about freedom and collaboration without taking an inventory of its negative externalities? Consultants warn of "peak advertising," nation-states warn about surveillance and espionage, and politicians look for ways to slow down the rate at which unprecedented monopolies gobble up the world. When we confront cybercrime, when net neutrality is abandoned, when we witness rampant repression and net censorship, and when we consider the rate at which internet governance is tilting away from the ideals that made it such a runaway success in its first half century, it is hard to resist seeing an end.

While nobody may yet see the net as a necropolis, despite all the dross and abandoned links that litter it, there are real-world cemeteries with websites, and there are internet-only cemeteries that commemorate the dead—the oldest one purportedly at https://cemetery.org.[95] There is also at least one website outlining a procedure for memorializing websites that are no longer maintained or whose webmasters are deceased; it not only announces such sites, it also offers a zipped download of their files: "at this site you will find sites of value that have died."[96] There is a Korean patent for a cyber-cemetery "to reduce inconvenience" in visiting the dead.[97] And some internet museums are no longer online—their sites deteriorated or moved, their servers stopped responding. The Virtual Museum of Computing (VmoC) at http://vmoc.museophile.com was available between 2001 and 2008, but no longer responds to my browser (though 139 snapshots of its link collections can be found via the Wayback Machine). The Swiss MuDa, Europe's first physical museum of digital art, recently closed forever despite years of growth.[98] There was an "open adaptive virtual museum of informatics history" in Siberia, hosted by the Ershov Institute at Novosibirsk State University, a Russian Online Museum of Computer History, and a European Virtual Computer Museum in Kiev focused on Ukrainian computer history.[99] There has been a Virtual Computer Museum as a "cultural knowledge project" in Russia since 1998 (https://www.computer-museum.ru), claiming over 2,000 daily visitors, yet declaring since inception that it would never be completed.[100] Dutch designers are compiling the Big Internet Museum, with an emphasis on memes.[101] A German website called Computer Archiv exhibits a selection of devices and documents, including an attempt to musealize the web itself.[102] Web museums like these can distinguish between unregistered users and registered ones, whom it may offer greater access.[103] But they are just as likely to disappear. A "webmuseum" is still at https://www .ibiblio.org/wm, though it started out as a pioneering site called Weblouvre. Developed in 1994 by Nicolas Pioch, it won a Best of the Web Award for multimedia, but when the Louvre found out, it recovered the domain and launched its own website, forcing Pioch to change domains. Discussed in recent internet history scholarship as a "research-based online presentation of web design history" active since 2008, now Webmuseum.dk no longer responds; another site on the history of web design is still extant at https:// www.webdesignmuseum.org. There is a notable delay between the advent of the computer age and the opening of computer museums, between the birthday of the internet and the first efforts to commemorate and musealize internet history: now the question is when a defunct machine or site should be commemorated (and the stipulated rest period for an individual grave needs to exceed that of decomposition). Monuments and memorials proliferate just as museums do, indicating that the threshold of historicization continues to expand. Our need for secured sources goes beyond canonizing the story of how we got here, and keeps producing the past.

As Kittler diagnosed, "computer simulations do not merely form user interfaces, they actually constitute a museum. More precisely, a museum that, as in ancient Alexandria, functions also as a library that has not gone through the modern separation of text and image, libraries and galleries."[104] Archives and museums orient themselves toward a stipulated future interest in that past, saving communicative processes for later edifying consultation and historical study.[105] But the utopian vision of a time to come when historical review will not be constrained sources always founders on the rapidly accumulating contemporary data about computing and the internet. As Bowker remarks dryly, "We are perhaps not quite at the point of witnessing the inaugural act for the archive of computer-mediated communication, but its prophets are many."[106] Warnings of information overload on the one hand and a digital dark age that sees historical records lost for future generations on the other hand are exaggerated, but questions of loss and preservation loom large in computing. Neither technical storage capacities nor our ability to process the meaning of exponential storage can keep up with the dynamics of the internet, despite various government and private initiatives to sift, index, and render searchable "all" data, whether for marketing or for security purposes—both have had to switch to metadata.[107] Could a radical vision of the museum of the internet exhibit just metadata? The Commission on Preservation and Access and the Internet Engineering Task Force developed standards for the identification of digital documents (URNs—uniform resource names) in addition to URL (uniform resource locator) addresses.[108] Metadata, or data about data, is the technical term for sender and receiver, size and date, and other types of information; as long as standards are agreed upon, they allow flexible search across multiple databases. Metadata are exciting not just to cataloguers but also led creatives and technologists to prerequisites for access. Categories are shifting and expanding, context requires updates, and there is no such thing as unambiguously "raw" data prior to labels.[109] Technical media make users forget their operation at the interface to create illusions of pure content: at moments of miscommunication metadata become perceptible. Technologies of data retrieval and digital processing supplement historical narrative by cross-referencing.[110] This is, of course, a native feature of the internet, and yet we are often too much in a rush to take time for collective remembering, or inversely we jump to the facile conclusion that the internet already does our collective remembering. If the latter is true, then the internet is always already its own museum, and no effort to commemorate, document, curate, and exhibit its past is needed; but if the former is an accurate observation, then the fact that there are now museums that seek to preserve and present the history of networked computing is striking.

While there cannot be an internet without computers, and the history of computing certainly appears (at least with hindsight) to bend toward resource sharing, remote access, and networking, it would be far simpler to musealize something that is no longer evolving and changing so rapidly: just wait to create the museum of the net after the end of the net. What we now take for granted emerged only from protracted experiments before congealing into tentative standards; as late as fall 1969, net pioneer Lawrence Roberts "struggled with the issue of network topology: the interconnection of nodes. He began simulating network topologies on a computer."[111] The pace of technical and cultural change driven by, and driving, computers is one of the fundamental problems in this nexus. The Australian Computer Museum was established in 1994 and amassed a significant number of devices, but a decade later found that properly maintaining hardware, software, and oral history since the 1940s represented insurmountable challenges; they passed along their collection to the Powerhouse Museum.[112] Other museums that started strong have either similarly faced warehousing and financing problems, or remained small and therefore less capable of representing the full breadth and depth of computing history; the Monash Museum of Computing History (founded in 2001) chose to collect and preserve only what reflects the development of computing at Monash University.[113] This tension between programmatic selectivity and systematic representation of context characterizes the computer history museum landscape.

As Gordon Bell recalls, his desire to collect the history of computing germinated as early as 1968 when he coauthored a book that "established a Linnaean-type functional taxonomy" for information processing components, which in his mind became artifacts to collect, as MIT began thinking about preserving groundbreaking computers like Whirlwind and its successor, the AN/FSQ-7 built for SAGE, as well as the Lincoln Labs TX-0.[114] SAGE is a seminal reference for networks in particular, as the first modems emerged from collaboration between Bell Labs and the Cambridge Research Lab of the Air Force to process and transmit radar data from remote sites to IBM 790 computers in the late 1950s (which also demonstrates that in computing, as in biology, lateral transfer is key, not a Linnaean order). The museum Bell initiated operated in Boston from 1984 through 1999.[115] To Bell's regret, his taxonomy was dropped when the museum moved to the West Coast, and its acquisition policy evolved away from the motive to "know, seek and obtain the first, mainstream, last, and interesting failures in each class."[116] Lured to Silicon Valley by industry interest, the organization moved to capture artifacts at their source.[117] While parts of the collection were deaccessioned (and are now kept by the Boston Museum of Science), the early years of the California museum coincided with rapid growth of online companies, making fundraising easier until the first dot-com bubble burst.[118] But instead of seeding a network of institutions devoted to computer history, the move out west was a separation, abandoning the opportunity to network. Across the Atlantic, the National Museum of Computing in the United Kingdom opened in 2007, adjacent to the historic buildings of Bletchley Park, holding the largest collection of functional World War II–era machines, including Enigma and Lorenz encryption devices, a working Turing-Welchman Bombe, a rebuilt Colossus, and the WITCH, the world's oldest working digital computer.[119] As STEM education "has not systematically embedded historical awareness into the curriculum," virtual field trips to the National Museum of Computing are proposed as a remedy.[120] Even as stout a defender of collecting and exhibiting historical computers in a museum setting as Dag Spicer admitted that "for the great majority of museum visits people will increasingly use the web rather than travel to a physical location, hence even real museums now integrate their holdings, exhibits, education, and outreach programs into web-based knowledge architectures."[121] Thus when, in November 2007, the Heinz Nixdorf Museums-Forum collaborated with Bletchley Park to reenact via radio the World War II operations of Enigma and Lorenz machines, those displays became operative for a brief operative window of interaction, sublating historical difference "in an equiprimordial rather than historical state."[122] A "virtual Lorenz" simulator is also extant online at https://lorenz.virtualcolossus.co.uk. Despite such rare moments of networking, the collection databases of museum holdings are rarely linked and cannot be cross-referenced readily (though there is a meta-finding aid called Museums Online for Swiss museum collections).[123] While some museums in the US and UK grant access to inventory lists, many restrict it to internal use, and most smaller collections offer none. Even where museums share data, they tend to arrange their collaborations in a star topology, saturating the central node quickly when too many edges are added. While archivists agree that knowledge relies on interconnection, museum collection management systems lag behind the potential of networks.[124]

Computing history is rooted in a longer historical context of calculating machines, as documented in exhibitions and collections at the Arithmeum at the University of Bonn in Germany, the Museum of Mathematics in New York City, the Oxford History of Science Museum, or at museums of communication such as those in Bern, Munich, or Berlin (not to mention the history of automata and of clocks, which would shift the context from a history of technology mindset to a history of science mindset—we will come back to that). Babbage's envisioned Difference Engine #1 was the first automatic calculating machine to operate without human intervention in arithmetical processing; while an incomplete version of it was put together in 1832, a full version of it was not built in his lifetime. His Analytical Engine was likewise incomplete when he died in 1871. In 1991, to celebrate Babbage's 200th birthday, the London Science Museum exhibited a functional reconstruction of Difference Engine #2, with over four thousand parts, weighing almost three tons; working with engineering specs from Babbage's time, they had to add a gear to turn the handle, so one might argue that what they built is not in fact a faithful Difference Engine. In 1998, the Science and Industry Museum in Manchester built a replica of the 1948 "Manchester Baby" or Small-Scale Experimental Machine (SSEM), an electronic stored-program machine used as a test bed of tubes for random access memory.[125] Leibniz kicked off mechanization of calculations three centuries ago, long before Turing's theoretical and Zuse's practical demonstrations of computing's potential in the 1930s and 1940s.[126] But to the extent that informatics and computer science teach such roots, they rarely point to the didactic potential of museums or interactive exhibits that foster hands-on learning of a sort that simulation rarely replaces. The Computer Museum of America (opened in 2019 in Roswell, Georgia) seeks to "educate visitors on the past and future of computing."[127] Yet the history of computing is not nearly as prominent in the teaching of computer science or the history of communications as it perhaps ought to be, and museums are not nearly used as much in research as they might be—whether in terms of a frame of reference, as motivation for problem solving, as reflection on method, or as reminders that the distance between academia and industry is often not as great as we are told.

While experts in education, museum studies, and history agree that one can learn a lot in a museum, the disconnection between the prominence of digital media industries (including in education itself) and the representation and investigation of their history in educational settings is palpable. As Liu points out, "elitism has become the ground of critique against the academy as well as the museum," mitigating claims to our attention.[128] Granted, "museums emphatically demand something of the observer."[129] Their offerings need to go beyond the simple consolations of time lines or listicles of great personalities and great machines. Consider the representation of computer history at the National Museum of American History in Washington, DC, which runs the gamut from a reconstruction of a section of Babbage's Difference Engine to several components of Bush's Differential Analyzer and from components of a Univac to a Harvard Mark 1, among a couple

thousand items in their collection.[130] Instead of selecting devices representative of American history, they show items that have accumulated a certain
reputation. "Imagine the loss, 100 years from now, if museums hadn't begun
preserving the artifacts of the computer age. The last few decades offer proof
positive of why museums must collect," the museum advertises—yet they
frame their computer collection as "business machines" rather than devices
engaging with knowledge or learning. And when the National Museum of
American History hosted a "summit exploring the past, present and future of
the internet" in 2015, its emphasis was on American business pioneers: no
mention was made of adding relevant artifacts to its museum collections, as
if nothing could be learned from the history of the net.[131]

Learning as conscious activity leading to changes of behavior expands
the human capacity for inventing and reasoning; it stimulates discovery,
abstraction, and experience. And this is where an institutional framework
offers more stability than ad hoc online communities for the adequate
representation of historical knowledge. As De Kosnik pointed out (drawing on Williams's critique of "selective traditions" in archives), institutions
"grant priority to the culture that supports the narratives and identities of
the dominant group."[132] She endorsed the formation of "rogue archives" as
one potential alternative, arguing that they offer opportunities for nontraditional voices to participate in archiving. While fan-based archives offer an
interesting approach to institutions of cultural heritage, they define themselves in opposition to traditional institutions. Observing that "popular
enthusiasm for educational applications of computer networking outpaced
scholarly research on their educational value," museums offer factual and
procedural knowledge mediated not by reduction to the most popular
events and objects, but by embedding them in context.[133] Museums support
both formal instruction and informal learning processes, guided tours and
self-directed exploration. Fans and collectors cannot come close to achieving what museums as formal institutions of cultural memory do. Whether
one may think here of the Internet Archive or of file-sharing communities, the "rogue archives" De Kosnik praises (as constantly available with
zero barriers to entry) keep running into legal troubles that serve as potent
reminders that fan archives succeed only so long as they serve as free advertising or free labor.[134] Historical, theoretical, and applied museology show
that cultural patrimony deserves sustained attention that elevates idiosyn-
cratic impulses for collecting and sharing to exacting standards of public (or

otherwise broadly defined) sustainable access to permanent exhibits that explain and maintain the relevant material and immaterial evidence for the benefit of current and future generations.[135] A museum is distinct from private curiosity cabinets, corporate self-reflection, or fans' hoarding. To the extent that one may expect verified original exhibits that can be recognized as authentic, museums not only collect and exhibit, they acquire up-to-date expertise in conservation and maintenance, in research and didactics; museums consider the real thing pivotal to telling their stories (though today they may consider the process of creating NFTs from their collection, simulating ownership and authentication).[136] Computer preservation suffers, perhaps more than other subject areas, from technical obsolescence and format drift, balancing protecting valuable artifacts with the futility of exhibiting complex devices inaccessibly—as their appeal and relevance are rarely discerned from looking at some artifacts' outside.[137]

By 2005 the ZKM in Karlsruhe managed to restore a Zuse Z22 from 1957 (415 vacuum tubes, 2,400 diodes, two magnetic drum memory devices, ferrite core memory, external cooling system, key panel, oscilloscope, teleprinter, paper tape puncher/reader) to full operation, making this rare device (serial number 13) the oldest fully functional and authentically preserved vacuum tube computer worldwide.[138] The Technikum in Kelkheim likewise presents historical computers that are fully operating; the same emphasis characterizes the collection of the Living Computer Museum in Seattle.[139] This is not to deny the importance and utility of models and simulations. As simulation is a cultural technology supported by computing, it is entirely apt to deploy it in support of computer history.[140] Software emulation offers "logical replication as distinct from physical replication," and the current best hope for sustainable emulation is the FPGA (field-programmable gate array).[141] Sites devoted to digital art have begun to offer Emulation-as-a-Service frameworks.[142] Historians harbor legitimate worries about this: Gerard Alberts, for instance, confessed to being horrified that "one can no longer distinguish between original machinery and software or emulation software"—but it can serve as a record of interactions that otherwise became inaccessible.[143] The practical reproducibility of historical computers raises not only historicist questions. "When antique computer hardware is exhibited in a museum, its essential time- and bit-critical processes remain excluded."[144] When extant artifacts are too valuable, too damaged, or too fragile to demonstrate interactively, models and simulations are invaluable, and software emulators have made great strides—the Living Computer Museum, for instance, offers emulations of the Apple II, the Macintosh SE, and others.[145] From its inception, the Heinz Nixdorf MuseumsForum planned to balance around thirty hands-on models with the same number of multimedia installations and simulations (including emulators for Apple II, C64, MS-DOS 1.x, Windows 1, etc.).[146] On the hardware side, the Italian Roberto Guatelli distinguished himself by building a number of working replicas of seminal devices that were originally associated with da Vinci, Pascal, Leibniz, Babbage, Hollerith, and others.[147] Faced with this tendency of museums to exhibit something "fake but true," we may complain that "museums of the history of technology are presented as materialized architectures of memory; however, they actually reveal not the past but rather always only the presence of things," whether or not the technical media on exhibit are nonfunctioning.[148] Nonetheless, models, simulations, or videos of interactions with devices can provide insights, even if understanding the history of mechanical, electromechanical, and digital devices in human communications benefits from hands-on experience.[149] Physical models are still an important form of hands-on active learning not fully comparable to more expensive simulations.[150] Rapid prototyping technology offers educational benefits while eliminating logistic difficulties of complex simulations or aging emulators; the explicitly didactic Konrad Zuse Computer Museum in Hoyerswerda demonstrates how mechanical models for teaching kinematics and dynamics or ball-and-stick models of complex molecules for teaching chemistry are gradually replaced with educational simulations.[151] Engaging physical models is not only good for active learning, it helps with learning disabilities relating to visual spatial perception. Some argue that hands-on interactions with models may help avoid gender bias due to differences in spatial cognition. The benefits of such models not only accrue to students of biology, math, aeronautics, engineering, and so on, but are just as plausible in teaching the history of technology.

Too often the story of computing is told merely as a "great inventor" story or a "great machine" story. For decades, the history of computing seemed to pursue a realization of the Turing machine, or more broadly build upon ideas developed over centuries by mathematicians such as Leibniz and Boole, Babbage and Lovelace, Gödel and Turing, or the like; a more robust historicization over the past decade gave rise to a critique of various implicit claims.[152] Science and technology studies argued that computer history ought to be seen not as a lab of models but as a series of transformations that can only be explained if we consider the interest and expertise of the people who shaped computing. Others pointed out that the history of humanity is intricately entangled with the history of technology in general and the technology of information in particular. Histories of technology tend to skew toward novelty, but here the epistemological value of history is emphasized instead. Many "new ideas" are actually older—networking and resource sharing, miniaturization and portability, hypertext and web, emulators and virtual reality, and so on. Nonetheless, there are new approaches—presenting the computer as a "digital machine," historicizing the conceptual inventory of computing, not to omit the inversion in the question of how the world got into the computer.[153] Historians tend to be fascinated primarily with genesis, emergence, and innovation, while museums are just as concerned with the aftermath. One important consideration at this juncture (which we had promised to return to earlier) is the distinction, subtle but consequential, between an art museum and a museum of technology. Unlike an art or design museum, you may think a computer museum appeals not to subjective aesthetic judgment but to objective comprehension.[154] However, the most cursory visit to any museum of technology reveals that they rely as much as any museum on aesthetic representation (images, drawings, charts, historical reconstructions, videos, simulations) to reconstitute a horizon of continuity and help explain the withdrawal of perceptible processes into boxes. They do not in fact exhibit merely specific isolated objects, like a chip or a cable or a computer box: they exhibit symbolic relations. In either case, the basis for museum success is the creation of aesthetic communication, whether for its own sake or for the sake of intellectual appreciation. Hence Lewis Mumford, with his conviction that museums are the pivotal artifact of our time, described an axiomatic transformation of museums from storehouse to powerhouse.[155] Underneath lurks a distinction between discourses supporting the mission of either type of museum: the history of technology (or perhaps more broadly the history of science) may or may not hold the same notions of collectability, representative sampling, acquisition, and deaccession that a curator of artworks does; either way, the method of disposal is more difficult than the decision whether or not to remove something.[156] This has not stopped computer museum founders from simulating exactly the discursive setup they perceived in art museums. While Gordon Bell's framework for a computer museum in Boston was a

list of "firsts" he coveted, asking what computers might be considered the
Mona Lisa of such a collection, most scholars subscribe to neither a great-
man theory nor a great-machine theory of computer history, just as art
history is no longer written in that heroic mode; neither computer history
nor art history is the story of exceptional flashes of genius. If the history of
science is the history of our world made by our tools, and the history
of technology is the history of our tools made by our world, they do not
relate to each other as the study of theory and of practice. If both differ
from the history of art (which itself is differentiated from the history of
aesthetics, art being clearly older than the discourses around aesthetic communication), nevertheless, "a curious set of parallels has evolved," Thomas
Elsaesser pointed out, between "the museum as a site of aesthetic distance
and reflection, and scientific instruments of calculation, of mathematics as
means of measuring and monitoring"—including the internet.[157] Both are
now expressions of a society of control, relying on data mining and self-
censorship, sensors and metrics—which makes the museum an apt site for
the confrontation of computing with its own history, up to and including
that of networked computing.[158]

Museum studies observe in granularity how moving objects draw more
attention than static exhibits, so fully functioning models of historical computers, and detailed emulations of software with a look and feel faithful to its
period, increase the attraction of an exhibit, and museum pedagogy is constantly monitoring demographic variables (age, education, gender, attention, visit duration) as controls for the success variables (the holding power
of individual artifacts, galleries, special exhibits, visitor feedback, and demonstrated learning effects). Exhibit effectiveness can be measured by changes
in audience behavior and evaluated on their consistency with stated aims
or objectives.[159] Of course, "the acquisition of facts and information cannot
be separated from the feelings, values, actions and locations associated with
those facts," and most certainly it hinges on curiosity and interest; but that
does not mean that the multidimensional experience of learning is as effective online as it is in our sensory environment.[160] The hook that arouses our
curiosity risks being snuffed out in an avalanche of impulses vying for our
divided attention online; museum pedagogy revolves around carefully calibrated attention.[161] Our interest can be drawn via sensory, intellectual, or
emotional pathways, and our pursuit of what is on offer depends on a balance of demands on our attention with our capacity to absorb information;

if this results in a sense of improved knowledge or skill, that is valuable feedback for the museum visitor.[162] Intrinsic motivations for a museum visit include, but should not be limited to, the exploration of a building and its exhibition layout, a perception of its special status that sets it apart from quotidian spaces, a sense of respect for the importance, value, or attraction of the exhibited objects and interactions, and a sense of discovery, surprise, curiosity, or even spectacle. Extrinsic motivations include, but are not limited to, exploration and discussion together with others, competitive or communal enjoyment of the visit, and a period of time that is set apart from our ordinary life experience, in terms of the multiple demands on our schedule or on our attention. This need not mean that one must invest a quiet and focused tour in a museum with the auratic status of a temple's formal atmosphere that suppresses our social instincts. The museum gaze signals a suppressed desire for touch and interaction; it aims for sublimation, not passive alienation.[163] Granted, there are barriers to access and to knowledge acquisition: the price of entry, restricted opening hours, overwhelming or under-explained exhibitions, a sense that this is not a family-friendly space, anything that inhibits exploration at an individual pace.[164] In those terms, the internet promises to help lower access barriers to museums.[165] Over 80 percent of museums let visitors comment publicly on their websites, three-quarters trawl social media to see what is said about their exhibits, and half of them routinely crowdsource feedback about new ideas or plans.[166] Yet all this increasing integration of museums and the internet only compounds the challenge of a museum of the internet.

For it is evident that "there really is no single model of just how the Internet works and what should be done at the physical level and what should be left to programs," as the lower layers of a protocol are implemented in hardware or firmware, and "many models exist for information infrastructures—the internet itself can be cut up conceptually in a number of different ways."[167] Academia has become keen to look at the internet's predecessors to mine its prehistory for explanations of where the actually existing internet may have failed to live up to the hype; this encouraged counterfactual thought experiments in computer historiography.[168] Having informed discussions about the future of the online world depends on preservation of sufficient historical materials about earlier systems as well as on a comparison mindset. Internet historian Marc Weber reminds us that "the commercial networks of the 1970s—Telenet, Tymnet, General Electric

Information Services (GEIS), the corporate-facing side of CompuServe—were more significant at the time than the research-only ARPANET and the experiments that eventually led to the Internet," and that Americans may better recall the BBS system of the 1980s and the multimedia CD-ROM of the 1990s, while French scholars may be more aware of the Minitel as a first mass-market web of the 1980s or of the datagram-based packet-switching research network CYCLADES of the 1970s.[169] An ancestral vision media historians like to invoke is science fiction author H. G. Wells's 1937 "World Brain" essay for the *Encyclopédie Française*, envisioning a "permanent world encyclopedia" of "the whole human memory" as "a world synthesis of bibliography and documentation with the indexed archives of the world." With hindsight, we need to draw distinctions between phantasms of archival totality or libraries' classificatory zeal and the internet, which due to its design remains unstable. "The starting point for revisionist histories of networking," we are reminded, "is an acceptance that the Internet is flawed, dangerous and ephemeral."[170] It may promise the world's knowledge and supplement database or library interactions, but fundamentally it is something different.

The Mundaneum in Mons, Belgium, is a unique museum that lays claim to making the story of the internet in part a Belgian story.[171] It was founded by Paul Otlet and Henri La Fontaine to revolutionize how documents are classified and connected. Their Office International de Bibliographie aimed to create a universal search engine for knowledge based on cards sorted by Melvil Dewey's universal decimal classification system. In 1934, a decade before Vannevar Bush published his ideas about a memex, four decades before Ted Nelson began working on his fabled Xanadu and Doug Engelbart sketched out his NLS online system, Otlet published a magisterial work of synthesis, the *Traité de Documentation*.[172] Part of its pacifist, internationalist, universalist mission was a scholarly setup providing automated electro-mechanical access to microfiche data linking all the world's knowledge.[173] Envisioning a range of affordances in the 1930s that we now call the web, video conferencing, mobile telephony, and cloud computing, the workstation uncannily anticipated communication formats that are now part and packet switch of our understanding of the internet.[174] Otlet's project of a Universal Book was to manifest connections each document has with all others and to open this referential structure to annotation and restructuring by each user. Since 1895, Otlet envisioned a master bibliography of the world's libraries but found one fatal flaw all systems shared—it stopped at bibliographical metadata; Otlet wanted to penetrate that boundary, to link up the substance, sources, and conclusions of all books. He imagined the *réseau* would eventually be accessible by phone lines, retrieving facsimiles projected onto a flat screen. It foretold what Vannevar Bush called for in 1945 with his memory extender: a reference network based not on classification but association.[175] Museum scholars pointed out that the rediscovery of Otlet in the 1990s as a forefather of the internet "coincided with new understandings of media and of museums in the light of developments in new media and computing."[176] The pivotal importance of Otlet to our current interpretation both of the features and of the bugs of the net notwithstanding, visits to the Mundaneum reveal this prolepsis; despite multilingual documentation at the core of the project, it draws fewer visitors each year to Mons, and despite efforts to balance the authentic character of the original exhibits with contemporary elements, the overall impression hovers between nostalgia and neglect.

This situation is radicalized when we consider net art as one use case for computer-savvy exhibition spaces. An argument could be made that the audience for net art far exceeds visitor numbers at any museum, yet "some net artworks cease functioning in less than five months."[177] A hybrid expression, drawing on both the history of computing and the history of art, is museum representation of computing as art. This is not the place to sort through art-world groupings and aesthetic arguments. If it sometimes seems as if museums are still having the same debates about the role of computing that they had in the 1960s, this need not imply a basic incompatibility between museum practice and networked communications; nonetheless, many people still seem to tacitly agree that art belongs in art galleries and art museums, not in science or technology museums, even if that art is highly reliant on computers and the internet. C@C or "computer-aided curating" was one of the earliest curatorial endeavors on the web, initiated 1993 to ask why it was easier to get an entire museum collection on the internet (albeit in thumbnail format) than to get a single work of net art into a museum space; the site stopped working in 1995.[178] A decade ago, a thought-provoking touring exhibition called *Collect the WWWorld: The Artist as Archivist in the Internet Age* explored the impact of computer-mediated communications on visual arts, including work by Ryder Ripps, the founder of an online collection of images, animations, sounds, and videos titled *Internet Archaeology*.[179] The flip side is illustrated by net art that deliberately plays on impermanence: collaborative work like *The Impermanence Agent*, a software art installation that washes away gradually in the course of your exploring it, or works like Mark Napier's *Digital Landfill*, Garrett Lynch's *Things to Forget*, and William Pope L.'s *The Black Factory*.[180] Even as such art about the internet was made and shared on the internet, the discussion about how to preserve the net and its native art scenes for later generations raised thorny questions. As Wolfgang Ernst warns, an "archival language has yet to be developed for digitized networked artworks," though enthusiasts have set out to try and formulate it.[181] Flying in the face of the idea that the internet automatically opens things up for individuals, consider that the *Rhizome Artbase*, a pioneering archive of media arts since 1999, went through three main phases: (a) open submission, 1999–2010; (b) filtered submission, 2010–2015; (c) closed/by invitation only, 2015–2020.[182] Often the people bringing museum exhibits online are not curators but archivists or educators, and instead of an exploration of the net as an exhibition space, they follow models of collection management.[183] Another issue is that a museum is not simply a repository but provides context that helps tell stories: you can see different things next to one another and can process their juxtaposition with others; this can be done in a digital environment but does not always have the same impact.

Despite all these problems, it may still be feasible to argue that the internet sort of acts as a museum of computing. If a museum is defined as an institution that collects, documents, preserves, exhibits, and interprets evidence and information to make it widely accessible, then arguably the internet has come to simulate those functions. Until the museum reconfigured computing and the internet as special (re)collections, the net of computers itself served as the form of historic retention.[184] Once attention is calibrated toward the mediality of computer-mediated communication, we participate in the musealization of the net. Inversely, computer museums increasingly rely on replica hardware and emulated software, simulating the heritage they curate. But there are major forces obscuring those histories. Before the privatization of the internet backbone and the commercialization of the web, the understanding was that computer networks served basic research; before the black-boxing of apps and operating systems, for several decades of bootstrapping and experimentation, the understanding was that computing served scientific needs—but we tend to forget that now. Of course, the internet has a history, and it obviously would not exist without computers, but by the same token it obscures infrastructural history. Enormous investments in a past to be restored, maintained, and defended are symptoms of doubt about our present.[185] Excavating the media archaeology of this rich heritage is becoming ever more complicated. Even those who believe that "the internet is by nature a kind of museum" worry that museums of the internet, preserving and elevating artifacts of the defining techno-culture of our times, make interactive computer-mediated communication homogeneous and exclusionary.[186]

As computer museums establish a (shrinking but distinctive) difference between their holdings and candidates for addition, they simultaneously maintain a significant distance from quotidian technology. This is one way they fail to capture major developments of the actually existing internet. The exploitation of the domain name system, the monopolization of search engines and browsers, the withdrawal of governments from regulatory policy, the ascendance of platforms (and the dominance of platform lobbyists), and the complete capture of mobile devices by surveillance, all point in directions rarely represented in museums. Computer history museums are less likely to thematize open-source software, hacking, or computer activism than the sanitized version pleasing corporate sponsors. "By the patronage of the museums, the ruling metropolitan oligarchy of financiers and officeholders establish their own claims to culture: more than that, they fix their own standards of taste, morals, and learning," as Mumford observed.[187] Computer museums offer this paradoxical compensation for the destructive sweep of modernizing: the shocking progress of technical media provokes a selective conservation financed by profits from innovation. The impulses for aestheticizing historical technology originate in how museums help us react to industrial innovation by differentiating, though musealizing technology can create a false sense of continuity. Arguably, the fundamental impulse for the appearance and proliferation of computer history museums (and of the musealization of the internet) since the early 1990s is that this allows institutions to neutralize the history of computing, to create a semblance of digital culture as settled, historicized, closed. Yet the ideological dimension of museum exhibition invalidates the idea that its objects can be neutralized. For the museum's primary functions of preservation and exhibition pivot around a translation from the primary language of computing into the secondary language of history. Musealization as a selective process produces surplus value, and the discourse around the history of computing and the history of the internet creates cultural capital. Under the guise of preserving, protecting, and restoring computer history, these institutions do not in fact rescue it from the abusive treatment of mercantile interests—it is how those museums manufacture history in the image of what they pretend to withdraw computers from, namely the very social forces that brought computers into the museum and are continuously bringing the museum onto computer networks: museums replicate the tensions of capital, with its fits of accumulation and expenditure, stockpiling and liquidation.

3 FakeBit: Let It Bleep, Keep It Sample

In the ubiquitous streams of our audiovisual media sensurrounds, a note-worthy yet still academically neglected gaming culture is the enduring popularity of 8-bit music, the sound of retro-gaming.[1] At demoparties around the globe, programmers showcase artistic audiovisual works and compete in chiptune genres.[2] Whether we think of *Information Chase*, the six-pack of GameBoy-inspired tracks by Bit Shifter, the *MeanTime* EP by 8BitWeapon, or go back to a Dubmood collection, the chiptune scene remains creative, delighting in limitations of storage space and expressive power from earlier technical eras.[3] Media history documents how every technology of repetition seems to accelerate forgetting but also aids cultural memory—and new media generate not just hype but also nostalgia.[4] This holds equally for art projects like the tour of arcade and console games that is *ROM CHECK FAIL* or for commercial games like *Mega Man 9*, playable on Nintendo Wii. Here the aesthetics of the NES era is called up in detail; a legacy mode emulates the low tact rates and flickering screens, and above all the limited sound palette of its ancestors. One illustration of technostalgia are retro text editing apps like Cathode and Blinky, downloads from the Apple Store. Among the colorful and graphically animated present of the Apple interface culture, there are apparently many users with a real longing for emulators of Unicode terminals and text editors with the slowed-down and angular charm of flickering pixels. While Cathode even offers you a choice between different technology generations, Blinky affords you the capability of turning images into ASCII "text art" and of playing with burn-in and fade as if our screen was back in 1976 again. And if you decline to pay for Cathode, the effects grow weaker over the course of time, static and flicker increase until you reset the app. However, what both apps neglect is the acoustic dimension of the same retro desire.[5] The perennial media-historical hit

"Daisy Bell" accompanies that dimension since 1892, from Alexander Graham Bell's phone demo to Donald Duck in 1950 and on to the first IBM 7090 singing lessons in 1961 at Bell Labs in New Jersey, famous since Kubrick's *2001: A Space Odyssey* (1968), not to omit Steve Dompier on his Altair before the Homebrew Computer Club in 1975.[6] The same song also appears on television in *Futurama* and in pop songs that sample or cover it. Technostalgia is central in cultural reflection about video game culture, whether in Ernest Cline's *Ready Player One*, in films like *Scott Pilgrim vs. the World* (2010), or in the Videogames Live summer concerts first organized by Tommy Tallarico, where symphony orchestras play cover versions of the tracks gamers came to love.

It may seem counterintuitive to talk about a widespread current of nostalgia and retro styling in a new medium like gaming that has been so pivotally characterized by rapid technical advances. But there is a serious retro movement, with its own conferences and journals and record labels.[7] As always with nostalgia, we recognize it as an expression of resistance to inexorable technical progress: "progress did not cure nostalgia but exacerbated it," as Boym writes.[8] Though it may seem rather obvious, the spatial, textual, interactive, and ludic affordances of games have changed quite a lot since the first agglomerations of computer sounds, animations, and controls. Nostalgia is of interest here because it is a kind of memorial construct—a yearning for a past experience or situation that in most cases never existed.[9] One might go further with Jameson and speak of a "desperate attempt to appropriate a missing past"; indeed, the retro sounds discussed in this chapter can occasionally give that impression.[10] Why would gaming seek to recuperate a missing past? Because while computer museums and game museums have sprung up around the globe, few have managed to keep old hardware and old software functioning well enough to allow a full interactive experience of what earlier technology not only looked, but felt and sounded like. Examples include the Strong Museum of Play in upstate New York, the Computer Game Museum in Berlin, or the National Videogame Museum in Frisco, Texas.[11]

Even after mere decades of gaming, the difference between early and current games can seem enormous; but the point in retro-gaming is rarely the painstaking reconstruction of exactly the same limited audiovisual palette and maddening haptics that one would have encountered decades earlier—it is rather the pursuit of a highly selective vision of pure, simple, unadulterated enjoyment suggested by an earlier era. It is often less about forensic computing or emulators than it is about other inventive modes of simulating a historical interactive situation.[12] The appeal of retro modes in gaming culture appeals to an often imaginary but culturally constitutive moment to which we can date our fascination with gaming, as Fenty suggests: "The nostalgia felt for video games is not nostalgia for a past state before the trauma of the games disrupted us, but a desire to recapture that mind-altering experience of being in a game for the first time."[13] The retro bent, as seen in merchandising, in new retro-like titles, in film adaptations and fan fiction, is perhaps most pronounced in the mainstreaming of iconic game lore—whether from 1970s arcade gaming, home computer games on Commodore or Atari from the '80s, or console titles from Nintendo or Sega from the early '90s. As scholars have noted, much of the attention here continues to go to titles like *Pacman* (Midway Games, 1980), *Donkey Kong* (Nintendo, 1981), or *Legend of Zelda* (1986).[14] The NES afforded the sound for *Legend of Zelda* with its 11-bit Ricoh RP2A03 up to 2,048 frequencies: a lot compared to the more limited capabilities of the TIA chip with 5-bit yielding 32 tones, or the POKEY with 8-bit and 256 frequencies, although the NES programmers ended up using only 57 frequencies for *Zelda*. Yet the fact that these continue to hold an undeniable attraction not only to their aging first fans but to several successive generations can be explained in part by the pop cultural expansion of merchandising, and in part by newer titles that expand on the original intellectual property. Moreover, the sounds of gaming have been appropriated for other media formats, including television, cinema, advertising, and pop music, since the late 1970s; one infamous example is Nelly Furtado's 2007 pop song "Do It," which was based directly, though without permission, on the Amiga track "Acidjazzed Evening" by Janne Suni and its Commodore 64 chiptune cover by Glenn Rune Gallefoss—a controversy that agitated the likes of MTV and *Rolling Stone* and even led to a lawsuit against Furtado's producer Timbaland.[15] Concomitant legal issues raise doubts about fans or pirates shouldering the full burden of preserving digital heritage.[16] In this chapter, I will argue that from the moment we focus on gaming music instead of relegating it to the background, we introduce an element of nostalgia. That is because in gaming, much like in film, music is used non-diegetically to accentuate and enhance but not distract from the visual spectacle. And if we foreground those sounds, it is an act of nostalgia for an audiovisual

form of entertainment that valued music and endowed it with cultural dig-
nity, while in gaming for decades it was neither particularly complex nor
endowed with high production value. Computer and video games may be
conceivable without sound, but the vast majority count on a diegetic interface design that pivots on sound spaces and signals, not to mention non-
diegetic mood music. To get to that state of audiovisual integration took a
complex series of technical and aesthetic decisions.

Computers have always made sounds—"from the clicking of the beads
on an abacus and the early electro-mechanical analog computers to the
relays and audified bit streams of mainframes and the mini-computer
sound hacks at MIT in the 50s."[17] Even the pre-electronic era of computing was quite noisy, as the extant pneumatic, mechanical, or electromechanical switches in museums around the globe attest; *The Imitation Archive*
(2015) is a remarkable album of music Matt Parker made with the sounds
of a reconstructed 1943 Colossus, the world's first large-scale programmable electronic computer, at Bletchley Park.[18] A comparable recording
using the Bletchley Park Colossus by chiptune artist Pixelh8 (aka Matthew
Applegate) is titled *Obsolete* (2009).[19] Inverting the common attitude of
audiophile noise suppression, both harness the creaky sounds of venerable
computers reconstructed by the British National Museum of Computing in
soundscapes full of glitch, crunch, hiss (indeed, the hissing, beeping, and
grunting of early computers had diagnostic value: in the 1950s programmers would attach audio amplifiers to their machines for a so-called noise
probe, listening to the patterns of their calculations).[20] Of course, most
games are not silent, and indeed games play an important role in computer
sound developments—not only because the first dedicated sound chips
were developed for them, but because the increasing demands on games
provoked soundscape development.[21] By 1962 *Spacewar* on a PDP-1 came
with its simple register of sounds; *Computer Space* by Nutting Associates in
1971 offered different outer space and war sounds—"rockets and thrusters
engines, missiles firing, and explosions"—and with *Pong*, the commercial
sound effect of the early '70s took off.[22] Indeed, early gaming only had any
sounds if they were coaxed out of the hardware, as Atari programmer Acorn
reports about *Pong*:

> The truth is, I was running out of parts on the board. Nolan [Bushnell, one of
> Atari's founders] wanted the roar of a crowd of thousands—the approving roar
> of cheering people when you made a point. Ted Dabney [the other founding

member] told me to make a boo and a hiss when you lost a point, because for every winner there's a loser. I said, "Screw it, I don't know how to make any one of those sounds. I don't have enough parts anyhow." Since I had the wire wrapped on the scope, I poked around the sync generator to find an appropriate frequency or a tone. So those sounds were done in half a day. They were the sounds that were already in the machine.[23]

Pong not only had to overcome limited technology, but simulates the radar and sonar query, as Pias demonstrates in his media-archaeological discussion of audiovisual feedback.[24] Starting with *Space Invaders* (1978), programmers had some storage for sound samples, as, for example, in a descending sequence of four tones as a slowly accelerating signature of the extraterrestrials. Atari's *Asteroids* (1979) played two tones as theme; such elements are laboriously wrenched from the hardware.[25] By 1980, sound chips, also known as programmable sound generator (PSGs), became affordable, allowing continuous sound loops, as, for example, in the Namco/Midway title *RallyX*, which modulates a melody over six bars before it repeats. Since 1985, the 8-bit sounds of early gaming are at the core of a scene that continues producing popular tunes, as by *8bit Weapon*, *ComputeHer*, and others.[26] Whether emulated or generated on historical hardware, their synthetic electro sounds found their way out of net labels into dance clubs and festivals (like the Blip Festival in Tokyo, Pulsewave in New York, or BRKFest in Liverpool) as well as into art galleries.

Whether we consider these musical offerings a subculture, a nostalgic hobby, an anti-commercial statement, or a manifestation of media-archaeological research, let us take a look first at the factors affecting early video game music before returning to the question of how we interpret their recurrence in contemporary culture.[27] Most commentators agree with Montfort and Bogost in admitting that neither the frequency range nor the sonority of the Atari VCS promised anything particularly musical; generally, neither the melodic nor the harmonic capacities of early audio chips are very advanced, resulting in an emphasis on rhythm in chiptunes.[28] It is hardly surprising that many professional game audio experts relish and embrace new capacities (including generative audio since the nineties), even as the recalcitrant retro scene that luxuriates in the most infuriating hardware limitations is rapidly expanding.[29] But in some ways, sound in games did not change all that fundamentally despite all the technical progress since then; only recently, an accomplished game audio professional went on record with the complaint that "audio is always the lowest priority for game developers—always has been, always will be."[30] Similarly, even as one can make the case that audio is pivotal for a take on computing that is not held captive by superficial time lines of great designers or great machines, observers and practitioners of game sound complain about "a surprising dearth of literature that concerns the use of sound in games."[31] Although game scores can now be considered for a Grammy and indeed appear regularly on radio or in concert, neither musicology nor game studies pursue the study of game audio very systematically.[32] Although computer museums worldwide lure their audience not only with Turing and Leibniz, but also proudly with old slot machines and dusty game consoles, sounds belong to the largely unexplored secrets of computer game history: what makes it into the inventory of collections in Boston or Palo Alto or Cambridge, not to mention Karlsruhe, Berlin, or Paderborn, is only a very limited selection (see chapter 2). The Centre for Computing History in Cambridge, England, rents some of their consoles to nostalgic gamers— from *Pong* and Atari 2600 up to the first PlayStation, from Commodore 64, Sinclair Spectrum, and BBC Micro to Nintendo NES and Sega Megadrive. How do we explain the peculiar attraction these historical artifacts quite obviously are, not only for those who once played *Discs of Tron* on an Amiga 1000 and remember its primitive bleeps and clicks? Let us quickly retrace how it is even possible for computers to play music before we return to consoles and their peculiarly attractive limitations.

The availability of sonic environments of music, effects, and speech in games is a direct consequence of research in computer music, which also means a significant expansion of what is considered musical sound. What do we hear when we go to the Internet Archive and cue up a nerdcore track like "hc152 too bleep to bloop" by 8Bit Betty?[33] Remarkably, it matters neither for the in-game role of those sounds nor for their transfer into pop, dance, or even art music whether the sounds that accompany and define those games even exist beyond the world of play. As physicist Meyer-Eppler already stated in the early 1950s about radio broadcast: it is secondary how "such noises arose and whether they could have been heard before their electric stage in the form of sound energy."[34] Fantastic yarns like Ernest Cline's hit *Ready Player One* (and its cinematic adaptation by Spielberg) or Austin Grossman's *You* indulge in the fantasy that playful exploration of obsolete technology leads the retro-obsessed protagonist to victory, or at least extra lives.[35] But what does it mean when known songs by bands like Radiohead, the Stone Roses, or other pop groups are reproduced in minimal cover versions by the primitive machine known as Mr. Hopkinson's Computer as if they were a vintage game endboss singing in the shower? How do we get to the remarkable creolization of musical styles that is "8-Bit Reggae"?[36] The attraction of the 8-bit era for sound environments and music programming does not lie exclusively in its inherent limitations—it is also a question of game design, and many of these titles were essentially characterized by loops and repetitions, thus by incessant replay. Beyond that, it is probably undecidable whether the prominence of science fiction and fantasy settings for games is a reason for, or rather a consequence of, technical limitations—yet it is a fact that these games allow sounds for which there is no direct equivalence in our experiential world, so that low-fidelity effects are not only practical but credible. Futuristic and extraterrestrial concepts allow an unconventional sound design, and from this vantage point, chiptunes are both the promise of a technically easily accessible music and an expression of nostalgia for an age of playful access to new technologies.

We may trace the legacy of chiptunes (sometimes dubbed "micromusic") back to experiments at Bell Labs, at MIT, at Turing's Manchester University lab.[37] We know that a Zuse computer played 1-bit music in Germany as early as 1958, and that Peter Samson as a student at MIT used a lightpen to control a piece of music on a TX-0 in 1959 (a few years later he wrote a harmony compiler for the PDP-1 at MIT).[38] And though we have little information about the Christmas carols Alan Turing made his Manchester Ferranti play in 1951, when we think of computer music now, we mostly associate the concept with an almost infinite breadth of possible sounds.[39] Yet it took years until the suggestion that aroused Turing's amazement and Shannon's courage could at last turn into a veritable industry: "Shannon wants to feed not just data to a brain, but *cultural* things! He wants to play music to it!"[40] By the same token, the hypothesis of a real encounter of music and computer poses the question how this would be audible, how it would be heard, for gamers on the one hand and for media studies on the other hand. The media-archaeological distinction Ernst draws between acoustics and music usefully differentiates between listening and hearing, but in his reference to Wiener's mathematics of the interpolation and extrapolation of time series, he situates his media-archaeological analysis below cultural semantics, having little to say about the contingent turns of technical history and aesthetics beyond a mathematics of the sound or a communication theory of acoustics.[41] I would rather turn to the history of computer sound without drawing a distinction between sound and music just yet.

In 1956, Bell Labs engineers Max Mathews and John Pierce returned home after a piano recital in New Jersey and began to speculate about the possibility that a computer could tickle the ebony and ivory keys. Pierce, one of the inventors of the transistor and a pioneer in satellite communication, was Mathews's boss and had enough leverage to make sufficient computing cycles available. (After Pierce left Bell Labs, he worked briefly at the CalTech Jet Propulsion Lab in Pasadena, but then became professor of music at Stanford.) In short order, Mathews presented Music Compiler I, a piece of software for the production of structured synthetic noises—a potent ancestor of all synthesizers, nowadays the most popular of all musical instruments.[42] Several years later, version 4 was used for a demo of an IBM machine with punch card input and magnetic tape expenditure, 32 kB of memory, and a processor with less than 5 kHz. It performed the media-historical classic "Daisy, or a Bicycle for Two," a song by Harry Dacre also used by Alexander Graham Bell for a demonstration of the phone in 1892. In Mathews's cover version, it also appears on the 1961 LP *Music from Mathematics*, as its liner notes point out:

> The patterns of human speech are analyzed in the same manner as the instrumental sounds. The computer is then programmed to speak the desired words. On this band the computer not only was programmed to sing but also to simulate a Honky Tonky type of piano accompaniment that was popular during the era when this song was a hit.[43]

A personal demonstration of such algorithmic sounds at Murray Hill impressed Stanley Kubrick, who famously allowed his computer HAL to sing in the film *2001: A Space Odyssey*. However, for the recording of the song Kubrick did not use a Bell Labs computer but an ELTRO Information Rate Changer—a device that manipulates magnetic tape with two heads, as becomes clear when HAL's voice sinks lower the less storage space is available: this is clearly an analog media effect that would not happen in digital media but would have had to be programmed. Wendy Carlos, the sound engineer and composer for this scene, was only too familiar with the technology at the time, and in a 1971 interview confirmed the use of the ELTRO.[44] Since then we cannot be surprised to come across cover versions of the same song by pop bands like Blur or electronica outfits like

Rechenzentrum. It is also worth noting that the synclavier has been made since 1974, directly derived from the software developed by Max Mathews, and John Chowning at Stanford used it to develop the first Yamaha synthesizers and keyboards—now the most popular musical instrument. In short, both the generation of electronic sounds and the description of rules that make them recognizable as music are greatly expanded because of that Bell Labs invention.

As computer pioneer Ornstein reports with amusement in his memoirs, his first encounter with a computer making music was at a demo day at MIT, and the experience stuck in his mind even as he went from working at Lincoln Labs (where SAGE, the semiautomated ground environment, was developed) to Bolt Beranek & Newman (the consulting firm helping developed the early internet) and later to Xerox PARC (the influential skunk works where many enduring computing interface solutions were first developed):

> One day there was an open-house demonstration of computer facilities at MIT (not, of course, including the Cape Cod system, which was classified). A new core memory had been installed in MTC, replacing the one that had been moved to Whirlwind, and a program had been written that enabled it to play music (by carefully switching the inputs to an amplifier back and forth at just the right frequencies). This was my first encounter with, and must have been a very early instance of, the use of a computer to play music.[45]

Ornstein, who back then had a piano in his Lincoln Labs office, discovered that the TX-2 computer not only had the (in 1958) impressive storage capacity of 64 k but also an analog–digital converter, which meant it should be able to read and print analog sound signals; he soon became interested in the question of teaching a computer musical notation.

> Although it was many years before word processing would become commonplace, I suspected that a computer might be able to help with the problem of notating music, just as text processors now help writers of prose. My initial thought was that the computer should be able, by analyzing the sound, to decide what notes were played, and then print out a score. After all, musicians could do it; why not a computer?

This was the same machine that not only gave rise to Sketchpad, the revolutionary graphics program invented by Ivan Sutherland, but also important experiments in artificial intelligence that later led to the founding of the computer company DEC. However, Ornstein underestimated the physical properties of piano sounds, and overestimated the ability of the TX-2 to "hear" them; his research was probably more applicable to sonar, for which programs were written at the time.[46] A few years later, Ornstein returned to his earlier musings about frequencies and converters when he helped BBN put together the first routers for the ARPAnet. But his experiments from the 1950s really bore fruit when in 1980 he wrote to several American composers (among them Leonard Bernstein, Aaron Copland, and Samuel Barber) and asked them about their notation habits. Together with a student, John T. Maxwell III, he wired a synthesizer to a computer to analyze notation; at the time there was no MIDI yet, but they created the first functional notation program, called Mockingbird.[47] One of the more interesting results of Ornstein's research for our concerns is the fact that synchronization in computers becomes more problematic the faster the cycles are. Attempting to prove wrong anyone who prematurely claimed there could be a glitch-free circuit, Ornstein started publicly deriding any such designs as mere "move-the-glitch circuits":

> In every case we were able to determine to where, in the design, the ingenious designer had moved the glitch. In each case, the glitch persisted, and the presenter was brought into alignment with this new correct view of the universe. Our fervor approached that of religious zealots. It was our mission to stamp out anti-glitch apostasy wherever we could find it.

The problem of glitch, the unavoidable chance event introducing errors and distortions, is well known to computer users. But strictly speaking, even electricity needs to be considered a source of noise and error in music now. There is a common misconception that power delivery is ancillary in music production and reproduction, despite the fact that electronics, speakers, and cables are all sensitive to it. A related bias is that much of the noise that impacts a performance or a recording of a performance stems from external sources. But sound does not originate at microphones, nor is it simply captured equally by tape, CD, or LP. The voltage and current of amplified instruments, of recording equipment, and of reproduction equipment do in fact determine the sonic characteristics. If a power source in your audio reproduction chain is unstable, then the output will be too, regardless of the quality of the information supplied by the signal. Electromagnetic or radio frequency interference can come not only from nearby devices (Wi-Fi, Bluetooth, 5G, dimmer lights, microwave ovens, etc.), but also from the audio equipment itself. Modern electronics have complex circuits that produce high-frequency noise that is difficult to filter or shield off; as power supplies convert AC to DC, they generate switching transients that reflect onto the power line, unless complex isolation is designed for them. So while we got used to the fact that computers will buzz, hum, or generate heat, we tend to forget that musical instruments and stereo equipment do the same. And even if power utility noise today is orders of magnitude lower than it was just decades ago, it cannot be completely eliminated. Some genres have therefore reacted by a valorization of glitch and error, embracing the limits of technology.

It is an interesting question why, despite rising storage capacities and processing cycles, we witnessed what basically amounts to a cult of the glitch—and a cult of 8-bit game sounds.[48] How does acoustic material that remains far below the technically possible become an aesthetic choice? Why do tracks like "Come Back to Me" from the *Error Repeat* collection by Australian outfit little-scale hold sufficient appeal to be archived for posterity?[49] As elsewhere in digital culture, it is a matter of the transcoding of analog impulses into digital signals whose numeric representations are modulated and varied under the technical conditions of automation in order to satisfy the requirements of a particular channel. A hearing simulator connects the device under test to a microphone in such a way that the working load of the device tested is as close to the same as if used on a human ear. The need for modeling the correct impedance increases with the proximity of the device under test to the ear. Modeling the input impedance of the human ear becomes more important as the acoustic output impedance of the device being tested increases. This setup to measure frequency response curves and nudge them closer to the target distribution is used both in audio design and in reviews of audio devices, from microphones and speakers to headphones or hearing aids. Technical knowledge (about bandwidth and amplitudes sampled, bit rates and word lengths) has direct aesthetic consequences, cutting across telephony, music, television, cinema, and games. Music history nerds claim that the capacity of a CD was chosen to accommodate the recorded length of Beethoven's Ninth Symphony (at Karajan's speed), and it is documented that Stravinsky composed a serenade so it would fit on one 78-rpm side of vinyl.[50] Similar things hold true for game sounds.

Neither telephony nor games have the luxury of a lot of capacity, which helps explain the effort and creativity necessary to represent sound and music even under severely curtailed technical conditions in a recognizable, relevant, and entertaining manner. Among the many compression algorithms (from the Fraunhofer MP3 to Sony's ATRAC, Windows WMA, and Apple AAC), there are some that leave the data almost or completely intact, for instance, the open source compression Ogg Vorbis used for games like *Doom 3*, *Unreal Tournament 2004*, *Myst IV*, *Grand Theft Auto San Andreas*, or *America's Army*. Even with the rapid increase in available storage space, the room granted to sounds has not grown proportionately.[51] In fact, for quite some time game consoles did not provide any storage for prerecorded sound or music (whether in analog or digital formats) and had to rely on the existing limited hardware to generate them instead. The combination of a sound chip from the 1980s like the General Instruments AY-3-8910 with an ADSR Envelope Generator (for attack, decay, sustain, release) offers modulated sounds on the Sega Master System or the Sinclair ZX Spectrum. A similar chip of the same era, the Texas Instruments SN76489, served in consoles like the ColecoVision and Sega Genesis as well as in the BBC Micro Computer, while Nintendo's *Donkey Kong* from 1981 onwards used a DAC chip that performed digital analog conversion, and Atari's *Indiana Jones and the Temple of Doom* game could call upon several sound chips and a digital–analog converter. The Atari VCS or 2600 that still fires up the chiptune scene to this day features a chip known as the Television Interface Adapter, or TIA. For sound, it offers two channels, each with a 4-bit waveform selector, combining to generate up to sixteen different wave forms—though the most used are a sinus, two sawtooth, and one rectangular wave, plus a few percussive noises.[52] Depending on whether one uses the PAL or the NTSC version of an Atari VCS, the frequency filter makes composing for this platform risky, as one author of a sequencer kit for chiptune music warns: "Although each set contains notes that are close to being in tune, you can still end up with songs that sound pretty bad if you aren't careful."[53] The Nintendo NES offered five programmable sound gates, with two channels devoted to about eight octaves of sound range, another channel to low sounds, one to noise, and one even allowed samples (for instance, for recorded voice or short sound effects). Mostly the typical sound of a NES game uses one channel for a melody, one for harmony, and one for a bass line, occasionally combining with sound effects; usually the music is programmed in loops of eight bars each that simply repeat. Even a small shift between the two pulse channels also permits the generation of echo or vibrato effects, for instance, in the 1987 game *Metroid*.

When IBM introduced their first personal computer in April 1981, the platform offered the first time sound cards that could be swapped, and in the effort to keep up with successful competition from Commodore and Apple after 1984, the IBM PC had a sound card from Texas Instruments that had already proved itself in game consoles. The Sierra Online game *King's Quest* in 1984 was one of the first to fully deploy not only the graphical and textual capabilities of the home computer, but also its sound potential. Soon the development of the "adventure game interpreter" game engine for *King's Quest* also led to other popular game titles like *Police Quest* and *Leisure Suit Larry*. The Commodore NIC-20 and C64 as well as the Apple II were designed as game platforms from the start, so they had not only advanced graphics but better sound as well. Yet at the time the sonic possibilities of games were limited by the fact that games distributed on 5.25 inch floppies or on magnetic tape had less space left for audio the more the demands from game graphics rose. A floppy disc storing up to 170 kB usually left less than 10 kB for music and sound, while magnetic tape was slower than floppies or cartridges. The use of magnetic tape for program data offered a rare opportunity for software pirates: as binary data streams were stored as audible frequencies (1,200 Hz for a zero, 2,400 Hz for a one), but Atari used only the right stereo channel of stereo cassettes for 8-bit devices, other material could be stored on the left track.[54] This also allowed, though its implementation was rare, the looping of recorded material to the speaker of an attached TV set, so music could be heard while loading a program; the tape version of the 1986 game *Warhawk* permitted the player to listen to music while playing. On hardware like the Commodore C64 and the TRS-80, gamers later found a hack that pushed its sound capabilities beyond the SID chip by connecting the CPU to a cassette port and sending the data not to a recorder but to an amplifier, resulting in a sequence of bleeps.[55] But most gaming setups eschewed the slower tape media in favor of data carriers that were less easily copied or corrupted. One way or another, game designers had to tickle the maximum out of the available chipsets, which meant they were mostly restricted to simple loops. Only in the late 1980s would 16-bit chips permit games to deploy the FM synthesis pioneered by Chowning, for instance in the Sega Genesis MegaDrive, the Super NES, and later consoles, so the end of the 8-bit era and the availability of significantly more storage space finally allowed for sound effects and music that were no longer programmed for severely curtailed technical environments—and yet remarkably, it is 8-bit sounds that hold enduring appeal.

One fascinating aspect of this creative derivative of game culture is found in remix culture—specifically in the enduring popularity of remixing the odd and awkward sounds of original Commodore C64 games. The website www.remix64.com (devoted exclusively to the C64 and Amiga music remix community) explicitly directs voting members to evaluate each upload in three distinct categories: technical impression, artistic impression, and nostalgic impression.[56] Regarding that third category and its distinction from the second, it should be mentioned that a recurring and controversial discussion topic is how close one may get to the original, or what the properties of the original are that one should try to approximate; in certain cases this can make the result predictable, resulting in a lower score on the artistic scale, while in other cases the nostalgic score falls short of the artistic one if greater freedom in remixing is claimed. For the title music of typical 1980s games like the C64 game *Cybernoid* (Hewson, 1988), which sold more than 22 million times, the remix64 site offers at least two dozen versions.[57] This popularity seems not at all stunted by the fact that the central sound chip of the Commodore C64 could only produce three mono channels— quite the opposite: the very limitation of the hardware is what made the 8-bit sound popular enough to become part of pop, TV soundtracks, the dance floor, or art installations.[58]

Just like musicians seeking to harness computers for music, game composers quickly adapted to the problematic aspects of the systems they used and "learned to use musical patterns that avoided the notes that sounded 'off,'" as McAlpine points out.[59] For example, the Atari VCS produced nine notes reasonably well, so the console's Television Interface Adapter's 1-bit tone generator restricted the acceptable choices, even though it offered two 4-bit volume registers (amounting to sixteen levels of volume).[60] When Atari introduced the 5200 "Super System," it hoped to convey the sense that it was twice as powerful as the VCS (which had been renamed the 2600); while its graphics relied on the Alphanumeric Television Interface Control (ANTIC) and the Graphics Television Interface Adapter, for sound and controller input it used a separate chip, the Pot Keyboard Integrated Circuit (POKEY), supporting up to four audio channels. Its tone generation and control was similar to that of the TIA, but the POKEY operated two sound channels at 16-bit precision (or one 16-bit and two 8-bit channels).[61]

Since POKEY sounds became "classics" of the chiptune world, soon enthusiasts emulated one on a modern microcontroller to take those old Atari
chiptunes into the contemporary environment.[62] While the POKEY could
have competed successfully against the sound interface device (SID) in the
Commodore 64, it was soon phased out; yet both the SID and the POKEY
remain centerpieces of the chiptune scene. Enthusiasts have been collating
chiptune music at sites like ASME and HVSC to keep the sounds of the 8-bit
era playing on modern hardware.[63] Meanwhile, the first Sinclair to feature a
dedicated onboard sound device was the ZX Spectrum, launched in the UK
with the promise that it "can make sounds of an infinite variety."[64] Users
soon found that in fact it offered one channel of 1-bit playback across a ten-
octave range—effectively not much more than a beep. Moreover, the loops
of the typical game music generated shifting pulse widths that affected timbre and volume, resulting in what McAlpine describes as "an undesirable
roughness to the sound."[65] Whereas the SID in the Commodore 64 was far
more accommodating, it too had its limitations, and composers who ran
up against them would soon decide to use what happens at those limits.
Many programmers were oddly content to put out "out-of-tune sounds and
filters that produced only quiet."[66] The Nintendo NES, in turn, used a Ricoh
RP2A03 CPU that integrated the audio processing; it afforded five channels
of sound, and Nintendo exercised stricter quality control than the competition over its games. The Nintendo sound became a hallmark, and Nintendo
stuck with that style even after newer consoles and computers introduced
more sophisticated multichannel sound capacities. The SNES, for instance,
with its combination of an 8-bit coprocessor and a separate digital sound
processor that could mix eight channels in 16-bit stereo, still featured game
titles that intentionally harked back to the audio style of the NES era, and
arguably this adherence to an 8-bit house style continued with many of the
most successful titles for the GameCube and Wii.

  In the 1990s, fans of the vintage game sounds began to write and share
music in bulletin boards and other online communities, whether using
Amiga or Atari or other devices to generate trackers; this demo scene soon
developed live events as well.[67] The scene also shared software to emulate the legacy chips. The first commercially released tracker was quickly
cloned.[68] Even today, demoparties feature tracker music competitions for
tunes written with the aid of sequencer software.[69] Soon ProTracker, for
instance, produced Amiga music from the early 1990s, while Nerdtracker

(running on MS-DOS) generated Nintendo NES sounds. If you wonder how (rather than why) someone might make a PC sound like an older console, this can be readily achieved by emulators that model the capacities and limitations of that legacy 2A03 chip (for a discussion of emulation, see chapter 1). Trackers like ReNoise are now accepted as an inexpensive alternative to music software and "can reproduce a wide range of chip types by adjusting some of the electrical parameters of the simulation."[70] Just as interestingly, the demo scene in Poland, Finland, and Germany has recently found acceptance by UNESCO as intangible cultural heritage.[71]

There are, however, several controversies around the authenticity of chiptunes, and many participants in the demo scene consider the use of emulation anathema; to those purists, emulation can only yield what they call FakeBit.[72] Anything not composed on original hardware but using sound chip emulation is considered the equivalent of performing folk music without the traditional folk music instruments. At first glance, this desire for authenticity may be comprehensible, but as McAlpine comments, the reality is more complex—the Amiga, for example, did not in fact have a dedicated sound chip but already used samples:

> Alongside software models like those built into Nerdtracker, hardware emulators like the SwinSID chip, a direct pin-correct replacement for the original SID, and Papilio, a type of user-programmable integrated circuit that offers hardware modelling on a gate-by-gate basis of a range of classic PSGs, provide a range of options that take emulated sounds astonishingly close to those of the original chips.[73]

Nonetheless, many musicians feel uneasy about the use of emulation to capture (an approximation of) the authentic 8-bit sounds.[74] Some point to the tactility of using authentic hardware; others resist the easy lure of kitsch. When one finds elements and timbres from (or reminiscent of) chiptunes in pop music such as the Black Eyed Peas song "The Time (Dirty Bit)" from 2010, critics tend to object to the samples and how they are used. If FakeBit is defined as "music which used the sound of 1980s chipmusic but is completely produced with regular modern samplers, synthesizers and sequencer programs," then only the listener can decide whether the derogatory sense of the fake is in evidence or not.[75] If, of course, FakeBit is the practice of sprinkling some digital cool over an otherwise unremarkable pop production, then the unease of the purist 8-bit musicians, coders, and gamers may be more readily understood. Nonetheless, McAlpine has a point when he reminds us that the history of music is replete with cover versions—Liszt and his piano transcriptions of various popular works being a striking nineteenth-century example.[76] Inversely, it smacks a little of the romantic sentiment of the lone creator if we expect musicians to generate everything from scratch with now-obsolete hardware and software, despite newer and easier tools like Cubase being available. A range of new synthesizer plugins allows newcomers to emulate the sonic characteristics of 8-bit era sound chips, whether the 2A03 from the NES, the AY-3-8912 from the ZX Spectrum, the SN76489 from the ColecoVision, or the P8245 from the Magnavox Odyssey. These game consoles each had their recognizable acoustic signatures and limitations, so having them (and a dozen others) readily at hand in software can be intoxicating. By the same token, that ease of access arguably diluted chiptunes; one might say that FakeBit is not defined by the tools used to create it but by the relative lack of effort in generating its sonics, and that is what will still today distinguish a careful approach to these legacy sounds from a quick and dirty rush for something that sounds similar.[77]

When the scene vigorously debates the difference between "8-bit sound" and what some deride as "FakeBit" sound, this criticism is often directed toward mainstream appropriations—as in the notorious example of pop singer Beck's 2005 song "Hell Yes," which he also released in a so-called 8-bit remix version under the title "Ghettochip Malfunction."[78] Quite apart from the fact that Beck's song and remix in turn had sampled other recorded music, the charge against claiming this for 8-bit music is that its sonics were not in fact derived from the original console hardware, but resulted from synthesizer approximations—in fact, an entire album was released the same year as 8-bit remix by Beck himself, but met rather mixed reviews because its FakeBit sheen was so cynical. This raises difficult questions for chiptunes: Whose ears reliably differentiate between a piece of music in which the sounds are generated and mixed in real time (as was necessary before the advent of mass storage for prerecorded sound) from a piece of music designed to sound that way, though actually using prerecorded sounds? And how pure a distinction can be drawn given that even the most rudimentary and ostensibly canonical examples of 8-bit music likewise are not only electronic music made with the sound chips of older devices but often combined with modern equipment and vocals? "When I load the VICE emulator on my Mac and use it to run an old program for the Commodore Pet, what computer is running that program?"[79] Can we trust even those ears immersively trained in the chiptune scene to distinguish between Amiga and Sony and C64 sound chips and their proper sonorities? Probably not entirely, since we know, for instance, that Atari VCS television interface adapters depend in their timing on the color system (PAL or NTSC) and the frequency of the mains voltage (50 Hz or 60 Hz) in American and European Atari setups, respectively, meaning the same game would sound (and look) somewhat different depending on the location of its being played. Moreover, chiptunes are often put together in a composing interface that loops samples, rather than deriving them purely from original hardware (and programming in BASIC or Assembler). Such tunes can be made with a wide variety of tools; while each sound engine has its choice of editors, I recently came across Bintracker, a cross-platform, open source chiptune editor that can target any sound engine on any vintage machine.[80] In tackling thorny questions of 8-bit versus FakeBit, originality versus remixing, and technical versus aesthetic fidelities, the acoustic substance is not as readily secured as one might have hoped.

Like many born-digital communities, the chiptune scene embraces collaborative and sharing modes (including open licensing of tunes, but also access to tools). Remixing is a complex topic, and this is not the place to fully unfold the various overlapping discourses that are relevant to its appreciation. The emergence of recording and reproduction raises questions about originality and repetition; the policing of legal and aesthetic boundaries has various direct and indirect consequences with regard to genre, copyright, and distribution, and these consequences are discussed widely in terms of art, communication, digital humanities, music and sound studies, media studies and visual culture, cultural history and media anthropology.[81] By the same token, and despite its topical currency, it is clear that "remix studies" is not a settled discourse—straddling critical legal theory (including but not limited to copyright), political considerations (including but not limited to the digital divide), industry studies (including but not limited to distribution of media "content"), and spirited debates over the historical and future potency of innovation and creativity (including but not limited to the difficulty of defining and distinguishing improvisation or imitation, homage and derivative work in mashups). Consider C.P.U. Bach, an interactive music-generating program designed by Sid Meier and Jeff Briggs for the 3DO, released in 1994.[82] Though they became famous as Microprose game designers, this piece of interactive software is not a game—it neither presents you with a challenging path through a narrative (what Sid Meier famously defined as "a series of interesting decisions"), and there is no win condition. Nor can you use this program to write your own music; instead, you assist the program in creating Bach-style music by selecting from given variables (seven moods, sixteen Baroque forms, twelve musical instruments, and four different graphics—from a kaleidoscope-style visualizer to a gallery of scrolling nature photographs). The resulting music is not prerecorded; C.P.U. Bach sought to demonstrate the power of computers to create music with a limited amount of user input.[83] Yet in the end, this demonstration of computational permutation is a mere remix of Baroque styles. Little wonder, then, that generations of gamers would instead embrace the limited palette of 8-bit consoles in pursuing chiptunes as a far more free and creative endeavor, playing with computer-generated sounds.

The enduring popularity of chiptunes (whether presented as pursuing an aesthetics faithful to the earlier styles or developed further into chip-hop, chip-rock, glitch IDM, EDM, or chip-thrash, etc.), of game sounds used in other music genres, as well as of historical console and computer chip sounds in remix culture is the takeaway here. For the more our digital culture oscillates between the sovereign omnipotence of the machine and the all-too-human confusion of the user, the more readily we give up the fantasy of the perfect copy and turn toward the aestheticization and historicization of contingency and error. So we make music with the by-products of digital progress, sounding out what can still be done with the extant hardware and software long after their hype has flagged.[84] Complaints about "FakeBit" game culture also comprise the creation of games like the puzzle adventure *La-Mulana* (2005) that mimic retro platforms, in this case a Windows (and later Wii-Ware) title that invokes the Japanese MSX hybrid console computer of the mid-1980s.[85]

In retro-gaming audio exploits we recognize three distinct models: computer synthesis, chiptune, and FakeBit. Each of the models optimizes for aesthetic engagement as it turns numbers into sounds, though they deal with the right to access and modify software and hardware differently. While they seem to follow a historical and technical progression, in fact their aesthetic and compositional principles commingle and recycle each other, forming a recursive discourse. Faced with this, the retro scene has developed a kind of comparative philology—collecting, restoring, and describing revisions of software for different platforms. Yet in many cases the commercial source code is hard to find, and one has to face copy protection, code obfuscation, and other endemic issues in software. The demo scene prizes the technical specificity of particular platforms: there are creative as well as scholarly projects systematically comparing the affordances of sound processors like the TIA (Atari VCS), AY-3-8912 (Amstrad CPC), SID (Commodore 64), POKEY (Atari 800 XL), and pulse modulation with the aid of the Z80-CPU (Sinclair Spectrum).[86] Differing not only in frequency range and channels, but also in the number of filters used and in the type of waveforms available, these are in many ways obsolete parts, and therefore increasingly hard to obtain, maintain, and program, inevitably leading to the growing use of emulators, synthesizers, and other sampling methods. These recourses in turn can be scorned by the hard-core chiptune scene as derivative, as if the simulation of "originally" simulated sounds was audibly further away from the authentic experience; and even the best-equipped research collections and museums have to balance (playful) access with (scholarly) preservation, historical authenticity with museum pedagogy. Gaming culture turns the noise of computing—the electromechanical and digital processing of numbers—into acoustic phenomena open to aesthetic shaping.[87] People poke these sound chips to not merely enrich visual interactions, but to give it meaning in the first place: quantity becomes quality as sounds aspire to the condition of film music, of mood music, or even of music that stands on its own. In an industry fueled by a competitive race into ever new technological advances in support of greater immersion and interactivity, more detail and resolution, and deeply marked by continuous radical changes and planned obsolescence, it is remarkable how enduring the retro appeal of chiptunes and their real or simulated sounds has been and continues to be.

4 Troll Security: Espionage in Virtual Worlds

Are massively multiplayer online games and virtual worlds potential havens for activities that require a systemic response in the name of national security? This is the question raised—and as it belatedly turned out, rather extensively explored—by more than one secret service over the past decade. The rise of online gaming has not only changed the way we think about role-playing, but also transformed the strategy genre; beyond these genres, networked computing also spawned virtual worlds that are not strictly speaking games but venues for congregating, exploring, communicating, and commerce. They rely on data flows that are minutely logged and analyzed—not only by the publishers of such games and virtual worlds themselves, who have an obvious interest in monitoring them for operation and feedback, but also by secret services, including but not limited to the UK's GCHQ and the NSA in the US. Just what they see in online games and virtual worlds can be instructive for those of us interested in game studies in particular and in computer culture in general. "In December 2013, Edward Snowden released NSA documents from 2007 and 2008 that detailed the role of games and virtual environments not only in state intelligence gathering operations, but also their utility as an interactive influence medium."[1] In part, this is a logical step, since much like the telephone or other communication platforms, virtual worlds and online games enable conversations and transactions. As Zuboff and others have copiously documented, the current digital mediascape has become an exploitative one, as "unimpeded accumulation of power effectively hijacks the division of learning in society, instituting the dynamics of inclusion and exclusion upon which surveillance revenues depend"; surveillance capital in this definition is derived directly from the dispossession of our lived experience, which is scraped and sold to fund

"their knowledge and our ignorance about what they know."[2] More specifically, state agencies in several parts of our globe simultaneously began to
worry that virtual worlds "may be a potent means of spreading values and
ideologies," including by terrorist groups, as one government-sponsored
study of intelligence gathering in virtual worlds surmises:

> given that the more sophisticated groups of this type, including al-Qa'ida, have
> exploited the internet in very refined ways, they will likely soon seek to exploit
> newer virtual world technologies for recruiting, raising and transferring funds,
> training new recruits, conducting reconnaissance and surveillance, and planning
> attacks by using virtual representations of prospective targets.[3]

Thus the data-mining dragnet reached the playing fields of elves and
trolls—but despite focusing on *World of Warcraft* and *Second Life* as its pivotal examples, the report also discusses such virtual worlds for preteens as
Barbie Girls, *WebKinz*, and *Club Penguin*, along with more casual game environments like *MapleStory*, *There.com*, and *Spore*. The scope sought to encompass the history, demographics, and play characteristics of over 200 virtual
worlds and online gaming environments surveyed in 2008. Yet while systematic exploration and exploitation of virtual worlds by intelligence and
security branches of various governments has received some journalistic
coverage, the salient issues of secrecy and surveillance in virtual worlds
are rarely being addressed in academia.[4] Game studies has yet to rise to the
challenge of identifying salient issues: are avatars a serious national security
threat? Is the belief that we can role-play freely in online games impacted by
the Snowden leaks, cramping people's enjoyment of game environments or
impacting developers' considerations in game design? What does surveillance in online games mean for players and operators, what are potential
justifications or problems from the perspective of game design and game
play, and are there implications for the ludic, legal, and economic environments of virtual worlds and multiplayer online games? Let us retrace a
discursive formation here.

Vernor Vinge's 1981 science fiction novella *True Names*, a very early depic-
tion of a virtual world, stages conflicts between individuals and groups via
computer-mediated confrontations.[5] His protagonists role-play online while
being pursued by agents of the federal government into a full-immersion
virtual reality experience, here called the other plane; their skirmishes and
battles are decided in terms of access to computing power and networks.
Before long, the protagonists and their ilk are not only role-playing, but

competing with (and hiding from) the NSA and the military online; their software tools inevitably sieve government databases and other such online records for clues that might offer an advantage in digital hide-and-seek games. For quite a while, this science fiction progenitor of online gaming was considered a prototype of cyber-libertarian attitudes, espousing a defense of anonymous or pseudonymous action in networks, free from interference or regulation by any authorities or government agencies. Its subversive hacker-warlocks pass off what they pursue online as magic to the uninitiated, and live in fear only of being accidentally or maliciously connected to their true (real-world) names and identities, since those remain subject to taxation and policing. Vinge himself remembers chatting online, as early as the late 1970s, and playfully trying to trick others into giving away something about their offline identities.[6] He foresaw that strong encryption would trouble government agencies, and crypto-anarchists like "cypherpunk" Tim May ran with that argument in advocacy both for nongovernmental encryption and for secure digital payment systems.[7] Unfortunately, these arguments can also be said to have distorted and oversimplified debates over regulation and privacy online, presenting the policy issues as a crude choice between a total surveillance state and a libertarian anarcho-capitalist state. Yet even if the sci-fi story about hacking security agencies "from the Laurel end of the old ARPAnet" now feels nostalgically silly, the fact, of course, is that the NSA headquarters at Fort Meade (close to Laurel, Maryland) understood something crucial about Vinge's vision of "data that was not information and information that was not knowledge. To hear ten million simultaneous phone conversations, to see the continent's entire video output, should have been a white noise. Instead it was a tidal wave of detail."[8] At the risk of spoiling the plot, suffice it to say that the final antagonist in Vinge's novella turns out to be a simulation that grew out of an NSA software construct—a "developmental kernel" that "gobbled incredible data space" and prompted even its early programmers to use Frankenstein analogies, before somehow a copy of it was misplaced . . . all in all, quite reminiscent of things that happened much later to the same agency. It is hardly surprising, then, that a novella from the early 1980s should hold pride of place in movements that sought to claim cyberspace—including but not limited to libertarian subversives like Julian Assange, Dread Pirate Roberts, or members of Anonymous. In turn, the NSA has been fingered since around the same time as a place taking a pivotal role in shaping computer networks. In Kittler's delirious yet prescient warning that dates back to 1986, "The NSA as the collapse of strategy and technology would be information itself—No Such Agency. With the chance of forgetting us in the process."[9] Yet beyond the hype and fantasy this debate has all too long been imbued with, surely it is remarkable how prescient the novella was in its confrontation of the NSA and online gamers, whether we focus on human agency or on bureaucratic forgetting.

The high hopes for virtual worlds go beyond the historical development of simulations, from closed mechanical systems like the Link flight trainer to the Microsoft flight simulator game, from floor or tabletop planning games to computer chess, and from Fuller's Operating System Earth to Helbing's Large Knowledge Collider, as discussed in previous chapters. Of course, virtual worlds can bring together previously disconnected knowledge sources and cause "conceptual collisions" that are productive for generating insights.[10] By the same token, they can serve as an adversarial stage. However, until very recently most expert commentators on MMORPG play implicitly or explicitly assumed that "MMOs present a conceit that the virtual world is separate from the real world," as pioneer Bartle put it, and though "players are aware that their virtual world is part of reality, of course, but they so want for it to be separate that they are prepared through strength of will to treat it as if it were."[11] As a consequence, game designers rarely break this purported covenant with their players, but maintain (as well as they can) what anthropologists and psychologists after Goffman call frames, or game scholars after Huizinga have been calling the magic circle.[12] To insist on play is to suggest that "these actions in which we now engage do not denote what those actions for which they stand would denote"—yet to simulate counterterrorism in virtual worlds is to deny that very figure of thought.[13] Hence the intrusion of HUMINT and SIGINT methods into the virtual worlds of make-believe may at first blush seem like a rough disruption of the shared illusion gamers indulge in. Yet arguably, the penetration of state security and surveillance into this realm of make-believe can neither have come entirely unexpected, nor be considered completely incompatible with the nature of online games. It is an old cliché that espionage is "the great game," and it certainly could be argued that the surveillance and subsequent (or even real-time) big-data parsing of certain patterns in virtual worlds and online games is a kind of strategy game in itself, since it requires the highest possible quality of real-time information as well as lots of planning and foresight, and a mix of stealth and aggression to carry out the resulting plans.

If we define a virtual world as a computing environment offering a dynamic representation that invites and fosters immersive interaction (rather than merely audiovisual processing or haptic and kinesthetic processes), we may say that they stimulate the senses and activate cognitive processes in ways that enable and encourage certain exploratory, collaborative, or competitive interactions. As one scholarly definition has it, "virtual worlds are immersive, simulated, persistent, and dynamic environments that include rich graphical three dimensional spaces, high fidelity audio, motion, viewpoint, and interactivity," and they have "gained legitimacy in business and educational settings for their application in globally distributed work, project management, online learning, and real-time simulation."[14] Both those clusters of features and capabilities aroused the worry that led to a number of incursions by state agencies and their contractors into virtual worlds and online games. But as people share experiences or communicate synchronously or asynchronously, of course, these worlds also allow for antagonistic behavior, just as Vinge's fiction foretold—or, for that matter, William Gibson's digital deep throat in the 1987 novel *Count Zero*, dramatizing the difficulty of distinguishing between intrusive hacking and countermeasures, whistleblowing and betrayal, leaking and espionage.[15] Nonetheless, the realization that state security agencies found it necessary and justifiable to conduct covert as well as clandestine operations in virtual worlds and online games raises a number of provocative questions—both for game studies in particular and for media studies in general.

Television perpetuates this fear. In the first season of the Amazon streaming series *Jack Ryan* (2018), an adaptation of the character first developed for the potboilers of Tom Clancy, the Syrian villain Suleiman uses the chat capacity of an online video game to communicate covertly with his brother in France. Having detected this subterfuge, the titular hero later attempts to use the same game to trick Suleiman into revealing his plans by pretending to be that brother. The game shown does not resemble any known title, though it evokes the affordances of contemporary games. This plot point may have made it into the final version of the show because of an erroneous 2015 media report that the terrorists responsible for attacks in Paris that year were linked to each other through the PlayStation 4 network. That report has been debunked—not least due to the fact that it mentions the Belgian Interior Minister Jan Jambon's false claims, which came just days before the attack, that PlayStation communications were popular with Islamic radicals because they could be considered more secure than WhatsApp.[16] A few months prior to that choice piece of fake news, an Austrian teenager who had downloaded bomb-making plans onto his PlayStation was arrested—but there is no corroborated proof that Islamic terrorists ever coordinated their activities via Sony PlayStation networks.[17] Nonetheless, the *Jack Ryan* plot renewed speculation about the security threat posed by online gaming.

Similarly, a TV series from Norway that became an international success under the title *Occupied* (*Okkupert*, 2015/2017/2019) is a tense three-season political thriller that takes place in the near future. Here the story is inspired by climate change, as Norway's ruling Green Party government declares a goal of energy independence on a national scale; however, fossil fuel–dependent nations prove reluctant to change. The US has left NATO, and the EU allows Russia to take control of Norway to keep the supply of oil and gas flowing (the show's creator, thriller author Jo Nesbø, had come up with this concept in 2008—before Russia annexed Crimea). While the plot encompasses assassination attempts and conspiracy theories (a hacker creates a social media app with hidden malware that lets him access the prime minister's office email server), an interesting twist for our nexus here is that the resistance, made up mostly of politicians and active military as well as some hackers, regularly uses a video game to communicate, apparently using the PlayStation 4. In season two, the in-game communications among insurgent forces plotting a coup d'état are detected, apparently by accident. Soon the security service seeks access to live chat sessions inside an online first-person shooter (a game that looks very much like *Frontline Commando: D-Day* but is not credited by the Norwegian production). Both the fictional "Free Norway" (Fritt Norge) resistance movement in the show, and some of the music used in several episodes, are clearly meant to evoke the Norwegian resistance to German occupation during World War II, so it is no surprise that the game used should also be set in that war. This period, of course, is one of the more popular ones in the FPS genre, so it would not be conspicuous if people have such a PC game on their computers—though in the show, some politicians pretend it is not they but just their teenage kids who play.

The Norwegian series is critical both of the US and of the EU, and managed to enrage Russia, while the American series is jingoistic and simple in its view of American actions abroad.[18] But as different as their ideological framings may be, these internationally distributed television shows demonize online gaming, suggesting that states ought to develop appropriate surveillance capacities.[19] This is a direct challenge to the way online games have been operating, namely under the pretense that make-believe and leisure are separate from work-related communications, that one can act anonymously or pseudonymously online, and that network operators facilitate but never police such activities. As online gaming became a commercial juggernaut to rival streaming music and movies, it should be obvious that this is not just about designing games, but also about their networks as games depending on robust defenses against lag and jitter. Therefore, chief information officers and their equivalent working for developers and distributors of online games are as crucial to the gaming experience as artists and writers, programmers and animators behind a game's design. As gradual integration of artificial intelligence provides players with realistic environments, the procedural generation of in-game content hinges as much on the processing power of your console or computer as on the efficiency of the network connecting it to those of other players and of the game's operators.

It took four and a half years for the Office of the Director of National Intelligence (ODNI) to comply with a Freedom of Information Act request filed by Steven Aftergood on behalf of the Federation of American Scientists in Washington, DC. Aftergood is one of the most important voices in the debate around overclassification; he had requested a copy of a report, including a DVD, resulting from a July 2008 ODNI Summer Hard Problem (SHARP) on virtual worlds and their implications. Citing the National Security Act of 1947, the ODNI denied the DVD in full, and released only a heavily redacted version of the report of the discussions held in San Jose, California, between July 13 and August 8, 2008, ostensibly to protect the names and identifying information of ODNI personnel involved with the summer program called "Cyber Space Spillover: Where Virtual Games Get Real." However, as the call for the session explicitly states, "the goal for this intensive four-week study is to engage external (non-government) experts on an intractable program of significant national security interest"—so the majority of participants would not have been ODNI personnel. Indeed, the

composition of the study group was to involve thirteen government analysts and seventeen external experts who came together "to examine the
intent and culture behind the use of virtual world technologies" through
research, simulation, lectures, and peer-to-peer intellectual exchange.[20]
According to the redacted ODNI report that the FAS eventually was able to
post, thirty-six people participated in the SHARP program, some of them
providing material beyond the scope of the report that was appended to it.

While parts of the report deal with basic aspects of virtual worlds, from
the combination of graphics and networks and the formation of online
identity to issues of virtual world economies and griefing, other parts address
the "potential threats of compelling worlds with no social norms," "virtual wars," and the "exploitation of virtual worlds by political and religious
extremists and terrorists." Forms of communication of interest to the ODNI
in virtual worlds include messages typed and thus broadcast to avatars in
the area, but also billboards, posters, and other advertisements, music or
movies that can be broadcast in virtual worlds, and, of course, nonverbal
communication methods, including but not limited to gestures. In fact,
gamers in *World of Warcraft* suspected as early as June 2008 that the NSA
might be reading their in-game chat logs.[21] Concerns raised by the SHARP
report range from securing the network infrastructure used by games to
securing avatars against manipulation, securing computers and game
devices, and controlling access to files and programs relevant to the virtual worlds in question. Remarkably, the report foresees the rise of input
and control devices beyond the keyboard, mentioning motion sensors,
haptics, touch screens, and interactive wearables such as glasses that com-
bine a head-mounted display, GPS, and computing capability; it also considers consequences of distributed and location-independent storage. One
interesting question raised is what the result might be of allowing users to
move across virtual worlds the same way they move from one website to
another. An appendix to the 2008 SHARP report purports to offer examples of extremist presence in and nation-state manipulation of the virtual
world. In a moment of candor, the report also concedes plainly that "so far,
cyber-terrorism and cyber-warfare have been overrated threats, at least with
respect to terrorist groups." Nonetheless, the assertion is that virtual worlds
could be plausibly used for information gathering, networking, recruitment, fundraising, and training—from the sharing of manuals to elaborate
staging of simulated actions.

While in retrospect it may seem quaint to see the ODNI's excitement about virtual embassies in *Second Life*, there is undeniably some potential in trading virtual currencies, and consequential questions also continue to be raised about the energy footprint of virtual worlds, both as measured in communications bandwidth and in their electricity use; some estimates made it look as if a *Second Life* avatar consumes as much energy as the average Brazilian in 2008—and server farms offering the low-latency connections preferred by gamers continue to see surging demand.[22] Despite the clarification that game operators of course "monitor avatar activity and identify risky behavior," authorities began to worry that money laundering might be enabled by virtual worlds, and credit card fraud, identity theft, and tax evasion surely remain concerns of law enforcement agencies looking at online culture.[23] In addition to these economic sides of virtual worlds, intelligence agencies also look at other potential exploitation of online games. "On the darker side," the proposal for the 2008 SHARP program suggested, "virtual worlds are ideal training grounds for criminals and would-be terrorists, and searches of the Second Life web site reveal the presence of virtual terrorist groups."[24] The concern here is that reconnaissance and actual attacks could be rehearsed on the simulated locations, including monitoring of responses. Indeed, law enforcement in the UK, in Australia, and in the United States assumes that virtual worlds can help terrorists train in the same way that flight simulators assisted the 9/11 terrorists who practiced flying (but not landing) airplanes. "Virtual fencing" for online worlds may be needed, as an undersecretary of homeland security for intelligence and analysis put it in a presentation to the Washington Institute Policy Forum on May 6, 2008.[25] There is even the concern that terror groups might use virtual worlds to "engage in propaganda, recruitment, coordination, training, and information gathering," including also recruitment of those who might translate their messages into certain languages and act as messengers between such groups and the media.[26]

Despite the fact that a national security brief in 2008 clearly acknowledged that fears of threats are overblown ("even though some users may engage in clandestine activity, products employ electronic tools that automatically look for risky behavior by avatars"), there was sufficient interest in virtual worlds and online games to launch investigations.[27] An unclassified US government project to develop ways to spot terrorists who use virtual worlds was a data-mining project code-named Reynard, described as "a seedling effort to study the emerging phenomenon of social (particularly terrorist) dynamics in virtual worlds and large-scale online games and their implications for the intelligence community."[28] To do so, the program needed to establish a baseline of "normal" in-game behaviors and then determine the feasibility of automatically detecting suspicious actions in the virtual world. According to the 2013 Program Summary, Reynard was a study of approximately 15,000 players from nine countries in twelve multiplayer online games and virtual worlds, which started in 2009 and ended in 2012, aiming to "determine behavioral indicators in the realm of Massive Multiplayer Online Games and Virtual Worlds that are predictive of Real World characteristics of the users."[29] Research indeed found objective behavioral indicators for over a dozen characteristics, allowing for a high degree of accuracy in prediction; some of the reports were presented at academic venues, including SIGGRAPH 2011, CHI 2012, and the IEEE Conference on Computational Intelligence and Games in 2010. It is probably safe to assume that overall, Reynard did not live up to its original promise; in a report to Congress on data mining, ODNI outlined that "if it shows early promise, this small seedling effort may increase its scope to a full project," but instead it ended soon after.[30] Moreover, nothing in Reynard hinted at the full extent of eavesdropping in games and virtual worlds that NSA and GCHQ engaged in (and might still do).

Only the materials leaked by former NSA contractor Snowden brought to light a far more extensive trove of documents about the interest of intelligence agencies in online games, compiled by the contractor SAIC.[31] This file predicts "if virtual world technology enters the mainstream, criminals and US adversaries will find a way to exploit this technology for illegal and errant behavior." Headquartered in California but with a major presence in Washington, DC, SAIC promoted its ability to support "intelligence collection in the game space," warning that militant groups might try to use them since they could provide them with a powerful platform to reach core target audiences. Since tracking cell phones and calling cards—let alone social media and virtual worlds—is a different matter from tracking Soviet airplanes, former NSA Director Hayden in 2000 had announced an initiative named Trailblazer that was going to replace Cold War technologies for collecting intelligence with modern information technology. SAIC was a major component of Trailblazer, as were several other major intelligence and defense contractors, including Boeing, Northrop Grumman, and Booz

Allen Hamilton (where Snowden used to work). As the cost of Trailblazer mounted while it dropped further and further behind schedule, the ambitious plan for an integrated signals intelligence capability came under fire, leading to an investigation by the Department of Defense inspector general.[32] SAIC had won an initial $280 million, twenty-six-month contract to design the Trailblazer system; four and a half years and more than a billion dollars later, it was abandoned. It appears that much the same happened to the ambitious venture into virtual worlds.[33] Though one terror scenario proposed by the Pentagon for *World of Warcraft* made some headlines in 2008, it focused on human intelligence in online games (pointing out that "most spy agencies' employees aren't exactly level-70 shamans"), whereas much of the signal intelligence activity in and around virtual worlds remained unknown until after the Snowden documents became available.[34]

Under the joint GCHQ and NSA effort to spy on gamers in virtual worlds and multiplayer online games like *Second Life* and *World of Warcraft* and in online gamer communities including Xbox Live, analysts not only created their own game accounts to eavesdrop on militants who may rely on features common to games, such as voice and text chats, financial transactions, and other interactions among avatars and online characters; "feedback loops require that we give proper recognition to the avatar as an embodiment of the player's actions and experiences in very particular ways."[35] They also arranged to collect and store communications data from inside virtual worlds that had previously not been sifted for potential threats. The obvious implications for player privacy raised eyebrows, although it is not easy to establish how many gamers may have been monitored or what activities were in fact captured for analysis. Since many players of *World of Warcraft*, for instance, are US citizens (who are not supposed to be targets of NSA surveillance unless an intelligence court specifically permits targeting them), the legality of the program is in question. Blizzard, Microsoft, and Linden Labs declined to comment to the press about the extent of the espionage on their games, but their customers were irate.[36] Describing them as "target-rich communications networks," a 2008 NSA document titled "Exploiting Terrorist Use of Games & Virtual Worlds" alleges that certain terrorist target selectors (such as email addresses or internet protocol addresses) were associated with Xbox Live, *Second Life*, and *World of Warcraft* accounts. This in itself does not prove that the games were used for anything related to terrorism—but it led to surveillance, coordinated at GCHQ's Menwith Hill station, of engineers, scientists, embassy drivers, and other targets identified by a "network gaming exploitation team." According to the report, GCHQ was able to shut down a crime ring that sold stolen credit card information in *Second Life*. Meanwhile, the NSA sought to establish the intelligence value of *World of Warcraft* accounts related to Islamic extremist groups, nuclear proliferation, and arms dealing; also targeted were Chinese hackers and Iranian nuclear scientists. When this scheme was revealed in early 2014, journalists had a field day pointing out that intelligence agencies had again exaggerated the threat—to the point where a special group had to be created to avoid collisions between CIA, FBI, and Pentagon spies in games. As in any intelligence operation, it is practically impossible to tell whether there were any concrete counterterrorism successes due to game surveillance and data mining. Indeed, it seems quite likely that groups intent on clandestine communication might find easier environments to operate in than online games, whose players are most certainly tracked in a number of ways by the companies operating them.

Despite drawing on experts from industry and academia, these studies for the intelligence community do not always demonstrate a solid understanding of online games and virtual worlds. One worry the 2008 SHARP report articulates is that terrorist groups might, for instance, create an "Osama bin Laden" avatar that would then remain active (preaching, issuing new fatwas, recruiting) "for centuries to come, as the fidelity of his likeness would be entirely believable and animated in new ways to keep him current and fresh."[37] Let us parse the significance of this scenario. Would the Republican Party create an animated Ronald Reagan to address their conferences for decades to come? Would a Mother Teresa avatar or a Dalai Lama character keep the attention of the faithful for centuries? Then again, of course, this type of casting for posterity is nothing new in the film industry. The SHARP report cites stunts as a reason to use digitally animated replicas of actors, but the transfer to a game avatar of such contributions is perhaps far-fetched. Consider the three techniques that are currently used to digitally animate someone's likeness, or even "re-cast" film or TV actors after they have passed away. The simplest is the juxtaposition of older and newer footage. Outtakes of Larry Hagman's performance as J. R. Ewing from the TV soap opera *Dallas* (1978–1991, 2010–2014) allowed him to appear in episodes not actually filmed until after his death. However, in the case of *The Sopranos* (1999–2007), the same trick lacked emotional depth. Livia Soprano was played by actress Nancy Marchand, who died in 2000, and HBO soon decided to give her character an off-screen death. A second approach, rotoscoping, allows clever montages using footage from different eras, showing living and dead performers together in the same shot. Notable examples include Bruce Lee in a recent Johnny Walker ad, or Natalie Cole's Grammy-winning duet with her late father Nat King Cole. A Coca-Cola ad from the same year featured Elton John and put the deceased Humphrey Bogart, James Cagney, and Louis Armstrong in his audience. The third and most complex technique involves the computer re-creation of someone's likeness (facial expressions, skin textures, and hair modeling) to create synthetic actors. One landmark of this technological feat was *The Lord of the Rings'* Gollum (2001–2003). Computer graphics fleshed out the character as played by actor Andy Serkis, who wore a motion capture body suit. Oliver Reed died of a heart attack before finishing his role in *Gladiator* (2000), but computer graphics allowed his image to be re-created. The same is being done with Philip Seymour Hoffman's character in *The Hunger Games: Mockingjay—Part 2*. None of this can come as a surprise, given the development of computer graphics, from the early line graphics of the 1960s to the two-dimensional surfaces with simple lighting effects that give the illusion of 3D in the 1970s and '80s (1982's *Tron* is one of the earliest efforts to create a feature-length film on a computer). Other milestones include the wireframe spaceships in *Star Wars* (1977–1983) and the particle rendering that has propelled Pixar to success since *Toy Story* (1995). But just as important has been the demand for immersive graphics in computer gaming, which has driven innovation in chip design and animation software. Over the past few decades, cross-fertilization between computer graphics and film and television has accelerated—from *Jurassic Park* (1994) and the game *Doom* (1994) to movies like *Wall-E* (2008) and the game *Mass Effect 3* (2012). Simply put, without the rapidly scaling demands of computer games, today's special effect movies simply would not be possible. But does this mean that avatars function the same way in games? One last example might help sharpen the argument here. As anyone who watched *Furious 7* (2015) will notice, the movie pivots on competition between the old and the new—between a predator drone and a '60s muscle car, between an omniscient surveillance chip and urban street savvy. The film can be seen as a sentimental tribute to Paul Walker, the actor who died in a car crash before filming was complete. The accident meant the franchise's filmmakers had to resort to work-arounds to finish scenes featuring Walker. This was made possible by combining footage from outtakes with the construction of a "digital mask" of the dead actor's features, which was projected onto motion captured by Paul Walker's brothers Cody and Caleb, who have similar builds. This is why the film is poignant also in its juxtaposition of new and old questions about what audiences expect from film stars. In movies as in virtual worlds, the real question is how the acting profession and the audience will react if this practice were to become more commonplace. Whose body and whose face is up there on the screen? Who holds the rights to these images, to these performances? Tom Cruise was recorded performing in a motion capture suit for the movie *Oblivion* (2013), but after it opened in theaters, Cruise acquired the rights to all data recorded during his performance. It is unknown whether he did this to enable future use or to prevent future use, but less established actors might not have as much clout in this kind of decision. And then there is the question of what will prove acceptable to the fan base of an actor (and of a movie franchise). To what extent are the re-animators of Paul Walker bound by public perception of the actor? And to what extent are they constrained by available technology? Will other filmmakers resort to casting from the beyond, and how will audiences react? Ultimately, the technical and emotional range of what can be done with someone's posthumous digital recreation will be defined—and limited—by our living memory of the actor's onscreen performances. In the case of a reclusive terrorist, his voice and image would presumably carry weight only because of the perceived authenticity of his message, not because of the perennial look of his digital replica. It seems rather far-fetched for the ODNI to seriously argue that jihadists would pay a lot of attention—for centuries, no less—to an avatar controlled by someone who is quite evidently not Osama bin Laden.

As Hayles mused, "our narratives about virtual creatures can be considered as devices that suture together the analogue subjects we still are as we move in the three-dimensional spaces in which our biological ancestors evolved with the digital subjects we are becoming as we interact with virtual environments and digital technologies."[38] But after all this, are avatars really all that uncanny? The uncanny, Weber notes, is "a certain undecidability which affects and infects representations."[39] Freud's essay on the uncanny lists doubles, dolls, automata, alter egos, a tropology of the weird, subverting distinctions between fantasy and reality; and the uncanny is routinely tied to technology.[40] But today, we are fascinated less by mechanical ducks, chess automata, or music machines than by interactions on connected screens. One obvious contemporary illustration of the double or doppelgänger are avatars in online games—their eerily animated verisimilitude is often uncanny.[41] And just as in the fantasy fiction Freud cites, in most multiplayer online games the avatar serves as "insurance against the destruction of the ego" and "an energetic denial of the power of death"; few games feature perma-death, most allow players to return right after a temporary failure. Players have no fear of these dolls coming back to life again and again—they desire it, as Freud knew in discussing death drive and repetition compulsion.[42] The avatar is just another dancing doll or automaton—but unlike playing with dolls, which rarely gives rise to national security concerns, the reach and feature set of online gaming gave rise to interesting symptoms. And the detailed logging of communications and actions in online games is a direct challenge to the ethics and politics of interactive culture, leading to the vertiginous feeling that many players in games and virtual worlds might in fact be spooks. Moreover, the uncanny is not merely about undecidability, but as Weber continues, involves and implies a second movement, "which expresses itself in compulsive curiosity."[43] Or, to put it differently, "Secret services are the only real measure of a nation's political health," as le Carré wrote, "the only real expression of its unconscious."[44] We should also note, however, that this is said by the fictional villain of the book—the Soviet mole, Bill Haydon.

Another odd twist in observing the US government's efforts to drum up support for systematic surveillance and intrusive data mining in virtual worlds is the fictional scenario offered by a related study from the Urban Warfare Analysis Center (UWAC) in 2008, titled "How a Boy Becomes a Martyr: The Dangers of Web 2.0 Technology."[45] This six-page document (the fifth in a series of reports on future urban warfare) details how a sixteen-year-old boy in Detroit (who lacks a stable home life, is socially awkward at school, and finds solace in online friendships) might be led toward becoming a suicide bomber for an Islamic extremist group. Pivoting on the simplistic idea that the teenager might "advance to a higher stage in his online community" by reading up on radical Islam, the scenario shows its protagonist steering his avatar through virtual worlds that harbor terrorist cells, joining others in a "virtual hajj to Mecca, complete with real-life replicas of the Kaaba and the Mosque of the Prophet Muhammad." This in turn leads him to jihadist videos of propaganda and martyrdom; soon, his contacts convince him that he was chosen among many other new followers to carry out an attack, which to the fictitious Detroit teenager is supposed to feel like a victory. With the aid of his radical online friends, he begins rehearsing in the detailed virtual world a suicide bomb attack at a professional basketball game. There may or may not have been an actual Hamas island in *Second Life*, and Facebook may be far more popular today than MySpace at the time this fear-mongering scenario was concocted, but the implication of the outline is plain: virtual worlds and social media have to be watched closely for signs of exploitation by murderous zealots. Notably, the scenario offers no solution for countering or overcoming the suggested seductive potential of online recruitment; yet despite its reductive and stereotyping portrayal of a gullible teenager, what it might have inadvertently surfaced is that by the very same token, virtual worlds and social media are just as potent as means of countering extremist ideology, whether through responsible news coverage or as a medium for political debate.[46]

The same tension is reproduced in the aforementioned SHARP report on spying in virtual worlds, which asserts on the one hand that "the culture that seizes the technological high ground in these spaces will have the advantage in spreading its world view," while on the other hand immediately conceding that "virtual culture exposes nuanced views of identity and personhood that lurk within rich, vivid, and compelling 3D online interactions." Either way, the report asserts that other countries have already recognized how well virtual worlds spread memes and communicate ideas and emotions. Significantly, it also makes certain assumptions about the transfer of values and patterns from online to offline behavior. While acknowledging research on serious games and their use in training, advertising, simulation, or education, and admitting that "how successful they are in achieving those objectives is unclear," the report nonetheless implicitly assumes that role-playing in particular has a seductive potential for influencing its players. Inversely, it also alleges that if players are hiding behind screen names and avatars, they may demonstrate a willingness to engage in behavior they might not in real life. But either way, at stake is not merely the issue of games with ideological objectives or themes, such as *America's Army* (US Army, 2002) or *Special Force* (Hezbollah, 2003), *Hostage Rescue* (Iran, 2007), *Quest for Saddam* (US, 2003), *Under Siege* (Syria, 2005), or *Kuma War* (US, 2004); more broadly, the question broached by online play is whether among the thousands or millions of innocuous playful interactions in milquetoast fantasy and role-play games, there might be nefarious activities that are not observed because they use the throng as a cover. The SHARP report acknowledges that "much of the information in the public domain about the alleged terrorist exploitation of virtual worlds has been speculative rather than based on substantive evidence." This leaves open the possibility that there is information not in the public domain that might substantiate suspicions, but nothing in the report would harden such suspicions.

One complaint advanced by the 2008 SHARP report was that "once a pioneer in virtual worlds technologies, the United States is no longer leading the race to adopt next-generation internet technologies." Thus the governmental response does not stop at analysis of game data, but also extends into modeling and developing new workspaces that enable and support big data parsing.[47] As one news outlet reports, "the ODNI's Intelligence Advanced Research Projects Activity (IARPA) program is planning to begin a project called the Analysis WorkSpace for Exploitation (A-SpaceX) that will examine how virtual worlds can be used to create the workspace of the future for analysts."[48] Little information about such data-oriented workspaces is publicly available, although it is plausible that it would be easier to cope with big data sets from online virtual worlds in a specific analytical and technical setup. A "framework for designing with virtual world technologies" by the IBM Almaden Research Center for the Air Force Research Laboratory Information Directorate points out that such technologies "can be used to radically transform how intelligence analysts encounter data, frame their stories, and review their analyses with both their customers and other analysts"; the final deliverable is supposed to be "applicable to blended reality solutions in which virtual world applications and real world applications are tightly integrated."[49] Data mining inside virtual worlds and social media certainly demands particular skills, and the SHARP report speculates that online games may indeed train people for a certain kind of pattern recognition, and that "the increased number of people with the skill of recognizing patterns in complex systems may mean that there will be a larger pool of individuals from which to draw intelligence officers and analysts." Elsewhere in the same report, the crowdsourcing of intelligence is proposed as a solution, via "outreach programs that enlist users as educated observers and reporters" to survey current and emerging systems more effectively.

While the SHARP report quite correctly surmises that "as virtual and gaming worlds increasingly become part of everyday experience, governance in those environments will assume greater importance," there is still no clear consensus as to what precisely the right calibration of such governance is: how much is left to the players, how much is a matter of regulation for the common good, how far does the authority of the developer and publisher extend, and to what extent are real-world laws and regulations relevant? Can virtual world communities effectively police themselves, or do they require agencies that can enforce laws (beyond contractual or business relations)? For this is patently not only a matter of property, but of privacy and personhood. Yet as China and South Korea (where online gaming culture is more advanced than in the US) have found, governance of virtual worlds raises a number of specific challenges. In China's case, limits on free speech and freedom of expression are not easy to embed in online environments, and as a consequence, the Chinese government seeks to control the software framework that is the condition of possibility for commerce and communication. In South Korea's rich culture of competitive online gaming, we may recognize its advantage of central government support for the infrastructure that has enabled and accelerated its virtual world platforms.

If it is true that "the intensification of contemporary surveillance can be seen as an elaboration of late nineteenth-century new media and the proliferation of evidence-producing communication technologies," that need not imply that the digital dragnet differs in quantitative and qualitative ways from prior discursive formations.[50] We do not have to summon the full extent of current criticism of big data and surveillance capitalism to be skeptical about secret agencies engaging in virtual world traffic analysis and data mining.[51] Knowing that for their purposes of mapping connections, traffic analysis is more powerful than content analysis, and knowing that they usually (though not always) focus on metadata—that is, the connections on the social graph rather than the individual semantics in communications—we may assume that automated analysis of in-game communications and interactions can take different forms; in some cases it might be simple content filtering—searching for the occurrence of particular phrases according to statistical filters—or it might be traffic analysis, sifting through patterns including but not limited to message length, frequency, paths, and so on, without examining the message contents. Traffic analysis is feasible even where contents are encrypted, mapping connections between participants and drawing conclusions about their relations. Advocates of doing so in computer-mediated communication networks like multiplayer online games argue that this can be understood as the electronic surveillance equivalent of what the police call a Terry stop: basically a quick frisk (without having to show probable cause) to check whether or not suspicions are verified or falsified. Only where they are not falsified would the monitoring continue. While legal scholars have long been arguing about the legislative framework for electronic surveillance in general and the uneasy relation between the 1978 Foreign Intelligence Surveillance Act and the US Constitution in particular, the crux of the argument is a shift from intense monitoring of selected individuals to wholesale data mining.[52] Nonetheless, as people disagree whether the NSA has the legal authority to do what it does, "even the most strident opponents concede the need to identify and monitor the communications of terrorists and stop them before they can act," and this requires an understanding of communications networks.[53]

We therefore must ask whether there can ever be a reasonable expectation of privacy in computer games. On the one hand, players knowingly engage with a machine (a console or computer or handheld device) that is designed to track, aggregate, and interpret user input, and connect that machine to others like it in order to facilitate interactions between players as well as between players and machine entities. On the other hand, players still tend to engage with the game and each other on the assumption that games are a sacrosanct space for activities that are part and parcel of their personal sphere, an aspect of their freedom of expression, of their freedom of association with others, and of their right to privacy.[54] If you are a US citizen, your Fourth Amendment rights cover constitutionally defined private domains, not only your physical residence and personal belongings but also your family, sexual and marital relations, your conscience, and your communications. However, if you enter into an end-user license agreement with an operator of online entertainment software, you agree to abide by terms of use that explicitly grant the other party access to any and all information regarding everything to do with the game and your activities in it. A player might be sitting home alone, assuming the privacy of their residence and their belongings extends into the sphere of the game, while those with a vested interest in tracking, aggregating, and evaluating in-game interactions would emphasize not only the contractual nature of the game but also that the location of the game servers and other infrastructure is on their business premises and thus not part of each gamer's private sphere. Thus, while there are numerous assumptions of protection regarding role-playing using an alias or avatar, they are countered by the socializing and exploring that are part of the same game world. Yet arguably, what is at stake in the multiplayer gaming context is not only the individual rights of a player, but the collective nature of play. Here it is worth pointing out that privacy can be formulated as an indivisible collective good like clean air, not to be sacrificed to business efficiency or law enforcement. Many examples of proposed privacy legislation have failed because they focused on the individual, instead of focusing on the benefit to society.[55] That collective benefit would extend to supporting the right to anonymous speech, the freedom of association, and a measure of protection against intrusive authority. Two garden-variety objections should not go unmentioned here: there are those who argue that privacy must yield to the collective good that is security, implying that privacy is somehow a selfish value—as if undermining people's rights in the name of security is not also destructive of what it purports to defend. Second, a common rebuttal of concerns about pervasive surveillance is the sentimental argument that in a small town, people can live happily together knowing a great deal about one another. But nostalgia for supposedly simpler times (before communications technologies alienated us from each other) is misleading: what people knew about each other in that fictitious village would be embedded in a rich social context, whereas online it is not; power differentials in that fictitious village would be small, whereas the power differentials between players as end users of entertainment software and game developers or operators (or indeed nation-state level security services) are considerable; and in the fictitious village, knowledge would be reciprocal, while secret services operate in secret.

What difference would it make if a nonplayer character in an online game performs not only tasks that help along an overarching game narrative by providing dialogue, plot points, directions, or other in-game information, but simultaneously serves as an agent of state security, eavesdropping and recording, tracking and monitoring, aggregating and analyzing? If we assume that privacy in this context of online gaming is, in part, defined by the degree of access others have, and, in part, by the amount of control we have over personal identifying information, it allows us to present the stakes in balance. Nissenbaum defines privacy as "neither a right to secrecy nor a right to control but a right to appropriate flow of personal information."[56] Exactly what is appropriate is determined by the full set of our expectations as shaped by organizing principles of social life. In the game context as in our social lives in general, those organizing principles are shaped by competing forces and constitute a set of trade-offs. One obvious zone for the flexible negotiation of how personal information flows is the interaction between you and your avatar, your name and your gamer tag, and so forth, whereby online games offer numerous choices regarding how you represent your age, race, sex, social status, marital status, and so on, without having to conform to the realities of your life outside the game. This flexibility, however, never means that games are a zone where anything goes; they have their lore and narrative, their social code and their look and feel—sometimes carefully guarded by way of trademark or business property, sometimes collectively negotiated by way of convention.

Seen this way, it might be the case that individual targeting is not the main worry—the real problem, as identified by observers across the political spectrum, from Julian Assange to Dan Geer or from the EFF to Apple, is a culture that aggregates any and all personal data. Nissenbaum is surely not the only informed observer who wants to "stop the slide down the slope and prevent a society from throwing away privacy in tiny bits."[57] For, faced with certain consumer choices, many people still opt for credit cards over cash, EZPass over conventional toll payments, caller ID over call blocking, store loyalty cards over cash, and traceable search engines over self-directed web surfing. But the question is whether those decisions are in fact free choices, or whether they are not the result of coercion. Who willingly lives without a cell phone, credit card, or search engine? Here it is important to remember that "privacy's moral weight, its importance as a value, does not shrink or swell in proportion to the number of people who want or like it, or how much their want or like it."[58] We may distinguish descriptive accounts of privacy from normative ones that assert it is something good, worth having, and deserving protection. Beyond this protection, however, there may well be a realm of other morally justified values we hold that make up our conception of personhood. In practice, this becomes a question of being able to withdraw from public scrutiny; if there is no such sphere of privacy, we run the risk of losing not only our freedom of expressing ourselves (say, in games) for fear of criticism or reprisal, but also our freedom of thinking and feeling about our game any way we like due to internalized censorship.[59] These risks are clearly visible in social interactions online, and they are arguably exacerbated in the game environment, since the general expectation of a playful interaction includes assumptions of appropriate and inappropriate play; examples might be play that adheres to the game's lore versus behavior that breaks that share of reference (in naming conventions, social references, in-game speech, etc.), fair play versus cheating, and so forth. In short, players may—naïvely or not—feel justified in an implicit horizon of expectations that does not normally allow for systematic eavesdropping or sustained suspicions.

Inversely, the paranoid "assertitude" of spies that there must be something untoward going on in virtual worlds clearly hinges on the axiom that one *cannot not* attribute one's own mental constitution to everyone else. Since they cannot possibly know the contents of another person's consciousness, they must jump to certain conclusions—if it is their business to ferret out other actors' intentions, they must intuit that your intentions are not so different from their own. Thus if they engage in clandestine behavior, then you probably do too. . . . If big data traffic analysis kills both privacy as impossible-to-observe and privacy as impossible-to-identify, then arguably what is left is merely the capacity to misrepresent yourself. Hence online games and virtual worlds became prime suspects in their pivotal reliance on avatars and on role-play.

But even if this argument turned out to be overblown, what about the worry about the sheer scale of virtual worlds and online multiplayer games? That attack also rather quickly fell apart. State agencies and their contractors had vociferously urged that the rapid growth of virtual worlds necessitated the rapid deployment not only of human intelligence, due to issues of scale, but also of signals intelligence that would sift through everything, due to issues of scale. But this point is a potent reminder of what is actually true of such network activity. As popular as they were at one point, *Second Life* and similar virtual worlds have not grown nearly as much as pundits predicted, neither among the teen and role-play market nor for the vaunted business angles (including but not limited to virtual meetings, education or training, corporate communication and marketing, etc.). Consulting firm Gartner had boldly predicted in 2007 that by 2011, 80 percent of active internet users would "lead a second life" in a virtual world.[60] As this type of prediction failed to hold true, and massively popular games like *World of Warcraft* saw the number of regular participants recede, qualitative as well as quantitative analysis provided handy reminders of the nature of networks. The greater the reach of a network, the lower its saturation with information; conversely, the more differentiated the information, the smaller its area of distribution. The more a medium correlates noise with profit and profit with noise (even and especially at the highest levels of production value), the more vacuous it tends to become—and this was clearly the case in virtual worlds and other online games. Rather than provide cover for nefarious congregation, they waxed and waned according to their primary characteristic—entertainment.

This is not to deny the potential importance, to the military, of information operations conducted during times of crisis or conflict to achieve or promote specific objectives online, but it is almost assured that virtual worlds and online multiplayer games are not very effective as secret venues for miscreants. And the disclosure of various agencies snooping on virtual worlds and online games (regardless of whether via Snowden's exfiltration or via Freedom of Information Act suits filed) seems to have harmed neither the games nor the agencies in question. Interestingly, several commentators like to claim that Snowden leaked because of his exposure to video games.[61] Indeed, Snowden's autobiography states, "It was *Super Mario Bros* that taught me what remains perhaps the most important lesson of my life," but the massively multiplayer online type does not get nearly as much attention there.[62] Despite strong trends toward pervasive networks of sensors (in the so-called "internet of things"), crowdsourcing, and "big data" pattern analysis, all of which empower corporate and state operators to gather information on people, the same technologies have also allowed amateur astronomers and other lay observers to follow spy satellites, drone strikes, or extraordinary rendition flights. In short, while media technology has made it easier for government agencies and large corporations to hoover up any and all traces of individual human behavior, it has also by the same token enabled whistle-blowing and leaking, which used to be far more onerous.[63] Under the conditions of networked culture, the "half-life" of secrecy may have changed:

> Secrets that would once have survived the 25 or 50 year test of time are more and more prone to leaks. The declining half-life of secrets has implications for the intelligence community and other secretive agencies, as they must now wrestle with new challenges posed by the transformative power of information technology innovation as well as the changing methods and targets of intelligence collection.[64]

Yet for secret agencies investigating virtual worlds and games, this need not mean that intense eavesdropping on online communities is a worthwhile investment of time and resources. Nothing proved that these new venues are potential hot spots for troublemakers, and nobody was able to show any intelligence gain from the deployment of surveillance and data mining, as profitable as it surely is for certain players in the industry.[65] The "International Strategy for Cyberspace" signed by President Obama in 2011 warned that the "low costs of entry to cyberspace and the ability to establish an anonymous virtual presence can also lead to safe havens for criminals," but it does not mention games or virtual worlds.[66] Neither the "National Strategy for Trusted Identities in Cyberspace," dated April 2011, nor the "National Strategy for Information Sharing and Safeguarding" from December 2012 discuss games or virtual worlds.[67] Nonetheless, the push to get the surveillance of virtual worlds to a point where it joins the trove of validated open source intelligence continues, for instance, with face recognition applied to avatars—as if there were not technically far easier ways to track people's behavior online.[68] Swire even goes so far as to worry about the sociology of IT professionals as a systematic threat to intelligence agencies, since the government is unable to impose ideological screening for libertarian views. Science fiction author Stross worries that it is not only an ideological but a generational gap that might soon plague the security services. About millennials, he writes: "The machineries of the security state may well find them unemployable, their values too alien to assimilate into a model still rooted in the early twentieth century. But if you turn the Internet into a panopticon prison and put everyone inside it, where else are you going to be able to recruit the jailers?"[69]

Perhaps more worrisome than the balance between keeping and spilling secrets—which may or may not change substantially despite technological transformations—is the fact that a regime of classification has allowed the share of information that is marked secret to swell in proportion. As a consequence, it can hardly surprise us when there are millions of people in the United States with a security clearance, half of whom are at top secret or higher, according to the director of national intelligence.[70] Only about a third of them are government employees; the rest are contractors or "other." The National Science Foundation and other grant agencies remain keenly interested in the potential of virtual worlds and online games.[71] And indeed, experts continue to explore "the potential of virtual worlds for decentralized command and control," as one recent study of "operation-alizing c2 agility" has it.[72] With the question of such potential posed once more, the idea of securing a game-based virtual world for command and control operations is an obvious concern, especially if the software and the networks deployed are often open architectures. The Snowden documents gave selected insights into some NSA activities, but we also know that the CIA, NRO, FBI, DEA, and local police all engage in ubiquitous surveillance using the same sorts of eavesdropping tools, and that they regularly share information with each other. While it seems unlikely that virtual worlds and online games are still a major target, the quixotic goal to know and track everything that is communicated has obviously not changed. This is because of the fundamental asymmetry in cybersecurity: an offender only has to find a new method of attack, while the defender bears the cumulative cost of forever defending against all attack methods discovered. State agencies therefore have to worry that the cost of finding a new attack is lower than the cost of defending against all potential attacks discovered to date.

It is an idle question whether states need espionage; no sizable nation can do without it as long as the others engage in it. But this does not settle the question of methods, nor the definition of targeting. It is unclear whether the Snowden leaks are crystallizing any legislative changes to surveillance in online environments; certainly the agencies have been arguing that oversight has been improved and no further changes are necessary. In Britain, oversight and accountability for surveillance is remarkably recent, with regulatory systems dating to the RIPA Act of 2000. The European Court of Justice in 2014 found that the data retention of the British Investigatory Powers Act breached the directive of the European Council of July 12, 2002, concerning the processing of personal data and the protection of privacy in electronic communications. Whether these kinds of rulings have consequences for what GCHQ and its partners do after Brexit remains to be seen. Some in the British press charged that the Security Service (MI5), the Secret Intelligence Service (MI6), and GCHQ (which has more employees than the other two services) acted in bad faith, but that momentum has not been maintained.

Pervasive clandestine and covert surveillance of online games and virtual worlds is arguably in direct contravention of international human rights law. Article 12 of the Universal Declaration of Human Rights and Article 17 of the International Covenant on Civil and Political Rights both

clearly state that "No one shall be subjected to arbitrary or unlawful interference with his privacy, family, home or correspondence, nor to unlawful
attacks on his honor and reputation," and that "Everyone has the right to
the protection of the law against such interference or attacks."[73] Even if one
did not hold that online games and virtual worlds belong to the sphere of
correspondence included in the declarations, the extent to which privacy is
implicated can be unfolded in some detail.[74] Technology as a challenge for
law enforcement and security is not an issue limited to internet communications; when in the 1990s the US sought to combat digital and wireless
communications that can hamper surveillance, Congress passed the Communications Assistance for Law Enforcement Act (CALEA), which requires
telecommunications carriers to assist with authorized electronic surveillance. It is unclear whether the developers and operators of online games
and virtual worlds were approached for similar assistance; at least Blizzard
is on the record as stating that they were unaware of the spying on *World of
Warcraft*. And it is clear also that different media technologies pose different
potential or real security risks. As one security guru observes,

> In the days of radio, there was Sarnoff's Law, namely that the value of a broad-
> cast network was proportional to N, the number of listeners. Then came pack-
> etized network communications and Metcalfe's Law, that the value of a network
> was proportional to N squared, the number of possible two-way conversations.
> We are now in the era of Reed's Law, where the value of a network is proportional
> to the number of groups that can form in it, that is to say 2 to the power N.[75]

It would be impossible to write the history of the internet without a history of its hubris, but whatever one may think of this kind of calculation
(which hinges on the uninterrogated assumption that each connection is
equally valuable), the facts remain: networked computers have been used
for playful exploration, in fictional modes and otherwise, practically since
their inception. Gamers have long suspected that networks are not neutral; it is no coincidence that the latest national security leak propagated
from Discord to 4Chan before spilling into mainstream media.[76] Despite
and because of a black-boxed infrastructure that has grown increasingly
complex, communities spring up whenever people congregate online,
information is traded, therefore also hidden and fetishized and encrypted
and decrypted. As long as we cast the infrastructural conditions of possibility of gaming in a shroud, we sow distrust and allow for conspiracy theories. As long as regulators and network operators invest in security through

obscurity, they provoke hacking and leaking. Media critic danah boyd calls leaking information "the civil disobedience of our age," arguing that revealing a secret is the strongest protest against secret courts, secret laws, and secret programs.[77]

One creative response to the Snowden leaks in general and their relevance to gaming in particular is a recent installation called "Secret Power" by the artist Simon Denny. With pieces like *Modded Server-Rack Display with Some Interpretations of David Darchicourt Designs for NSA Defense Intelligence*, it was first displayed in the Biblioteca Nazionale Marciana in 2015 when Denny represented New Zealand at the 56th Venice Biennale; it has since been acquired by MoMA.[78] In this show, Denny juxtaposed his installation art with graphics, charts, and other images from the Snowden leaks, which he argues had "retroactively become some of the most important artistic images created today."[79] Intrigued by the way the contemporary world is depicted in images used by NSA and other agencies, Denny had found examples of Darchicourt's work on freelancer graphics sites, and decided to commission new images (including a map of New Zealand) from the graphic designer in Maryland; Darchicourt had indeed worked as an NSA graphic designer for a number of years until 2012. Moreover, Darchicourt also created images between 1994 and 2012 for NSA's public-facing work, such as a series of "CryptoKids" cartoon characters, intended to educate children about the agency; they include Cy, "known to his friends as the best gamer on the block."[80] Simon Denny in turn went on to use Darchicourt's images for his installation in Venice without asking for permission, in case he would not give it; in fact, Denny has gone on record stating that using them without permission was crucial to the project.[81] Invoking the history of Venice in international espionage, Denny sought to offer a perspective on the visual culture of the Five Eyes intelligence alliance (which includes New Zealand) as illustrated by the documents leaked by Snowden in 2013 and 2014.[82] Part of Denny's "Secret Power" show was also on display at Marco Polo airport (which like any international airport is a contemporary citadel of state security), symbolically linking it to a Renaissance library known for its ceiling of allegorical images about the acquisition of knowledge. While Darchicourt said that he had not personally designed any of the Snowden PowerPoint slides, he confirmed to newspapers that he designed logos used internally at the NSA, for instance for the program POISON NUT.[83] Denny's Venice Biennale installation also cited imagery from leaked slides regarding various covert programs and TAO tools; in order to reveal something about the visual language of state surveillance, Denny not only installed them in modified server racks and office furniture—he also explicitly selected images that were lifted from online and gaming culture. Denny points out that the Snowden leaks featured images evoking the *Terminator* series' Skynet in the TREASUREMAP net mapping program, wizards used as icons for the phone-tapping program MYSTIC, and images evoking the game *Shadowfist* on slides describing QUANTUM (an NSA attack program that duplicates internet traffic).[84] In this iconography of surveillance, game culture comes full circle. Rather than relegate such expressions of networked culture to the margins, it is pivotal to reenter them into the way we remember and understand the history of computing.[85]

5 *Virtual U*: The Simulation of Higher Education

It may seem odd to see higher education administration modeled in a simulation game, but in the context of online education and rampant gamification it is surely not entirely unexpected. Despite considerable uncertainty, at least half a dozen trends can be readily identified for higher education in the twenty-first century. Institutions of higher learning see themselves in a global context of cooperation and competition. The growing influence of information technology on the creation, distribution, and absorption of knowledge has led some observers to predict a departure from traditional modes of communication and collective memory.[1] An increasing emphasis on interdisciplinary approaches also has both direct and indirect consequences for academic planning. The public–private interface is changing in the research and technology sector, and basic research now relies increasingly on private support. This has also accelerated the use of new performance assessments and priorities for intellectual inquiry; with the implementation of public–private partnerships come not only new performance indicators and benchmarking exercises, but also mutual agreements in teaching, research, and technology transfer. Finally, growing public concern about scientific and technological development, not just in areas like nanotechnology or stem cell research, increased political attention to parameters of universities' contributions to the public good. Telling the story of the transformation of knowledge work from tabletops to screens implies a history of management. A management simulation will therefore prominently exhibit the assumptions baked into its model about the system being modeled: as Bogost observes,

> In *Virtual U*, software technology structures the player's experience, both educating him or her on aspects of university management and reinforcing the

assumptions underlying such a structure. The game is an inspiring amalgam of software engineering, game design, management, and public policy, and in that sense it is a promising specimen of a critical network in practice.[2]

Universities have not been exempt from the inexorable rise of administrative technology.[3] Since the 1970s it has also shaped what some have called the cybernetic university, despite the apparent untimeliness of the phrase (because late in the twentieth century, cybernetics had seemed to fade away and merge into new perspectives).[4] One can quite plausibly interpret the computerization of academic administration as a reaction to growing pains in higher education and to functional differentiation under decades of neoliberal budget austerity. Still, some academic observers were caught by surprise by this cybernetic turn in higher education, since self-governance seemed so central and unbureaucratic an academic tradition.[5] The volunteer character of university administration had long remained unprofessional, and professors did not think of comparing their organization to corporate organizations and their metrics of efficiency and productivity. Education reformers deploy the plastic words of *excellence* and *efficiency* to foster a further McDonaldization of the university, with cheaper content, larger classes, fewer instructors, more online education, and a general dissolution of the standards and discursive fields that units had grown painstakingly over decades and generations.[6] For several reasons, the 1970s were a turning point in academic administrative culture. Buffeted by the demographic and political drivers of enrollment growth and budget austerity, university management is also transformed by information technology and by a rapid series of punishing reforms that reduce the autonomy of higher education as a social institution.

From the 1970s on, austerity politics hit higher education especially hard, and most institutions have never had a chance to recover since then.[7] European as well as American universities are notoriously underfunded, overenrolled, and structurally neglected; the so-called Humboldt model, imported from German academia to mold American universities, is in doubt.[8] As a consequence, universities met the new challenges of budget constraints, political pressures, and enrollment growth by adopting the ways of "new public management," including the installation of computerized administrative interfaces—they seemed to promise the institutional stabilization that would buffer academia against change management.[9] As computing took on new ways of collating, visualizing, and manipulating data, academic administration soon adopted them as well.[10] Soon operations research, systems engineering, and project management took hold also in academic administration.[11] Today we are used to the idea that resource and space management, personnel and time management, project management and strategy planning should rely rather heavily on computer models. But the conquest of academia by computing does not stop with the professionalization of central services and the rapid growth in administrative services; higher education in the eighties and nineties also saw computing introduced outside central administrative functions. Computing systems are now as critical for scheduling, announcing, and supporting lectures and seminars as they are for research projects, and not just for enrollment management, budget and finance, space management, and grant tracking—everything has become part of a large, interconnected database.[12] As a consequence, the legacy of (at least partial) academic autonomy—the partial self-determination of professors, departments, research centers, schools, and other parts of the university—have been hollowed out, since their functioning increasingly depends on being part of the integrated administrative systems that run the entire campus.[13]

While the *Sputnik* shock of 1957 led to a period of rapid growth of higher education in the sixties, it also brought about a much more explicit focus on political aims for higher education.[14] The resulting national research funding initiatives are one side of the resulting change; the rapidly growing emphasis on managerial structures has been part and parcel of the same effort since the seventies.[15] As the study of complex systems increasingly relied on computer models, it was only a matter of time until academic administration was included. The growth of systems modeling was made possible by machines that could instantiate observed or posited characteristics of natural or social systems. As early as 1975, Owen Gaede designed *Tenure*, a simulation of the first year of secondary school teaching, for the PLATO computer system.[16] As methods for modeling and simulation were refined and found commercial applications in games, since the 1980s experts have asked, "Wouldn't it be nice if you could drive the future before you wrote the check?"[17] The question is always whether organizational simulation adequately models an organization's culture, a set of key characteristics including its values, policies and norms, and the behaviors of key constituencies. This challenge to simulation was soon met by interactive computer models proposing powerful tools for predicting the performance of complex dynamic systems. While there is always a risk that necessary abstraction or approximation makes models lose precision or omit variables, or inversely that the rich data of a simulation model make us forget about assumptions baked into the model, increasingly we expect experts to be trained on simulations, and simulations in turn to be trained by experts. What makes learning organizations complex is that they face difficult dynamic decisions—responding to contingencies without complete information. Simulation models seek to reveal the result of interacting dynamics, and create synthetic scenarios that can be analyzed, whether in real time or after a few run-throughs.

Advances in organizational simulation were inspired also by the visions laid out in Apple's Knowledge Navigator (1987) and Sun's Starfire (1994), both inheriting elements from Alan Kay's work on the Dynabook.[18] The Knowledge Navigator is widely credited not only with predicting assistants like Siri, Alexa, or Cortana, but also with advances in data visualization and interface culture. Surely it is no accident that the now famous video for the Knowledge Navigator features a tweedy professor dispatching his chores with the aid of new technologies. The infamous video follows a distracted professor who returns home and turns on his computer in the form of a tablet the size of a large-format book. A software agent appears as a bow tie–wearing butler on the screen to inform him that he has several calls waiting. He ignores several from his mother, and instead uses the system to compile data for a talk on deforestation in the Amazon rainforest. While he is doing this, the computer informs him that a colleague is calling, and they then exchange data through their machines while holding a video conversation. The Knowledge Navigator video premiered in 1987 at Educom, the leading higher education conference, in a keynote by Apple CEO John Sculley, with demos of multimedia, hypertext and interactive learning. A decade later, science adviser and systems analyst Jesse Ausubel publicly presented his vision for "Simulating the Academy." Colleges and universities are complex and arcane, and "not well understood at a systems level even by those who live and work inside them," went his pitch. At the time a grant officer at the Alfred P. Sloan Foundation, Ausubel outlined his vision for a simulation of higher education administration:

> Lack of understanding mattered less when the academy was held in high esteem and resources flowed to it at rates sufficient to maintain internal stability. But times have changed, the gleam of the ivory tower has dulled. A growing number

of critics now believe that while educational services are central to America's successful future, existing colleges and universities are failing to adequately manage
their affairs.[19]

These structural transformations soon gave rise to the modeling of higher
education as a system of inputs and outputs with feedback characteristics.
Two years later, Stanford administrator William Massy announced that mis-
conceptions about higher education abound, and "these adversely affect
the higher education policy environment and institutions' ability to gov-
ern themselves." Since Massy and Ausubel had independently conceived
of a simulation as the proper response to that problem, they teamed up to
produce a university simulation game, together with Enlight Software of
Hong Kong (led by Trevor Chan, designer of games like *Capitalism* [1995]
and *Capitalism II* [2001]) as well as DigitalMill of Maine (led by Ben Sawyer,
cofounder of the Serious Games Initiative and the Games for Health Project), programmed in C++ for a Windows environment.[20] Claiming that "key
stakeholders appear not to recognize or accept facts about how colleges and
universities work," Ausubel and Massy proposed that "complexity in managing the system stems from lack of agreement or clarity among the stakeholders about purposes, measures of performance, and productivity." After
Ausubel and Massy pooled their experience and resources, their proposal
for academic administration simulations took the form of a commercially
available simulation game, playable on Windows NT computers and sold
as *Virtual U.*[21]

Before I turn to the actual game title (later also available in version 2.0
as a download, but now playable, after the demise of the Windows XP–
oriented program, only with an emulator), let me sketch the background
that led to the development of this remarkable simulation game. "The idea
is to give academics and non-academics alike a window into the complex
workings of a university, in the same vein as the hit game *Sim City* gave
players a feeling for the complexities of building and managing a city."[22]
Institutional research has long produced data and selected representations
of such data about higher education. Before we get to wonder who the
intended (or unintended) audience for such interactive software might be,
and before we take a look at its affordances and strictures, it is worth tracing the intellectual arc that led the Stanford administrator William Massy
and his collaborators to assemble a team that would implement such an
odd game.[23] Massy's efforts to formalize a cybernetic administration for

higher education can be studied in the massive tome *Planning Models for Colleges and Universities*, published in 1981.[24] Discussing at length the implicit or explicit mental models synthesizing as much of known facts as is possible within the given reference system, Hopkins and Massy state plainly that "planning models are products of modern decision science"— but at the same time they emphasize from the first page on that "we are wholeheartedly opposed to the notion of quantitative modeling as a substitute for the kind of qualitative decision making that is the essence of academic leadership."[25] Nonetheless, in almost 600 pages to follow, they present planning models for student enrollment, faculty workloads, sponsorship of research, fundraising, and the need for financial trade-offs, admitting that all of them involve institutional values and intangibles that must be built into models even though they risk being dominated by tangibles.[26] As Hopkins and Massy warn, models must not only be verified (or shown to have been constructed as their design required) but validated (to test whether the degree of approximation to the reference system is adequate). It is this latter concern that will guide my discussion of their work as it led to the development of Massy's model as a higher education simulation game, *Virtual U.*

This college simulator draws on three concurrent developments: management education games increasingly in use in management education, special purpose simulations developed for enterprises (from nuclear plants to military tactics), and commercial interactive entertainment software of the type that includes successful titles like *SimEarth*, *SimHealth*, and *SimCity*. These games use continuous computation, graphics, and sound to sustain user interest, and they make individual gamers play against the model. The guiding idea behind *Virtual U* was that administrators (and observers of higher education administration) have gaps in knowledge and credibility that "form major barriers to experimentation and reform," Ausubel and Massy argued.[27] Management science and operations research have long made their homes in universities, so it stands to reason that they would look at their own institutional support structures. But at what point are we assured that applying the tools of such disciplines to the campus that enables them is neither the occasional academic navel gazing or *pro domo* special pleading nor an ideological attack on ivory tower faculty from certain motivated actors? Indeed, in a study of "cybernetic administration" in higher education, Birnbaum explicitly warned that "external political or bureaucratic forces may point to obvious institutional shortcomings and demand correction, without understanding either the existing benefits for which they were a trade-off or the significant costs to be paid elsewhere in the institution for improving them."[28] Nonetheless, Hopkins and Massy point to a presentation by Dartmouth President (and mathematician) John Kemeny in 1972 that called for systematic modeling of colleges and universities. Kemeny mentioned faculty appointment and promotion rates, departmental allocations, academic program options, and the relation between endowment yield and capital spending. Notably absent from that first salvo was a representation of student enrollments, graduation rates, and attrition. Here I need to record a warning Hopkins and Massy issued already in 1981: While faculty staffing models may include aggregate factors such as age distributions, tenure ratios, or workload measures,

> there have been no successful efforts to model comprehensively the two most crucial areas of decision that must be faced by academic administrators. The first of these is the choice of academic disciplines in which the institution should try to excel: what mix of faculty appointments in particular subdisciplines and specialties will be needed to attain or maintain excellence? The second is the choice of criteria and measures for evaluating individual faculty members for appointment and promotion.[29]

Importantly, they concede that models and simulations of higher education are rightly viewed with alarm, since "some of the techniques that have been highly touted are in fact seriously incomplete with respect to academic and human considerations." They know, in short, that their models do not represent the reference system very well; faculty distrust of administrative modes therefore has less to do with lack of familiarity, and more to do with several major trends well recognized inside academia, but often misunderstood off campus, namely demographics, inflation, and increasing research specialization as drivers of academic cost that the universities and colleges have little or no control over.[30] While *Virtual U* makes an effort to model demographics, it is no surprise that it missed out on the major role played in the past two decades by international student enrollment in the US; notably, the simulation does not model inflation.

While it stands to reason that planning, programming, and budgeting can use spreadsheets, graphs, computer models, and predictive modeling, the management information systems required to track course demand statistics, enrollment trends, and long-term employment patterns lagged behind in the 1970s. Yet it was becoming evident that resource allocation needed to include these if it did not want to risk abandoning institutional values.[31] Interestingly, room scheduling was the problem that first invited computerization. As Hopkins and Massy note, a survey of ninety-six colleges and universities indicated that a third of them had begun to use computers first to aid with room scheduling. Later, analyzing an applicant pool's size and composition enabled the prediction of yield rates, and models soon sought to incorporate repeats, dropouts, and transfers. *Virtual U* operates with a market model for full-time undergraduates that classifies applicants into segments: blue chip, scholar, extracurricular, athlete, balanced, average, and stretch. Segment sizes and yield preferences are informed by longitudinal national data; depending on the player-president's input of priorities for the scenario, the admissions algorithm generates the ratios of applications, admissions, and matriculations for each segment. As university administrators, furthermore, Hopkins and Massy were also interested in optimizing staffing models—and while those had to reflect institutional values, they also needed to be responsive to enrollments or they would show gross inequities. Here they are among the first, as far as I can tell, to go beyond linear models and recommend Markov chains and cybernetic feedback processes.[32]

As the strategy guide to *Virtual U 1.0* boasts, it uses mathematical techniques that were quite advanced for simulations at the time: linear programming for faculty hiring, quadratic programming in student admissions and in the central budgeting engine, and Poisson probability models to determine sponsored research proposals and awards. The simulation game *Virtual U* lets you play as president of a US university. You choose how faculty spend time, allocate funds, and decide if you should give special admission to athletes. You set institutional and departmental budgets as a way to make decisions over hiring and compensation, as well as enrollment management and facilities, and so on. The first version was sold on CD-ROM and was playable on Windows 95 or 98; a downloadable version 2.0 for 2000 or Windows XP improved the model and added features. The game development product was supported by the Alfred P. Sloan Foundation, a fact worth noting in discussing research funds for higher education and university administration. *Virtual U* is now archived at the Stanford University website.[33] Data to drive the model, which draws heavily on a few decades of research by Massy and his collaborators on higher education policy,

were collected by the University of Pennsylvania's Institute for Research in
Higher Education, and by Massy's interlocutors at various research universities around the United States.[34] Massy admits, "while *Virtual U* is necessarily
a caricature of real academic life, it is grounded in authentic conceptual
structures."[35] As president, the player faces certain standard scenarios, such
as balancing a budget, increasing faculty salaries, improving pedagogy, boost-
ing research, winning athletic competitions, controlling tuition increases,
enrolling more minority students, and so forth. In addition, presidents can
also confront chance events, for instance, a governor making a sudden
change in higher education appropriations, Congress adjusting research
funding, or serious scandals or accidents on campus.

As the *Virtual U* strategy guide makes clear, the simulation operates on
seven computing modules. They are basically invisible to the player, but
they critically limit what the simulation permits you to explore. These
seven modules are enrollment management, faculty hiring and retention,
academic operations, nonacademic operations, physical plant, resource
allocation, and endowment asset allocation. Each of them is programmed
to work behind the scenes to inform the gameplay. For instance, enrollment management consists of application submissions, admission offers,
and matriculation decisions; the module always assumes that fewer people
matriculate than receive admission offers, and it also has implicit assumptions about checks and balances in financial aid (merit-based for academic
excellence, need-based for economic diversification, and universal aid for
doctoral students). The faculty hiring module runs calculations in the background that limit what the player-president can do in any given academic
year of gameplay; it handles the probability of promotion of faculty from
one rank to another (including age, service length, and research productivity), and it implicitly models the aging and departure of faculty. Interestingly, the nonacademic operations module reflects assumptions about
how investments in library and information technology affect morale and
work quality both of faculty and of students collectively; in addition, as the
strategy guide reveals, "IT performance also affects the number of courses
taught using distance technology and the University's attraction to distance
students."[36] Without rehearsing all details of the seven modules, what is crucial is that the president-player's inputs include a target, the relative importance of the target, and acceptable upper and lower limits for each variable.
The simulation then "sets its recommended values to minimize an index

equal to the weighted sum of squared deviations between these values and the targets." This index (called an objective function in the vernacular of modeling) determines the weights—so if your gameplay targets tuition growth at 2.5 percent and financial aid growth at 3 percent, with the financial aid target declared twice as important as the tuition raises, the part of the objective function dealing with these variables would be "1(tuition_ growth—2.5)^2 +2(aid_growth—3.0)^2." The model instantiates the accounting entities that require your gameplay to always steer between acceptable bounds, as if your staff impose consistency while carrying out your instructions as far as they can. As a consequence of these built-in modules, the simulation operates as a system of multiple interdependent variables, and each decision the player makes has knock-on effects: faculty morale depends on salary, teaching load, discretionary time, and performance. Faculty and student diversity influences minority morale and retention. Pedagogy, student quality, teaching load, and class size affect graduation rates. As Massy announced before the game was first released, these operate "through single or dual logistic response functions, classic s-shaped curves or stacked pairs of s-shaped curves, which have been parametrized judgmentally." Moreover, professors in the simulation will progress from year to year according to a Markov process, with transition possibilities to promote, depart, and continue in rank; the continuation possibility of assistant professors goes to zero after seven years, and the one for full professors declines as they pass age fifty-five.

The simulation knows only two issues that can delay a student's progression toward graduation—denial of entry into courses, or failure after the course has been taken; other (rather commonplace) student life issues are not part of the model. As Massy put it in 1999, "supply side effects derive from the faculty's preference for one or another teaching method, faculty size, and permissible teaching loads. . . . Departments have a preferred teaching method mix, which the president may seek to influence."[37] Were we to accept this reductive model, then we could not be taken by surprise when Massy also stipulates that "substantially larger class size limits for distance students stimulate a virtual learning environment." At issue here is not simply the fundamental question whether or not teaching, learning, and research are production functions that one can fully understand and model economically as market relations—raising broad objections, but also more subtle issues such as who the appropriate behavioral relations are with when we look at student demand, staff recruiting, or faculty retention; surely it is obvious that universities and colleges do not compete with other enterprises, and that many only see themselves competing with a small subset of other colleges and universities.[38] The *Virtual U* strategy guide and Massy's other publications on the game make it clear that the default settings require close attention to the trustees' annual evaluation letter, the year-end financial statements, and the budget.[39] While these are certainly among the preoccupations of a college or university president, they barely reflect on the highly visible role of such educational leaders in setting and articulating institutional values and communicating not only with trustees and politicians but just as much with alumni, parents, employees, and partner institutions. Those things are either too vague to be reduced to mathematical models, or too little understood.

This is partly the official motivation for marketing a simulation game like *Virtual U*: as renowned serious games developer Ben Sawyer, who worked on turning Massy's administrative vision into interactive software, told me, the team expected that the game would train department chairs and other part-time administrators to step up to full-time administrative roles in the cybernetic university.[40] Sawyer is not only a games consultant and developer, but also the founder of the Serious Games Initiative (a project of the US government's Woodrow Wilson International Center for Scholars), one of the leading organizations in the field of serious games. In 2000, he began producing the Alfred P. Sloan Foundation's university simulation game, *Virtual U*, which was an award finalist at that year's Independent Games Festival.[41] As the press noted admiringly at the time,

> Graduate programs for future leaders in higher education management at more than 35 universities already use the software. More than 15,000 faculty members and other representatives of more than 800 universities around the world have downloaded and used the first version of the software.[42]

In one of the most influential studies of higher education in the US, Clark Kerr, the long-serving president of the University of California, listed the following pivotal long-term directions: improve access, concentrate on core fields, keep faculty salaries competitive, maintain libraries and physical plant, preserve institutional autonomy.[43] Nonetheless, his successors, whether or not they play *Virtual U*, tend to see these five goals not as equally important but as trade-offs: federal funds for basic science compete with financial aid for students, deferred maintenance for the physical plant

competes with investments in new infrastructure, retention of star professors competes with a fair wage for other employees, laboratory sciences
compete with the liberal arts, and the professional schools compete with
the core campus disciplines. These choices are not always made explicit in
the *Virtual U* simulation game, but they can easily emerge from a casual
round of play.[44] One aspect foreseen better by Clark Kerr than by *Virtual
U* is the virtualization of instruction—Kerr wondered "whether or not the
greatly improved hardware and software for the new electronic technology may, at last, start to penetrate teaching as it has already research and
administration."[45] Remarkably, while many administrators today (including, prominently, the president of Arizona State University, Michael Crow)
continue to push the idea that online education must replace in-person
instruction, Kerr understood that

> the experience to date suggests that each new technology adds to but does not
> totally supplant prior technology—oral teaching added to apprenticeship experi-
> ence, the written word added to the spoken word, printing added to handwriting,
> and it seems likely that the chip will add to but not replace all the methods that
> have gone before.[46]

Online education all too quickly became positioned as a panacea—some
even proposed that the "Virtual University" serve as a conceptual model for
faculty change.[47] Despite the fact that dropout rates in online education are
as high as they ever were, eLearning is still touted widely.[48] And not surprisingly, when *Virtual U 2.0* became available as a free download, it not only
featured "more risk of being fired" but also a "new and expanded distance
learning model."[49] But here one may wish there was more of a direct link
between the role of distance education and the idea of firing institutional
leadership.[50] In a 1998 report, the consulting firm Coopers & Lybrand suggested that online technology could eliminate two significant cost factors:
the first is the need for bricks and mortar—traditional campuses are not
necessary; the second is full-time faculty. Would any savings or efficiencies
in online instruction be due mainly to increasing student–faculty ratios
and decreasing proportions of ladder-rank faculty? If one were to decrease
ladder-rank faculty numbers relative to student numbers, then surely the
university's character as a research university would be diminished. A
meta-analysis by the US Department of Education did find some benefits
in distance learning—not, however, due to any technology used, but only
insofar as online learners may spend more time on task than students in

face-to-face conditions. How would this redefine faculty workload? Asynchronous delivery models for online courses let students access materials and pose questions 24/7, so it is harder for instructors to manage their time devoted to the class. One of the largest and most successful universities for remote and online instruction, the Open University in the UK, educated hundreds of thousands of students over the past several decades using remote instruction, but it is not considered a major research university. The COVID-19 pandemic only accelerated the pressure on higher education to provide online access, even as students loudly denounced it as boring and awkward; though MOOC hype peaked long ago, their risible completion rates did not deter administrators from pushing for more Udacity, more Coursera, more Zoom, more Teams.[51]

In 1885, William Rainey Harper (an early pioneer of distance education who went on to become president of the University of Chicago) predicted that the day would come when "work done by correspondence will be greater in amount than that done in the classroom of our academies and colleges." By 1919, over seventy American universities offered correspondence programs, actively competing with about 300 for-profit correspondence schools. Yet though the universities initially promised high-quality courses taught by experienced professors, spiraling administrative costs soon made them resort to inexperienced and poorly paid instructors. Correspondence programs at UC Berkeley saw dropout rates of 70 to 80 percent. Still, in 1997, UCLA launched an "Instructional Enhancement Initiative" and started a for-profit subsidiary, The Home Education Network (THEN), headed by a former UCLA vice chancellor. The company subsequently changed its name to OnlineLearning.net, reflecting its abandonment of video-based programs, and UCLA soon unwound its contract with THEN due to quality concerns. In the late 1990s, NYU, Temple, and Cornell (among others) also set up online subsidiaries—NYUonline, eCornell, Virtual Temple—to tap into the seemingly limitless market in online learning. Virtual Temple closed its doors in July 2001; four months later, NYUonline shut down, after burning through $25 million. Nonetheless, the state of California recently pumped tens of millions of dollars into Calbright College, an "online community college" that even the state's own audit found to be overpaying its management while underserving its few students.[52] Faculty at the University of Arizona were irate about its agreement to acquire for-profit Ashford University to create a new University of Arizona Global Campus that sounds a lot like

Purdue University Global. Does following in such wasteful footsteps not seem ill-advised? When politicians consider the fallout from such attempts to disrupt higher education, they ought to consider less which dot-com lobbyist will fund their next reelection but focus on what factors into a quality experience.[53] Good course development is costly; quality courses always need to be updated regularly. Hedonic pricing does not apply here; a house bought a decade ago is comparable with new houses on the market, but a computer bought ten years ago cannot be considered comparable to one bought today. The same goes for courses in higher education, and curricular innovation fed by original research cannot be discounted. For decades now, it has been routine for people who wanted to podcast or to stream and archive video of their lectures to do so; yet this has never obviated the need for new lectures.

Let us also look at the way *Virtual U* scores gameplay. Simulations can keep running, but games imply a sense of winning or losing. As Bogost has it, "The simulation fever that reigns in *Virtual U* is its ability to represent and facilitate administrative change in academic institutions of all shapes and sizes."[54] While most simulations do not require a clear win condition, they do allow scoring mechanisms. Playing *Virtual U* means being evaluated in annual performance evaluations and, at the end of the envisioned interaction or chosen scenario, an ultimate score that can also be entered into an online Hall of Fame. The minimum threshold expected by the simulation is maintaining financial viability. A president's annual performance evaluation depends on four factors: academic output measures (graduations, publications), institutional performance indicators (effective teaching, maintenance of nonacademic operations), reputation (awards, grants), and financial status (debt or surplus).[55] The model is weighted so that institutional prestige, educational quality, the percentage of alumni who donated in the past five years, and scholarship are all equally important, and each twice as important as student or faculty diversity (though together they add up to as much). Particular scenarios allow bonus points. "Ultimate score = current trustee evaluation × (number of gaming years) + (current trustee evaluation — initial trustee evaluation) × 10 + total bonus points." Who would play this game? Who is it designed for? What do the developers allow, anticipate? Ausubel and Massy wrote in 1997, just before they tackled the realization of *Virtual U*, that the target market for a college administration simulator would be higher education administrators and faculty in leadership roles—a telling distinction, since it explicitly assumes that many full-time administrators are not in fact faculty members themselves.[56] What if regular faculty, not to mention students, were included (via models of meaningful shared governance) rather than simulated as input and output, respectively? The *Virtual U* strategy guide only has a minor place for the academic senate as a "collective voice" of the faculty, and does not recognize that meaningful shared governance lets faculty, not administrators, make most decisions about teaching and research. And despite the promise that subsequent versions of *Virtual U* would allow tailoring the data set and characteristics to different types of institutions (which would have made it more compatible with European or Australasian university types), that never happened. And despite an explicit admission in training materials for *Virtual U* that the majority of board members hiring, supervising, and firing college presidents have no meaningful experience either with faculty or with higher education administration, the way to keep score in the game is to get decent evaluations from the board of trustees (or at least not to get fired).

> Is there any way to truly fail at *Virtual U*? *Virtual U*'s board is fairly forgiving. Even several years of weak performance won't cause you to be removed from office. However, there is one thing that will cause you to lose at *Virtual U*—bankruptcy. Bankruptcy occurs if you continue to run deficits and carry the University beyond its line of credit for bank loans. This is why it is critical not to run a very high negative balance or deficit for the year.[57]

Even in 1997, the vision for the game was restricted mostly to a budget control vision, foregrounding "performance measures and the functions programmed into the game."[58] Indeed, in the end the question is whether *Virtual U* as it was developed and distributed is in fact an apt simulation that allows the player to explore higher education administration, or whether it merely boils down to a reductive and distorted model of academic administration that affords a modicum of gamification.[59] If (as game designer Ben Sawyer wrote to me in an email) the focus was on efforts to get administrators to play the game, and perhaps to get department chairs to start thinking about larger roles in administration, might one then stipulate that *Virtual U* was an effective training game? Is it a simulation that seeks to inculcate an open exploration of higher ed in the players, while at the same time allowing for an amount of contingency that allows students of higher ed to explore a virtual space for agency? Or is it more akin to a gamification title that strictly limits contingency because it has a restricted model of higher ed? To decide this, we need to look not only at the screens and decisions available in *Virtual U* and how they might compare to the interfaces used in current higher education administration, but also consider which of the assumptions baked into *Virtual U* actually hold up in university life as we know it.

> Simulations may be our best opportunity to create what Fredric Jameson calls "an aesthetic of cognitive mapping: a pedagogical political culture which seeks to endow the individual subject with some new heightened sense of its place in the global system." Playing a simulation means becoming engrossed in a systemic logic which connects a myriad array of causes and effects.[60]

In 1981, Massy asserted that a large part of a university's budget consists of faculty and staff salaries—he failed to mention the cost of their health benefits, which has risen far faster since then. But he was right to point out that wages are not the only source of pressure on the institution's budget.[61] While in his tome on *Planning Models* he correctly assumed that inflation would be a driver of all costs, *Virtual U* fails to incorporate it in its financial models—which is kind of like omitting the strategically crucial weather conditions from a simulator like *Civilization*.[62] Moreover, *Virtual U* sets out to model how productivity (whether measured in terms of enrollments, graduations, tuition revenues, publications, or grants) cannot simply increase without affecting other parts of the academic system negatively— if the student–faculty ratio deteriorates, this impacts pedagogy and student satisfaction as well as faculty morale, and if tuition increases faster than the wage rate in the economy, a university may risk pricing itself out of the market. Yet most preprogrammed scenarios you see offered in the game limit the time horizon in which such adverse impacts play out. Keeping faculty pay low, for instance, by adding auxiliary and part-time instructors, clearly affects educational quality as well as the reputation of the institution: and yet, in the decades since Massy clearly saw this, neither the simulation nor any real-world institution seems to have found good solutions to this. Various other assumptions in Massy's diligent research that clearly influence the game design have turned out to be wrong, despite his awareness that "much more needs to be known about prediction errors" in his model.[63] For instance, he surmised in 1981 that "it is doubtful whether the price of higher education can increase faster than wages indefinitely, even when significant sums are plowed back into financial aid"—yet this is precisely what has happened over the four decades since then.[64] Just as problematically, he asserted that "the university competes for many if not most of its staff employees in labor markets that are dominated by business firms"; in times of increasing specialization this has not held true, as staff require knowledge of legal precedents, federal regulations, financial aid systems, and other areas of expertise specific to academia.[65]

On this point, what explains the undeniable managerial bloat in education, and why is it not modeled in *Virtual U*, just as it is omitted in the apocalyptic scenarios and messianic PowerPoint presentations of neoliberal reformism? Surely a serious simulation of administration would have to consider the size and shape of the university's workforce overall, not just its faculty. One major area of concern for American academia is that although the overall higher education workforce nationwide is roughly stable, the number of faculty is shrinking. Meanwhile, the areas of the employee base that grew the most are administrative: student affairs (6.4 percent), business operations (7.1 percent), and "community, social service, legal, arts, design, entertainment, sports and media occupations" (6.6 percent). The picture at my own institution, the largest public university system in the world, is arguably worse. Almost 70 percent of the University of California's core funds (which constitute 19 percent of the overall UC budget) go toward salaries and benefits.[66] First, using information from the UC Statistical Summary of Students and Staff, let us compare two benchmark years, 1997–1998 and 2008–2009. During this period, full-time student enrollment increased by a third, from 169,862 to 226,040. The number of ladder-rank faculty only increased by a quarter, from 7,500 to 9,400. By comparison, the number of senior administrators classified as managers and senior professionals increased by 125 percent, from 3,651 to 8,230. Put another way, in 1997–1998, the University of California had one senior manager per 47 students and 2.1 faculty, while in 2008–2009, there was one senior manager per 27 students and 1.1 faculty. During this period, the number of lecturers increased by 54 percent, and the number of other non-ladder-rank faculty increased by 59 percent. Despite criticism of these trends when they were publicized statewide, the problem got worse: from 2011 to 2021, as UC student enrollments grew by 24 percent, faculty hiring lagged at 18 percent, while hiring in nonfaculty management positions jumped by 164 percent. As a consequence, the student–faculty ratio (one of the most meaningful metrics of the quality of an undergraduate education) rose further.[67] Other universities observed the same disturbing trends. At Yale, over the past two decades the number of managerial staff grew three times faster than the undergraduate student body (44.7 percent since 2003).[68] The University of Minnesota in the first decade of the twenty-first century added more than 1,000 administrators: their ranks grew 37 percent, more than twice as fast as faculty and nearly twice as fast as the student body.[69] Or take Auburn University as another example: between 2002 and 2016, Auburn added nearly 600 full-time employees, numbers published by the college show. The number of faculty grew by 10 percent while the number of administrators grew by 73 percent.[70] Ladder-rank faculty numbers nationwide have not kept up with student growth, while administrative hires far outpace student growth. Given that only ladder-rank faculty directly carry all three parts of a university's mission—teaching, research, and public service—their declining proportion raises questions about how well higher education is focusing on its core mission. Meanwhile, the rapid rate of growth in administrators provides ammunition to the universities' critics.

In responding to these findings, the UC's Office of Institutional Research argued that advances in technology require a more technically qualified workforce, but the bulk of the increase was in job titles such as managers (or directors) rather than computer programmers, engineers, or scientists. Another possibility is that professional and support staff are continuously reclassified as, or promoted to, more senior positions, yet the total number of lower-responsibility administrative jobs during this period also increased (by 36 percent, from 76,400 to 103,800). Indeed, the only major group of employees that did not keep up with student numbers was ladder-rank faculty. It has also been argued that the increase in senior administrators is due to an increased level of research at the university, as research expenditures increased by 74 percent in constant dollars during the period. Yet while the number of managers in the research functional area increased by 286 percent, from 220 to 850, the bulk of administrative growth was not in research support but in the institutional support functional area, a 106 percent increase from 1,160 to 2,390. One may also point to the role of hospitals, auxiliaries, and research as main drivers of employee growth at UC. Yet the number of non-medical center employees in the senior professional category, paid from general funds, increased by 125 percent, from 1,200 to 2,700, with earnings increasing, in constant dollars, by

192 percent between 1998 and 2008. Furthermore, one might note that UC campus administrations did not see a reduction in head count or budgeting commensurate with periodic budget cuts. These are alarming trends—the unarmed eye can see, from publicly available documents, that significant administrative growth in UC outpaced both student enrollment growth and faculty headcount. To make matters worse, in the decade since then, the trend exacerbated: between 2011 and 2021, UC administration continued to grow unchecked, while faculty hiring slowed down more. Management and senior professional hires increased by another 164 percent, while senate faculty increased by just 18 percent. Moreover, within these lagging ranks of senate faculty, tenure/tenure-track faculty increased by just 15 percent, while lecturers with security of employment increased by 187 percent. Obviously, UC has created irresistible incentives for bureaucratic proliferation that compound over time. Gamification has not dented this mission creep in higher education administration; but as the simulation does not model any controls for such employment trends, one cannot expect administrators training on the simulation to recognize their impact on their institutions.

Returning to tuition discussions: another major issue not modeled in *Virtual U* as a simulation of higher education administration is student protests. Formerly the last stand against neoliberal education reforms, they now almost seem nostalgic because they usually do not ask the pivotal question directly: what kind of university do we want? Many social forms that used to be ironclad modes of coping with uncertainty have become politically divisive—family, marriage, gender roles, class division, political parties, religious affiliation, the welfare state—yet one response remains a staple of all stump speeches about coping with our contemporary situation: we need education. To this extent, it is not the university as such that lies in ruins, but the pact between modern politics, academic science, and national culture.[71] In Europe, education reform fails to cope with national systems struggling to transform, and in the US, the role of the public land grant university has been all but abandoned for lack of political support, even as Asian and African countries seek to grow their education systems. As Beniger surmised, "synthetic life is certainly one of the possible products of the evolution of techno-bureaucratic control"; indeed, rampant gamification of education administration ignores what is unique in an institution built upon the fundamental unity of independent research, teaching, and service.[72] It would be a categorical error to confuse calls for autonomy in higher education with calls for a free market competition for the successor model to the public research university.[73] Such a crudely destructive substitution fails to realize the possibility that both research and teaching can and should be independent, in a meaningful way, both from state policy making and from industry interests, because both are inherently short-term, while fundamental research and effective student formation rely on a different time horizon.[74] By dint of its persuasive surface, *Virtual U* "threatens to perpetuate the assumptions that prevent critical networks from coming into being" and covers up the assumptions baked into its reading of educational administration.[75] Even the evangelist of disruption Clay Christensen warned that US universities must not lose their capacity for discovery, memory, and mentoring as their core defining features.[76]

Finally, already in 1981 Massy saw that "more effort is required in designing the appropriate interface between the user and the computer program."[77] So how does *Virtual U* stack up in the context of serious simulation games?[78] We know simulations can improve certain kinds of performance; we know simulations can be useful for training (which is different from learning). Yet there have not been a lot of studies that document whether simulation games do much for real learning. "A simulation is a representation of a source system via a less complex system that informs the user's understanding of the source system in a subjective way."[79] Game studies wondered for a while now what a state-of-the-art instructional video game would look like; the answers have been quite varied thus far. Gee's recommendation was to pick a domain of authentic professionalism, intelligently select the skills to be distributed, build a value system integral to gameplay, and relate instructions to specific contexts; too few games live up to this set of demands.[80] We have also come to accept that simulation games are not focused on entertainment.[81] As Bogost read it, "training simulation games such as *Virtual U* impart a more explicit pedagogy."[82] Serious games, a number of studies have found, tend to be more effective if regarded as a supplement to other instructional methods.[83] Other studies, however, found that games can decrease opportunities for peer interaction and communication with instructors, in some cases distracting students and hindering learning.[84] One study used *Virtual U* to examine the difference in academic achievement between students who did and who did not play it; adding the game to half the classes teaching third-year management students at an East Coast university in the US, identical tests were used and compared in terms of mean score as well as any differentiation by gender, ethnicity, or age. The result: students who used the game scored slightly better on average, but no differentiation by age, gender, or ethnicity was detected.[85] A review of *Virtual U* argued that it is a challenging game that is "realistic enough to be used as an educational tool. Just as *Capitalism Plus* is still used in business schools worldwide, *Virtual U* is being used around the US to train professional university administrators and education students."[86] Yet another review quips that it may seem impossible to "balance professors' dreams for a talented student body and a bigger research budget against students' desire for small classes and smaller tuition increases. And yes, the trustees want you to raise the institution's prestige and the alumni want to make sure the football team wins."[87] While it is fair to say that this simulation starkly models certain administrative trade-offs and managerial limits in higher education, surely the act of placating board members and political stakeholders is not the true hallmark of academic leadership, even as we now face a serious deterioration nationwide in shared governance of academia.[88] History may indeed, as Roszak already did before the computerization of the university, lay the blame right at the feet of higher education administrators:

> Inevitably, the administrative and financial forces that came to govern American higher education chose to be catered to, not combatted. And so service came to mean the indiscriminate adaptation of the university to every demand that monied interests and the general public could imagine making.[89]

Conclusion

In looking at how simulation plays a pivotal role in computer museums, university administration, digital music, and (playing games on) the internet, the chapters of this book illustrate how cultural techniques are practices demonstrating the framing of digital cultures as conveyed by means of media and institutions.[1] Simulation has rapidly grown to become one of these major practices across multiple fields of knowledge and communication. Moreover, the operations of technical media are quantitative as well as qualitative, and computing makes this obvious—hence this book argues that in digital culture we observe how techniques of working with information impact the experience of our media age. "Quantity has been transmuted into quality," as Benjamin knew a century ago. "The greatly increased mass of participants has produced a change in the mode of participation. The fact that the new mode of participation first appeared in a disreputable form must not confuse the spectator."[2] This is indeed what we can observe in internet-enabled cultural expressions, whether we think of online gaming or of how people play with the sounds of computer games. In retro-gaming sounds we can recognize, as the chiptune chapter documented, three distinct models: computer synthesis, chiptune, and FakeBit. Each of these models optimizes for aesthetic engagement as it turns numbers into sounds, transmuting quantity into quality. "All that is not information, not redundancy, not form and not restraints is noise, the only possible source of new patterns," as we know about the study of digital culture.[3] Notably, these three address questions of whether and how to access and modify software and hardware rather differently. And while they may seem to follow a historical and technical progression, in fact their aesthetic and compositional principles commingle and recycle each other, forming a recursive discourse. Feedback loops, as Hayles points out, "connect the material, operational, and symbolic into an integrated, recursively structured hierarchy."[4] These constellations are what the chapters of this study lay out.

Simulations are perfect illustrations of what Lyotard foresaw about a "circumverse" that aims for stable circuits, equal cycles, expected repetitions, and trouble-free compatibility by immobilizing our bodies in a libidinal economy.[5] That in turn means tackling the purported gulf between quantitative and qualitative approaches.[6] For it is evident that "certain design characteristics of digital games (e.g., the differences between a mainly qualitative or quantitative feedback) have a significant impact on the quality of narrative or interpretative perception of the visual presentations in the games."[7] If quality is a fundamental category of thought, then it is so not only in the sense of relative evaluation or comparison, but also in the sense of recognition in general. Moreover, we recognize development or progress when a new quality results from cumulative quantitative change. Without rehashing a long philosophical debate from Hegel and Marx into the twenty-first century, suffice it to say that quantifiable inflection points can have qualitative impacts; the distinction of analog and digital media offers ready illustrations.[8] At the risk of oversimplifying, one could even stipulate that most humanities or social science approaches focus on the way qualities result from quantitative changes, while most STEM models subsume the qualitative into more readily tractable quantitative attributes that can be counted, calculated, measured. (At a certain temperature, water becomes ice or steam; one neuron by itself does not think, but 100 billion may form a structure that can produce consciousness.) Our contemporary knowledge differs from prior ages of inquiry not only in quantitative terms—in turn, these tipping points from quantity into quality are what makes models and simulations such epistemic engines in contemporary academic endeavors. It is worth searching for points where quantitative data become qualitative evaluations—testing the efficiency and efficacy of models, measuring the pedagogical or political or therapeutic intervention of programs and proposals, observing social and cultural dimensions of technical innovations. There is a reasonable demand in academia for a comprehensible, reproducible manner of evaluation—not merely in an aesthetic sense (although that dimension is often implied), but just as plausibly in a political sense, in a social dimension, in a competitive sense, in the sense of technical proficiency. It would be disingenuous to maintain an artificial mutual exclusion of quantitative and qualitative aspects, despite the fact that they have been associated with methods and paradigms that appear to be separate. This is not simply a matter of interpretive or statistical analysis, or of economic information. Observers of digital culture cannot afford to ignore certain forces that are clearly shaping the industry, but they also must not forget to return to interpretive modes after acquiring relevant technical information. Qualitative studies generate hypotheses that can be tested in quantitative studies. We often seem to forget that simulations remain open to evaluation and that designers as well as players of simulations must continuously reflect on the assumptions baked into the models.[9] Investigating the cultural techniques of simulation, based on a critical vocabulary for the history of simulation, means engaging in the pursuit of histories of the *as if*, respecting both the performative and the constative properties of simulations.[10]

What can make simulations educational is the opportunity to tweak aspects of a particular model so as to facilitate insight; this can be seen in the chapter on online gaming, but also in the chapter on computer museums.[11] Half a century ago, Kuhn already warned that "scientific education makes use of no equivalent for the art museum or the library of classics, and the result is sometimes a drastic distortion in the scientist's perception of his discipline's past."[12] Nonetheless, there are now, as the museum chapter delineates, serious attempts in many places around the globe to musealize the legacy of computing. Indeed, with Turkle's book on *Simulation and Its Discontents*, we may hold that "citizenship in the twenty-first century calls for readership skills in the culture of simulation, the digital equivalent to knowing the *Who, What, Where, Why, and How?* of print media."[13] This hypothetical literacy includes not just a critical distance from scenarios and proposals for the future, but also crucially involves historical knowledge. The museum chapter highlights the consequential distinctions between museums of computing and other museums, particularly with regard to the technical challenges faced by institutions seeking to preserve a semblance of the historical look and feel of an obsolete assemblage. Inversely, some experts have come to feel that "highly technical definitions of digital preservation are complicit in silencing the past."[14] Museums of computing, however, have found intriguing ways to make the quantitative collection flip into a qualitative experience. As Kittler put it, "the museum is a hybrid medium that—historically or opportunistically, but in any case unsystematically—coupled its elementary storage functions to other media of processing and transferring."[15] At the same time, museum professionals insist that we ought to try and "think of museums as media in respects other than their communicative role," and the pandemic certainly accelerated expectations from museums and collections.[16] "The museum, as Malraux has taught us, is not a place but a history," and the pages of this project seek to unfold the nonlinear aspects of that history under the auspices of digital culture.[17] However, the rhetoric of digital media is sundered because it both promises salvation and threatens oblivion by the very same function: "Digital archives are allegedly H. G. Wells's World Brain and André Malraux's museum without walls, among other dreams, come true," as Chun observes, yet "at the same time, however, computer archives have been targeted as the source of archival decay and destruction."[18] Of course, media culture is rather adept at transubstantiating decay and destruction. In the retro-gaming audio exploits discussed in the FakeBit chapter, we recognize three distinct models: computer synthesis, chiptune, and FakeBit. Each of the models optimizes for aesthetic engagement as it turns numbers into sounds, though they deal with the right to access and modify software and hardware differently. While they seem to follow a historical and technical progression, their aesthetic and compositional principles commingle and recycle each other recursively. Faced with this, the retro scene developed a kind of comparative philology—collecting, restoring, describing revisions of software for different platforms.

Perhaps nothing is more emblematic of the representations and misrepresentations of computing and its dark sides than a destroyed hard drive on display in a curious show at the London Science Museum from 2019 to 2020. Why would this important museum of the history of computing display a hard drive that was intentionally destroyed with angle grinders and drills? And why would such a strange choice for a museum piece later travel to the Victoria and Albert Museum, to the Science and Industry Museum in Manchester, and to the British Library? It was a Western Digital hard drive used by the newspaper *The Guardian* to protect some of the files leaked by Edward Snowden. On Saturday, July 20, 2013, agents of GCHQ accessed the basement of *The Guardian*'s office in Kings Cross and proceeded to make sure the drive would never function again.[19] Under the title TOP SECRET: From Ciphers to Cybersecurity, the Science Museum exhibit was sponsored by defense contractor Raytheon and ostensibly set out to tell the history of GHCQ and its predecessor agencies.[20] A century of service in the shadows was laid out for the museum visitor, with copious artifacts relating to Britain's role in the First and Second World Wars, but rather less detail about GCHQ during the Cold War and into the present. The special exhibition was organized in three sections: a historical display, a selective gallery on contemporary issues (like the WannaCry ransomware incident at NHS in 2017), and an interactive puzzle zone intended, according to curators, to inspire people to be interested in secret communications. Alongside the destroyed hard drive, another contemporary object on display was a resin container resembling a petri dish, backlit and displayed under acrylic protection—a sampling of secret agency dust. For GCHQ grinds down everything that is classified (not only paper but machinery and circuitry), and even that dust is classified. Under protective acrylic guaranteeing proper distance and lack of access, however, and in the prestigious environment of top museums, even the garbage of computer history can be transubstantiated.

There is now even a playful simulation of the Snowden leaks: the Australian title *Need to Know* has players climb the ranks of the NSA-like Department of Liberty, while confronting "suffocating privacy invasions" and facing decisions about them.[21] Designed for Windows by Monomyth and initially crowdfunded via Kickstarter, it was published on Steam, the streaming game distributor operated by Valve. This title illustrates the three models intersecting at the core of my surveillance chapter: the romantic notion of the magic circle that pretends to insulate play against the conditions of its very possibility, the exploitative reality of surveillance in all computer networks, and the hardy yet embattled notion of privacy that would try to mediate between those two incompatible ideas. Modeling network surveillance seeks to optimize security at scale by pushing the tipping point of metadata into behavioral management, but at the risk of sacrificing the essential quality of play.

This goes just as much for management simulations and scenario games. Indeed, in engaging with the administrative simulator *Virtual U*, it becomes obvious that, as Bogost diagnosed the setup, "when we learn to play games with an eye toward uncovering their procedural rhetorics, we learn to ask questions about the models such games present."[22] As my close reading of the higher education administration simulator *Virtual U* elucidates, it seeks to model where quantitative administrative data tip into educational quality, optimizing for management. There are once again three competing models here—the service ethos of academic self-governance runs afoul of the increasing privatization of education and the rapid hyperspecialization in research; therefore it cedes more and more ground to the professionalization of administration, which in turn incentivizes administrative growth that soon looks like bloat.[23] The included/excluded third in this pairing is a dark vision of cybernetic management announcing itself as a way to automate homeostatic circuits of inputs and outputs regulated via positive or negative feedback, attempting to mostly take humans out of the loop and call on administrators only when a consequential decision becomes unavoidable.[24] As legendary university administrator Clark Kerr put it so memorably, "Universities are engaged in Faustian bargains—they leave the toughest decisions to the future and to external authority, and lose both quality and autonomy in the process."[25] Yet from a cybernetic viewpoint, "because of the unusual characteristics of academic institutions, attempts to improve the 'management' of colleges and universities may reduce rather than increase effectiveness."[26] The flip side of this vision of cybernetic autonomy is evident as the specter of online education and gamification thoroughly undermines the core values of higher education, including but not limited to the integration of teaching and research. "Whoever speaks of culture speaks about administration as well, whether this is their intention or not"—and to this extent criticism is sand in the smoothly administered culture machine.[27] But criticism of our technocratic era must not stop at pointing out the symbiosis of computing and the management of culture. Hence in my study of computing legacies I look at training simulations (like the higher education game *Virtual U*) not merely as symptoms but also as potential critique of digital culture.

Research on collective memory and memorial cultures is one of the main strands in the humanities, fomenting trans- and interdisciplinary discussions. Williams called culture "one of the two or three most complicated words in the English language."[28] A key question about culture is what affords its transmission, continuity, or maintenance. To state that media are the answer to that question is not sufficiently specific, but if we agree that culture is the memory of a human collective that is not inherited biologically but shared otherwise, this involves oral or written, visual or acoustic or audiovisual circulation, and technical media have significantly accelerated the differentiation of culture. By the same token, culture is not only about recollection of the past, but its interpretation in the current context. Media afford both the communication of material indications from the past and the communication across time and space of recent or current concepts; "without mass media culture would not be recognizable as culture."[29] Technical media are now pivotal in education, information, and entertainment, providing for cultural continuity. However, media themselves are not neutral carriers of information (of ideas, values, norms, identities); they in fact often constitute what they seem to encode. A memorial, a book, a painting, or the internet can influence the modalities of our thinking, perception, recall, and communication.[30] The question is what difference simulation as a cultural technique makes; the chapters of this project unfold this question in a series of case studies in computational culture.

Pointing out that the historical semantics of "culture" hark back to ancient craft and agrarian methods, proponents of the phrase *cultural technique* argue that culture is neither textual nor audiovisual, but "centering around techniques and rites, skills and practices that provide for the stability of lived-in space the continuity of time."[31] The operative processes that enable us to work with things and symbols are conceptualized and formalized only after the cultural practices they encompass have been habituated; arguably, humans had been producing pictures and sculptures long before considering them art, wrote long before conceptualizing text, sang and made music without knowing much about notation or music theory.[32] Other examples include calculus, money, and maps—visibly not merely representing but manipulating what they represent; this is what one may call a cultural technique.[33] Latour retraced the transition from ground to words for the representational strategy of science and described it as a "dialectic of gain and loss," recognizing in the process a reduction in materiality and particularity, and an amplification of universal standards and mobilization.[34] Parikka pointed out the connection between common references for media studies and those who study cultural techniques:

> As readers of Michel Foucault (technologies of the self), Marcel Mauss (techniques of the body), and British cultural studies (Raymond Williams et al.), we already knew about the close relation between bodily habits, modes of perception and (media) technologies.[35]

Not just any technique is included in this purview, however—with "cultural techniques" the focus is on symbolic work, on recursive or second-order techniques.[36] And Siegert reminds us that this emphasis was not a speculative indulgence: "it was archival obsession rather than passion for theory that made renegade humanities scholars focus their attention on media as the material substrate of culture."[37] The task in analyzing cultural techniques is to retrace by what processes they recursively formalize the practices that generate them—processes of selection, storage, and transmission in symbolic systems.[38] Cultural techniques make symbolic work possible: they tend to be recursive, self-referential, second-order techniques; that is to say, we can speak about what is spoken and tell stories about storytelling, we can paint painters or paintings, sing about singing. This is certainly the case when it comes to simulation, but it has also led people to worry that it is ever more difficult to discern base reality from simulations.

On the one hand, culture coordinates, or enables communication by generating synchronous horizons, and social theorists emphasize this regulation of time as social coordination.[39] On the other hand, culture makes continuity possible, or passes along knowledge and ideas diachronically from generation to generation, across time and space. In this book, the emphasis is less on descriptions of the sociopolitical moment as foregrounded by cultural studies, STS, or similar vantage points on computing in general or simulation as a computer-mediated technique in particular, but on excavating and interpreting their historical conditions of possibility and the conceptual strands emerging from a longer view. To the thesis that a grouping of media-historic facts already amounts to a socio-history of media is opposed the antithesis that such an account dissolves the technical specificities of computing, and thus risks erasing and forgetting the legacy of computing. Observers have been warning against purported amnesia as an effect of the digital. Institutions of cultural memory may store deep structures that enable the reproduction of patterns in a continuity of symbolic communication, of actions and interpretations; but by the same token they embody a break that distinguishes the past from the present, reconstructing and reproducing it differently in collective systems of referentiality and meaning.[40] Hence, here the emphasis is on how such institutions—libraries, museums, universities, archives—are seen to react to and cope with the advent of computing in general and the technique of simulation in particular. The aim is not merely a description of an assemblage that has sociopolitical significance, but an analysis of the conceptual apparatus that is embedded in techniques of simulation. A rigorous critique of values baked into the techniques of simulation is required if one suspects that technocratic society tends to present itself as an advertisement for its own unaltered continuation and the colonization of our life-world. Therefore this book looks closely at selected technical aspects without abandoning an interpretive ambition.

One of the problems with seeking to study recent cultural techniques is that we do not yet have a lot of critical distance from their constellations and impacts, and all too often media studies exhibit a short-term memory, focused only on the most recent past, at the expense of longer horizons. This is an endemic challenge to the nascent field of the history of computing, which still draws rather heavily on oral history as a primary source, or else tends to jump from the earliest beginnings to the most recent phenomena without due regard for what came in between. Instead of contrasting the biographical memory of eyewitness accounts with abstract listicles that musealize computing, the chapters of this study outline how communicative recall transitions into cultural memory in medium-specific ways— in music or in games, online or in higher education, in museums or in administration. All these situations are not merely case studies of simulation as a cultural technique characteristic of a "digital era," but challenge any extant constellations characterized by older media. The coding, storage, and circulation of knowledge about computing exhibit the differences made under the conditions of computing. These differences are less about the functions of media than about specific technical constellations. Yet the point is not to circumscribe distinctions between media (whether organized along the fault lines of verbal/nonverbal, analog/digital, storage/circulation, individual/mass media, etc.) as much as to foreground that there is a turn from medium-specificity to intermedial couplings. One consequence is that media used to allow neat distinctions between sender and message, receiver and communication, producer and user—yet, arguably, electronic media have significantly complicated the situation, and studies of digital media document that computer-mediated communication networks do not permit such simplifications.

Perhaps one rather unambiguous binary opposition is that of memory and forgetting, predicating the existence of culture on memory and defining it as something to be protected against oblivion. Cultures are not only defining themselves against the primitive or the barbarian but also against their disappearance; they insist on continuity and tradition and legacy because they fear oblivion and erasure. Yet the very idea of "digital culture" implies that "new" media displace and supersede older media, thus causing erasure and oblivion in the name of inscribing themselves. Digitization can extend and transform its predecessors, modify its gestures and traditions without making them unrecognizable. By the same gesture of interrogating oversimplified juxtapositions of forgetting and cultural memory, each of the chapters in this book presents a case study of how in the throes of archiving, protecting, saving, preserving, memorializing, and musealizing there is always a stealthy reentry of forgetting, and the way things are reinscribed actually reiterates an erasure. Chun warned against any discourse that "enables a logic of permanence that conflates memory with storage, the ephemeral with the enduring," worrying that "digital media's memory operates by annihilating memory."[41] The concept of cultural techniques implies that what they cultivate is (re)imagined as an archive, a recollection. Yet our digital era often seems to dismiss and erase history, hurtling recklessly into the future, and forgetting its own preconditions. As legendary computer scientist Alan Kay worried,

> Pop culture holds a disdain for history. Pop culture is all about identity and feeling like you're participating. It has nothing to do with cooperation, the past or the future—it's living in the present. I think the same is true of most people who write code for money. They have no idea where their culture came from.[42]

This notion of culture as continuity with the past that informs the present as it aims for the best future has indeed come under fire in some academic disciplines. If computational culture today is to be more than a pop culture, it needs to fully incorporate its own historical conditions of possibility; and if its legacy is to amount to more than simply the congealed content of educational privilege, it needs to reinsert the discontinuities and accidents and failures that it grew out of.

Contrary to Haraway's abstract of scientific and fictional discourses in Western cultures, it would be highly problematic to pretend that the humanities are somehow excused from contemplating the various forms of administrative clout and managerial control that are deeply embedded in digital culture. Haraway claimed that "the entire universe of objects that can be known scientifically must be formulated as problems in communications engineering (for the managers) or theories of the text (for those who would resist)."[43] While Haraway is not arguing that informatic control is always oppressive, it would surely be self-defeating for media history to restrict itself to notions of textuality and abandon technologies of the image, moving image, calculation, and animation. And if the potential for resistance were your exclusive angle, then surely the administrative impact of interactive computer simulations should be particularly relevant; as one book on simulation quips, "if you want to resist being simulated, simulation can arrange that for you."[44] Indeed, communication in and about simulations is one of the focal points of the present volume, as many people believe that it is in these areas that games, simulations, and case studies make their most valuable contribution to education. The use of models, of course, has a long tradition in education, from long before Francis Bacon's *New Atlantis* provided a "model for a college" to long after Descartes invited his readers to follow his model of thinking. The term is often enough taken literally, as when artists including Leonardo, Michelangelo, Dürer, or Galilei, but also the philosopher Leibniz drew and built fortification models in consulting on defensive modeling. Closer to our time, it was famously the Tech Model Railroad Club (a train set maintained in the 1950s and '60s with an elaborate communication system) that gave rise to the MIT hacker scene; and consider the long tradition of the model airplane—from before the Link Simulator to after the current generation of Microsoft Flight Simulator games.

Drawing a distinction between fiction and simulation, this project therefore comes down on simulation's side.[45] The point here is to interrogate models and simulations, especially networked ones. On the one hand, simulations are valuable for training; "reforms in undergraduate and postgraduate education, combined with political and societal pressures, have promoted a safety-conscious culture where simulation promises a means of risk-free learning in complex, critical or rare situations."[46] A pioneering example of modeling knowledge acquisition is Shannon's maze runner, Theseus, demonstrating that electromechanical relays used in the telephone system could simulate learning; a replica of Theseus was just presented by the Heinz Nixdorf Forum to the MIT Museum. Of course, soon after Shannon, Marvin Minsky would strive to distinguish simulation of human thought from artificial intelligence.[47] On the other hand, simulations have given rise to a deeply entrenched method of scenario planning that supports the dashboards, slide decks, and white papers of consultants. A particularly interesting nexus here is the use of simulations as catalysts for policy development in higher education.[48] Simulations as operating representations of central features can model stakeholders and limiting factors that circumscribe the range of available options, whether for university administrators, hypothetical faculty committees, or politicians. The chapter on the administrative training game *Virtual U* not only performs a close reading of simulating policy decisions in higher education, but in doing so also illustrates certain downsides of the simulation method.[49] My emphasis in these essays on simulation as a cultural technique is on dimensions that are more the purview of the historian, the philosopher, and the storyteller than of the engineer, the mathematician, or the dot-com executive. It would be an exaggeration to suggest that STEM fields overinvested in utopian views while the social sciences and humanities specialize in dystopian worries, though a penchant for critical objections is certainly undeniable. By the same token, the cultural formations coming to the fore in this book—games, music, museums, universities, the internet—remain pivotal to our understanding of what it is to be live and work under the technical conditions of computing.

This research project had its inception when I taught graduate seminars on models, games, and simulations at the University of California, Irvine (2011, 2017). In addition to those doctoral students, I am grateful for feedback I received at conferences or invited lectures. I presented research on simulation games that became part of this project at the Second International Media Studies Symposium of the German Research Foundation (DFG), Soziale Medien—Neue Massen, on February 3, 2012, in Lüneburg.[50] The chapter on museums I first presented at the Zukunftskolleg Institute of Advanced Studies in Konstanz, November 3, 2022. Material for the chiptune chapter I presented at Vanderbilt University on April 3, 2014, for a conference called Ubiquitous Streams: Seeing Moving Images in the Age of Digital Media in Nashville, Tennessee, as well as at the XII International Conference on Film Music Research at Hamburg University, July 22, 2017.[51] Material from my MMO espionage chapter was first presented in the lecture series mediaX @ Stanford on October 18, 2016, and in more detail at a conference on Surveillance, Form, Affect at the Education University of Hong Kong on December 9, 2016.[52] I first presented the *Virtual U* chapter at a joint session of the Center for Digital Culture and the Institute for Media Environments of Computer Simulation at Leuphana University, Lüneburg, on December 11, 2019. I should also disclose that some institutional information used in that last chapter was taken from a fifty-page report I wrote for the University of California Academic Senate headquarters in

Oakland. That report was presented to the Academic Council, to UC President Yudof and Provost Pitts, to the chancellors of the UC campuses, and to the UC Board of Regents in spring 2010, in turn provoking the institutional research response from the president's office mentioned in that chapter.[53]

Much of this work would not be presentable in its current form if it had not been for three visiting appointments that gave me time to develop the argument: as Professor Visitante, Ciencias da Comunicacao, UNISINOS São Leopoldo (Brazil) in spring 2018 and 2020; as a senior fellow for winter 2019–2020 at the Institute for Advanced Study on Media Cultures of Computer Simulation (MECS), a research initiative funded by the German Research Foundation at Leuphana University; and as a senior fellow at the Zukunftskolleg Institute for Advanced Study at Konstanz University, Germany, in fall 2022. The interdisciplinary nature of these excursions that took me, albeit briefly, away from my home campus duties have enabled workshops and conversations that spurred me to finish this project on models, games, and simulations.

Acknowledgments

I owe gratitude for their insights to Geof Bowker, Sybille Krämer, Catherine Liu, Claus Pias, and Erhard Schüttpelz. I have the UC Irvine Humanities Center to thank for publication support that helped defray copy-editing and indexing. Last but not least, I acknowledge the MIT Press readers and editors who shepherded this book into print.

Notes

Introduction

1. UNESCO Charter on the Preservation of Digital Heritage, https://en.unesco.org /about-us/legal-affairs/charter-preservation-digital-heritage.

2. Bernhard Serexhe, ed., *Preservation of Digital Art* (Vienna: Ambra, 2013); Howard Besser, "Longevity of Electronic Art," paper delivered at the International Cultural Heritage Informatics Meeting, 2001, https://archimuse.com/publishing/ichim01_vol1 /besser.pdf.

3. UNESCO Charter on the Preservation of Digital Heritage.

4. Narayanan Shivakumar and Hector Garcia-Molina, "Building a Scalable and Accurate Copy Detection Mechanism," in *Proceedings of the First ACM International Conference on Digital Libraries* (New York: ACM Press, 1996), 160–168; Timothy Hoad and Justin Zobel, "Methods for Identifying Versioned and Plagiarized Documents," *Journal of the American Society for Information Science and Technology* 54, no. 3 (February 2003): 203–215.

5. Zack Whittaker, "When the Cloud Fails: Why Universities Went Public Anyway," *ZDNET*, April 22, 2021, https://www.zdnet.com/article/when-the-cloud-fails-why -universities-went-public-anyway/.

6. Ben Jacobsen and David Beer, *Social Media and the Automatic Production of Memory: Classification, Ranking, and Sorting of the Past* (Bristol: Bristol University Press, 2021); Jessica Ogden, "Everything on the Internet Can Be Saved: Archive Team, Tumblr and the Cultural Significance of Web Archiving," *Internet Histories* 6, no. 1–2 (2022): 113–132.

7. Geof C. Bowker and Susan Leigh Star, *Sorting Things Out* (Cambridge, MA: MIT Press, 1999), 321.

8. "Actual computers—the ones we all use—are both more than and less than Turing-equivalent machines." Paul Dourish, *The Stuff of Bits: An Essay on the Materialities of Information* (Cambridge, MA: MIT Press, 2022), 75.

9. John Walker, "Introduction to *The Analytical Engine: The First Computer*," Fourmilab, n.d., http://www.fourmilab.ch/babbage; Charles Babbage, "On the Mathematical Powers of the Calculating Engine," in *The Origins of Digital Computers*, ed. Brian Randell (Berlin: Springer, 1982), 19–54.

10. John Walker, "The Analytical Engine: Is the Emulator Authentic?" Fourmilab, n.d., http://www.fourmilab.ch/babbage/authentic.html.

11. Sherry Turkle, *Simulation and Its Discontents* (Cambridge, MA: MIT Press, 2009), 71.

12. Claus Pias, "On the Epistemology of Computer Simulation," *Zeitschrift für Medien- und Kulturforschung* 2, no. 1 (2011): 52.

13. Jörg Dunne et al., eds., *Cultural Techniques. Assembling Spaces, Texts, Collectives* (London: De Gruyter, 2020).

14. Harun Maye, "Was ist eine Kulturtechnik?" *Zeitschrift für Medien- und Kulturforschung* 1 (2010): 112–135, with reference to Bernhard Siegert, "Kulturtechnik," in *Einführung in die Kulturwissenschaft*, ed. Harun Maye and Leander Scholz (Munich: Fink, 2011), 95–118.

15. Gwyneira Isaac, "Technology Becomes the Object," *Journal of Material Culture* 13, no. 3 (2008): 287–310.

16. Arup Foresight + Research + Innovation, *Museums in the Digital Age* (London: Arup, 2014).

17. Sarah Longair, "Cultures of Curating: The Limits of Authority," *Museum History Journal* 8, no. 1 (2015): 1–7; compare also Petrina Foti, *Collecting and Exhibiting Computer-Based Technology: Expert Curation at the Museums of the Smithsonian Institution* (London: Routledge, 2019).

18. Kenneth Hudson, *Museums for the 1980s: A Survey of World Trends* (Paris: UNESCO, 1977), 91.

19. Mieke Bal, "The Discourse of the Museum," in *Thinking about Exhibitions*, ed. Reesa Greenberg, Bruce Ferguson, and Sandy Nairne (London: Routledge, 1996), 145–158.

20. Lewis Mumford, *The Golden Day* (Boston: Beacon Press, 1957), 108.

21. Lejaren Hiller and Robert Baker, "Computer Music," in *Computer Applications in the Behavioral Sciences*, ed. Harold Borko (Englewood Cliffs, NJ: Prentice Hall, 1962), 425–451.

22. Abraham Moles, "La Musique Algorithmique, Premiere Musique Calculée," *Revue du Son* 93, no. 1 (1961): 28; Lejaren Hiller, "Computer Music," *Scientific American* 201, no. 6 (December 1956): 109.

23. James Newman, *Videogames* (New York: Routledge, 2004), 163, 165.

24. Bernard Geoghegan, "After Kittler: On the Cultural Techniques of Recent German Media Theory," *Theory, Culture and Society* 30, no. 6 (2013): 82; Eva Horn, "There Are No Media," *Grey Room* 29 (2008): 6–13.

25. Robin Hanson, "How to Live in a Simulation," *Journal of Evolution and Technology* 7, no. 1 (2001), https://philpapers.org/rec/HANHTL.

26. Sherry Turkle, "Seeing through Computers," *American Prospect* 8, no. 31 (March 1997), http://www.prospect.org/print/V8/31/turkle-s.html.

27. Eric Winsberg, "Simulated Experiments: Methodology for a Virtual World," *Philosophy of Science* 70 (2003): 105–125.

28. American Society for Cybernetics, *Cybernetics, Simulation, and Conflict Resolution: Proceedings of the 3rd Annual Symposium of the American Society for Cybernetics*, ed. Douglas Knight, Huntington Curtis, and Lawrence Fogel (New York: Spartan Books, 1971).

29. William Ross Ashby, "Simulation of a Brain," in *Computer Applications in the Behavioral Sciences*, ed. Harold Borko (Englewood Cliffs, NJ: Prentice Hall, 1962), 452–466; Geof Bowker and Ray-Shyng Chou, "Ashby's Notion of Memory and the Ontology of Technical Evolution," *International Journal of General Systems* 38, no. 2 (2009): 129–137.

30. https://www.piql.com/industries/technology-and-infrastructure.

31. John Woodwark, "Reconstructing History with Computer Graphics," *IEEE Computer Graphics and Applications* 11 (January–February 1991): 18–20; Nicola Lercari, "Simulating History in Virtual Worlds," in *Handbook on 3D3C Platforms*, ed. Yesha Sivan (New York: Springer, 2016), 337–352.

32. C. G. Lewin, *War Games and Their History* (London: Fonthill, 2012); Philip von Hilgers, *War Games* (Cambridge, MA: MIT Press, 2012).

33. Dourish, *The Stuff of Bits*, 6.

34. Gregory Bateson, *Steps Towards an Ecology of Mind* (San Francisco: Chandler, 1972), 143; Stewart Brand, *Two Cybernetic Frontiers* (New York: Random House, 1974).

35. Gordon Calleja, "Erasing the Magic Circle," in *The Philosophy of Computer Games*, ed. John Richard Sageng, Hallvard Fossheim, and Tarjei Mandt Larsen (New York: Springer, 2012), 87.

36. https://www.ietf.org/rfc/rfc1958.txt.

37. http://www.rfc-editor.org/info/rfc7169. Sean Turner is identified as working for International Electronic Communication Analysts Inc. in Fairfax on information security.

38. Wendy Hui Kyong Chun, *Control and Freedom: Power and Paranoia in the Age of Fiber Optics* (Cambridge, MA: MIT Press, 2005); Wendy Chun, *Updating to Remain the Same* (Cambridge, MA: MIT Press, 2017), 171.

39. https://tools.ietf.org/html/rfc1776. See https://hacked.com/former-cia-nsa-director
-kill-people-based-metadata/ as well as other coverage at https://www.techdirt.com
/articles/20140511/06390427191/michael-hayden-gleefully-admits-we-kill-people
-based-metadata.shtml or https://abcnews.go.com/blogs/headlines/2014/05/ex-nsa
-chief-we-kill-people-based-on-metadata.

40. Miroslaw Filiciak, "Playful Machines and Heritage: How to Prepare Future Cultural
Histories?" *Arts* 9, no. 3 (2020): 82–94, https://www.mdpi.com/2076-0752/9/3/82.

41. Edward Snowden, *Permanent Record* (New York: Metropolitan Books, 2019), 25;
Daniel Ellsberg, "Secrecy and National Security Whistleblowing," *Social Research*
77, no. 3 (2010): 773–804; Malcolm Gladwell, "Daniel Ellsberg, Edward Snowden,
and the Modern Whistleblower," *New Yorker*, December 11, 2016, https://www
.newyorker.com/magazine/2016/12/19/daniel-ellsberg-edward-snowden-and-the
-modern-whistle-blower; Jonathan Lethem, "Snowden in the Labyrinth," *New York
Review of Books*, October 24, 2019, https://www.nybooks.com/articles/2019/10/24
/edward-snowden-labyrinth.

42. Jill Lepore, "Edward Snowden and the Rise of Whistleblower Culture," *New
Yorker*, September 16, 2019.

43. See Stefan Hoeltgen, "Das magische Panoptikum: Technologien der Überwachung
zum Zweck des Spiels—eine computerarchäologische Analyse," *Paidia*, June 25, 2020,
https://paidia.de/das-magische-panoptikum.

44. Shoshanna Zuboff, *The Age of Surveillance Capitalism* (London: Profile Books,
2019), 498.

45. E. W. Martin, "Teaching Executives via Simulation," *Business Horizons* 2, no. 2
(1959): 100–109; Harold Guetzkow, Philip Kotler, and Randall L. Schultz, eds., *Simulation in Social and Administrative Science. Overviews and Case-Examples* (Englewood
Cliffs, NJ: Prentice Hall, 1972).

46. John Henry Cardinal Newman, *The Scope and Nature of University Education*
(London: Dent, 1903), 137.

47. Henk Becker, "The Emergence of Simulation and Gaming," *Simulation & Gaming*
11, no. 1 (March 1980): 11–25; G. A. Fine, "Fantasy Games and Social Worlds: Simulation as Leisure," *Simulation & Gaming* 12, no. 3 (1981): 251–279; Richard Chadwick, "Global Modeling: Origins, Alternative Futures," *Simulation & Gaming* 31, no. 1
(2000), 50–73; Edward Castronova, *Synthetic Worlds* (Chicago: University of Chicago
Press, 2005).

Chapter 1

1. George Box and Norman Draper, *Empirical Model-Building and Response Surfaces*
(New York: Wiley, 1987), 424.

2. Vilem Flusser, "On the Crisis of Our Models," in *Vilem Flusser: Writings*, ed. Andreas Ströhl (Minneapolis: University of Minnesota Press, 2002), 75–85.

3. Don Ihde, "Models, Models Everywhere," in *Simulation: Pragmatic Construction of Reality*, ed. Johannes Lenhard, Gunter Küppers, and Terry Shinn (New York: Springer, 2006), 79.

4. Clifford Geertz, *The Interpretation of Cultures: Selected Essays* (London: Fontana Press, 1973), 93; Eric Winsberg, "Sanctioning Models: The Epistemology of Simulation," *Science in Context* 12, no. 2 (1999): 275–292.

5. Willard McCarty, "Modelling: A Study in Words and Meanings," in *Companion to Digital Humanities*, ed. S. Schreibman, R. Siemens, and J. Unsworth (Oxford: Blackwell, 2004), ch. 19, http://www.digitalhumanities.org/companion; William Uricchio, "Simulation, History, and Computer Games," in *Handbook of Computer Game Studies*, ed. Joost Raessens and Jeffrey Goldstein (Cambridge, MA: MIT Press, 2005), 327–338; Larry D. Singell, "A Note on the Use of Simulation Games in Interdisciplinary Graduate Education," *Journal of Economic Education* 3, no. 1 (Autumn 1971): 61–63.

6. Theodor Shanin, "Models in Thought," in *Rules of the Game: Cross-Disciplinary Essays on Models in Scholarly Thought* (London: Tavistock, 1972), 1–22; Barry Hughes, "The International Futures Modeling Project," *Simulation & Gaming* 30, no. 3 (September 1999): 304–326; David Staley, "A History of the Future," *History and Theory* 41 (December 2002): 72–89; Peter Jenkins, "Historical Simulations—Motivational, Ethical, and Legal Issues," *Journal of Futures Studies* 11, no. 1 (August 2006): 23–42.

7. Flusser, "On the Crisis of Our Models," 75; Willard McCarty, "Knowing True Things by What Their Mockeries Be: Modeling in the Humanities," *Text Technology* 12, no. 1 (2003).

8. Evelyn Fox Keller, "Models, Simulation, and Computer Experiments," in *The Philosophy of Scientific Experimentation*, ed. H. Radder (Pittsburgh: University of Pittsburgh Press, 2003), 198–215.

9. David Alan Grier, "The Early Progress of Scientific Simulation," in *From Science to Computational Sciences*, ed. Gabriele Gramelsberger (Zurich: diaphanes, 2011), 57–63; Michael Williams, *A History of Computing Technology* (Los Alamitos, CA: Computer Society Press, 1997).

10. John von Neumann and Hermann Goldstine, "On the Principles of Large Scale Computing Machines," in *Collected Works: Design of Computers, Theory of Automata and Numerical Analysis*, vol. 5, ed. John von Neumann (Oxford: Pergamon Press 1963), 1–32.

11. Naomi Oreskes, "From Scaling to Simulation," in *Science without Laws: Model Systems, Cases, Exemplary Narratives*, ed. Angela Creager, Elizabeth Lunbeck, and M. Norton Wise (Durham, NC: Duke University Press, 2007), 93–124.

12. Paul Humphreys, *Extending Ourselves: Computational Sciences, Empiricism, and Scientific Method* (Oxford: Oxford University Press, 2004), 5; James Bailey, *After Thought: The Computer Challenge to Human Intelligence* (New York: Basic Books, 1996), 4.

13. Sergio Sismondo, "Models, Simulations, and Their Objects," *Science in Context* 12, no. 2 (1999): 247–260.

14. Herbert Simon, "The Science of Design: Creating the Artificial," *Design Issues* 4, nos. 1–2 (1968): 67–82.

15. Michael Zyda, "From Visual Simulation to Virtual Reality to Games," *IEEE Computer*, September 2005, 25–32; Roger Smith, "The Long History of Gaming in Military Training," *Simulation & Gaming* 41, no. 1 (2010): 6–19; Tim Lenoir, "All but War Is Simulation: The Military-Entertainment Complex," *Configurations* 8 (2000): 289–335; Tim Lenoir and Henry Lowood, "Theaters of War: The Military-Entertainment Complex," in *Kunstkammer, Laboratorium, Bühne: Schauplätze des Wissens im 17. Jahrhundert*, ed. J. Lazardzig, H. Schramm, and L. Schwarte (Berlin: De Gruyter, 2003), 432–474.

16. Geoffrey Winthrop-Young, "Cultural Techniques: Preliminary Remarks," *Theory, Culture & Society* 30, no. 6 (2013): 6.

17. Geoffrey Winthrop-Young, "The Kultur of Cultural Techniques," *Cultural Politics* 10, no. 3 (2014): 387.

18. Mark Hansen, "The Ontology of Media Operations, Or, Where Is the Technics in Cultural Techniques?" *Zeitschrift für Medien- und Kulturforschung* 8, no. 2 (2017): 170, citing Gilbert Simondon, "Culture and Technics," *Radical Philosophy* 189 (January–February 2015): 17–23.

19. Bernhard Siegert, *Cultural Techniques* (New York: Fordham University Press, 2015), 15; John Durham Peters, "Strange Sympathies: Horizons of German and American Media Theory," *Media and Society* 15 (2007): 131–152.

20. Winthrop-Young, "Cultural Techniques," 3.

21. W. J. Mitchell, *The Reconfigured Eye: Visual Truth in the Post-Photographic Era* (Cambridge, MA: MIT Press, 1992), 117–135; Martin Newell and James Blinn, "The Progression of Realism in Computer-Generated Images," *ACM 77: Proceedings of the Annual Conference*, Seattle, WA, October 16–19, 1977, 444–448; Michael Potmesil and Indranil Chakravarty, "Synthetic Image Generation with a Lens and Aperture Camera Model," *ACM Transactions on Graphics* 1, no. 2 (1982): 85–108.

22. Bernhard Siegert, "Media after Media," in *Media after Kittler*, ed. Eleni Ikoniadou and Scott Wilson (Lanham, MD: Rowman & Littlefield, 2015), 79–91; Friedrich Kittler, "Towards an Ontology of Media," *Theory, Culture & Society* 26, nos. 2–3 (2009): 25.

23. Claus Pias, "On the Epistemology of Computer Simulation," *Zeitschrift für Medien- und Kulturforschung* 2, no. 1 (2011): 29–54.

24. David Gaba, "The Future Vision of Simulation in Healthcare," *Simulation in Healthcare* 2, no. 2 (2007): 126–135.

25. Sybille Krämer and Horst Bredekamp, "Culture, Technology, Cultural Techniques—Moving beyond Text," *Theory, Culture & Society* 30, no. 6 (2013): 25.

26. J. C. R. Licklider, "Interactive Dynamic Modeling," in *Prospects for Simulation and Simulators of Dynamic Systems*, ed. George Shapiro and Milton Rogers (New York: Spartan Books, 1967), 289.

27. Michael Woolfson and G. J. Pert, *An Introduction to Computer Simulation* (Oxford: Oxford University Press, 1999).

28. John Holland, *Signals and Boundaries: Building Blocks for Complex Adaptive Systems* (Cambridge, MA: MIT Press, 2012); Richard Nance, "Personal Reflections on Over 50 Years in Computer Simulation," *International Journal of Parallel, Emergent and Distributed Systems* 35, no. 2 (2020): 118–131.

29. John von Neumann and Arthur Burks, "Theory of Self-Reproducing Automata," *IEEE Transactions on Neural Networks* 5, no. 1 (1966): 3–14; John Raser, *Simulation and Society. An Exploration of Scientific Gaming* (Boston: Allyn and Bacon, 1972).

30. Abraham Moles, "Die Kybernetik, eine Revolution in der Stille," in *Epoche Atom und Automation: Enzyklopädie des technischen Zeitalters*, vol. 7 (Geneva: Kister, 1959), 7.

31. Peter Galison, "Computer Simulations and the Trading Zone," in *The Disunity of Science: Boundaries, Contexts, and Power*, ed. Peter Galison and David J. Stump (Stanford, CA: Stanford University Press, 1996), 118–157; Peter Galison, *Image and Logic: A Material Culture of Microphysics* (Chicago: University of Chicago Press, 1997), 689–780.

32. Fritz Rohrlich, "Computer Simulations in the Physical Sciences," *Proceedings of the Biennial Meeting of the Philosophy of Science Association* 2 (1990): 507–518; Paul Humphreys, *Extending Ourselves: Computational Science, Empiricism, and Scientific Method* (Oxford: Oxford University Press, 2004).

33. Mary Morgan and Margaret Morrison, "Models as Mediating Instruments," in *Models as Mediators: Perspectives on Natural and Social Science* (Cambridge: Cambridge University Press, 1999), 10–38; Soraya de Chadarevian and Nick Hopwood, eds., *Models: The Third Dimension of Science* (Stanford, CA: Stanford University Press, 2004).

34. Samuel Weber, *Targets of Opportunity: On the Militarization of Thinking* (New York: Fordham University Press, 2005), 103.

35. Norbert Wiener, *Cybernetics, or Control and Communication in the Animal and the Machine* (Cambridge, MA: MIT Press, 1985), 39.

36. Gregory Bateson discussing Ralph W. Gerard, "Some of the Problems Concerning Digital Notions in the Central Nervous System," in *Cybernetics: Circular Causal*

and Feedback Mechanisms in Biology and Social Systems, ed. Heinz von Foerster, Margaret Mead, and Hans Teuber (New York: Macy Foundation, 1950–1955), vol. 7, 26–27.

37. Bernhard Siegert, "Coding as Cultural Technique," *Grey Room* 70 (Winter 2018): 7–8; Liam Young, "Cultural Techniques and Logistical Media: Tuning German and Anglo-American Media Studies," *M/C Journal* 18, no. 2 (2015), https://doi.org/10.5204 /mcj.961.

38. Bernhard Siegert, "The Map Is the Territory," *Radical Philosophy* 169 (2011): 15.

39. Jon Dovey and Helen Kennedy, *Game Cultures: Computer Games as New Media* (London: Open University Press, 2006), 5.

40. Wolfgang Iser, *The Act of Reading: A Theory of the Aesthetic Response* (Baltimore: John Hopkins University Press, 1978), 67.

41. Katherine Hayles, "Cybernetics," in *Critical Terms for Media Studies*, ed. W. J. T. Mitchell and Mark Hansen (Chicago: University of Chicago Press, 2010), 145.

42. Gregory Bateson, *Steps towards an Ecology of Mind* (San Francisco: Chandler, 1972), 411–412.

43. John Durham Peters, *The Marvelous Clouds: Toward a Philosophy of Elemental Media* (Chicago: University of Chicago Press, 2015), 19.

44. Norbert Wiener, *Cybernetics: or, Control and Communication in the Animal and the Machine* (Cambridge, MA: MIT Press, 1948), 18.

45. David Mindell, *Between Human and Machine. Feedback, Control, and Computing before Cybernetics* (Baltimore: Johns Hopkins University Press, 2002), 316, 321.

46. Hayles, "Cybernetics," 155.

47. Jon Dovey and Helen Kennedy, *Game Cultures: Computer Games as New Media* (London: Open University Press, 2006), 108.

48. Thomas Kuhn, "A Function for Thought Experiments," in *L'aventure de l'esprit* (Paris: Hermann, 1964), 307–334.

49. Jule Charney, "Impact of Computers on Meteorology," *Computer Physics Communications* 3 (1972): 117–126.

50. The US Air Force Test Pilot School's platform called VISTA (Variable Stability Inflight Simulator Test Aircraft) is a research and training vehicle developed to fly and behave like virtually any (other) aircraft to demonstrate control system concepts to test pilots and engineers. Maintained and operated by Calspan personnel at Edwards Air Force Base, the X-62A VISTA is a highly modified F-16D jet that mimics flight characteristics of other aircraft—an in-flight simulator.

51. J. M. Rolfe and K. J. Staples, *Flight Simulation* (Cambridge: Cambridge University Press, 1986), 14–17.

52. Eric Winsberg, "Sanctioning Models: The Epistemology of Simulation," *Science in Context* 12, no. 2 (1999): 275–292.

53. Dirk Helbing, "The FuturICT Knowledge Accelerator: Unleashing the Power of Information for a Sustainable Future," CCSS Working Paper No. CCSS-10-003, https://papers.ssrn.com/sol3/papers.cfm?abstract_id=1597095.

54. Eric Winsberg, "Simulated Experiments: Methodology for a Virtual World," *Philosophy of Science* 70 (2003): 105–125.

55. Elon Musk's Terranea Resort talk in Rancho Palos Verdes, http://www.recode.net/2016/6/6/11840936/elon-musk-tesla-spacex-mars-full-video-code; Andrew Griffin, "Elon Musk: The Chance We Are Not Living in a Computer Simulation Is One in Billions," *The Independent*, June 2, 2016, http://www.independent.co.uk/life-style/gadgets-and-tech/news/elon-musk-ai-artificial-intelligence-computer-simulation-gaming-virtual-reality-a7060941.html; Alex Hern, "Elon Musk: Chances Are We're All Living in a Simulation," *The Guardian*, June 2, 2016, https://www.theguardian.com/technology/2016/jun/02/elon-musk-tesla-space-x-paypal-hyperloop-simulation.

56. Martin Shubik and Garry Brewer, *Models, Simulations, and Games—A Survey*, RAND R-1060-ARPA/RC, May 1972; Garry Brewer, *Gaming: Prospective for Forecasting*. RAND Report P-5178, February 1974.

57. Hemda Ben-Yehuda, *All the World's a Stage: The Theater of Political Simulations* (London: Routledge, 2021).

58. Paul Dragos Aligica, "The Challenge of the Future and the Institutionalization of Interdisciplinarity: Notes on Herman Kahn's Legacy," *Futures* 36 (2004): 67–83; Louis Menand, "Fat Man: Herman Kahn and the Nuclear Age," *New Yorker*, June 27, 2005, 7; Virginia Campbell, "How RAND Invented the Postwar World," *Invention & Technology* (Summer 2004): 50–60.

59. John Rolfe, Danny Saunders, and Tony Powell, eds., *Simulations and Games for Emergency and Crisis Management* (London: Routledge, 2020).

60. Stephen Sloan, *Simulating Terrorism* (Norman: University of Oklahoma Press, 1981).

61. William Bogard, *The Simulation of Surveillance* (Cambridge: Cambridge University Press, 1996), 27; Jennifer Whitson and Bart Simon, "Game Studies Meets Surveillance Studies at the Edge of Digital Culture," *Surveillance and Culture* 12, no. 3 (2014): 309–319.

62. Michael Ward, ed., *Theories, Models, and Simulations in International Relations* (Boulder, CO: Westview, 1987); Nigel Howard, "The Present and Future of Metagame Analysis," *European Journal of Operational Research* 32, no. 1 (1987): 1–25.

63. James Der Derian, "The (S)pace of International Relations: Simulation, Surveillance, and Speed," *International Studies Quarterly* 34 (1990): 301; James Der Derian,

"The Simulation Triangle," in *Critical Practices in International Theory: Selected Essays* (London: Routledge, 2009), 228–238.

64. Thomas Allen, *War Games: The Secret World of the Creators, Players, and Policy Makers Rehearsing World War III Today* (Chicago: McGraw-Hill, 1987).

65. Herbert Simon, *The Sciences of the Artificial* (Cambridge, MA: MIT Press, 1998), 4; Francis Bacon, "Of Simulation and Dissimulation," *Essays 1597–1625*, ed. M. J. Hawkins (London, J. M. Dent & Sons, 1972), 17ff

66. Gabriel Deshayes, "L'Esthetique de la Simulation," *Revue d'esthetique* 2, no. 2 (1949): 254–273; Henri Lefebvre, *Metaphilosophie* (Paris: Minuit, 1965), 63ff and 228ff; Guy Debord, *La societé du spectacle* (Paris: Champ Libre, 1971), 9; Gilles Deleuze and Felix Guattari, *Mille Plateaux* (Paris: Minuit, 1980), 121; Jean Baudrillard, "La precession des simulacres," *Simulacres et Simulation* (Paris: Galilée, 1981), 11.

67. Gilles Deleuze, "Platon et le simulacre," in *Logique du Sense* (Paris: Minuit, 1969), 302; Gilles Deleuze, "Renverser le platonisme (les simulacres)," *Revue de Metaphysique et de la Morale* 71, no. 4 (1966): 434; Michel Foucault, "Theatrum Philosophicum," *Critique: Revue generale des publications françaises et etrangères* 282 (November 1970): 886ff.

68. Daniel Boorstin, *The Image* (London: Weidenfeld & Nicolson, 1961).

69. Paul Roth, "Simulation," in *Encyclopedia of Computer Science*, ed. Anthony Ralston (New York: Van Nostrand, 1992), 1204; Jochen Venus, *Referenzlose Simulation?* (Würzburg: Königshausen & Neumann, 1997).

70. Jean Baudrillard, *Simulations* (New York: Semiotext(e), 1983), 111.

71. Baudrillard, *Simulations*, 103; Andreas Huyssen, "In the Shadow of McLuhan: Jean Baudrillard's Theory of Simulation," *Assemblage* 10 (1989): 6–17; Brian Massumi, "Realer Than Real: The Simulacrum According to Deleuze and Guattari," *Copyright* 1 (1987): 90–97; Manuel de Landa, "Virtual Environments and the Emergence of Synthetic Reason," *Flame Wars: The Discourse of Cyberculture*, ed. Mark Dery (Durham, NC: Duke University Press, 1994), 793–815; Slavoj Žižek, "Cyberspace, or the Unbearable Closure of Being," in *The Plague of Fantasies* (London: Verso, 1997), 127–167.

72. Friedrich Kittler, *Discourse Networks 1800/1900* (Stanford, CA: Stanford University Press, 1990), 369.

73. Friedrich Kittler, "Fiktion und Simulation," in *Kanalarbeit: Medienstrategien im Kulturwandel*, ed. Hans Ulrich Reck (Basel: Stroemfeld, 1988), 269–274; Eric Winsberg, "Sanctioning Models: The Epistemology of Simulation," *Science in Context* 12, no. 2 (1999): 275–292.

74. Claus Pias, "On the Epistemology of Computer Simulation," *Zeitschrift für Medien- und Kulturforschung* 2, no. 1 (2011): 29–54; Michel Foucault, *Security, Territory,*

Population: Lectures at the Collège de France 1977–1978 (London: Palgrave MacMillan, 2007), 10.

75. Eric T. Lofgren and Nina H. Fefferman, "The Untapped Potential of Virtual Game Worlds to Shed Light on Real World Epidemics," *The Lancet: Infectious Diseases* 7 (September 2007): 625–629.

76. Ran Bailer, "Modeling Infectious Diseases Dissemination through Online Role-Play Games," *Epidemiology* 18, no. 2 (March 2007): 260–261; Richard Gordon et al., "Halting HIV/AIDS with Avatars and Havatars: A Virtual World Approach to Modelling Epidemics," *BMC Public Health* 18, no. 9 (November 2009): 1–13.

77. J. C. R. Licklider, "Interactive Dynamic Modelling," *Prospects for Simulation and Simulators of Dynamic Modelling*, ed. George Shapiro and Milton Rogers (New York: Spartan, 1967), 281–289.

78. Myanna Lahsen, "Seductive Simulations? Uncertainty Distribution around Climate Models," *Social Studies of Science* 35, no. 6 (2005): 895–922.

79. Jaideep Ray and Cosmin Safta, "Data-Driven Epidemiological Inference and Forecasting," *Sandia News*, March 2021, 46–51; Philipp Sarasin, "Smallpox Liberalism," in *Abwehr: Modelle—Strategien—Medien*, ed. Claus Pias (Bielefeld: transcript, 2008), 27–38.

80. Angela Zou, Robby Huang, and Kathleen Wang, "ECE5760 Advanced Microcontroller Design," Cornell, 2022, https://people.ece.cornell.edu/land/courses/ece5760 /FinalProjects/s2022/az292_kw456_lh479/az292_kw456_lh479/index.html.

81. Using three out of five rotors $= 5 \times 4 \times 3 = 60$. Two ring settings $26 \times 26 = 676$. Message setting $26^3 = 17,576$, and multiplying these three means $712,882,560 = 2^{29} =$ key space of rotors. The ten plugboard cables $= 150,738,274,937,250 = 2^{47} =$ key space of plugboard. The total key space is $2^{29} + 47 = 2^{76}$.

82. The 76-bit, 29-bit, and 47-bit estimates are actually rounded down; 100,000 operators working for twice the age of the universe (13.8 billion years) can check $.87 \times 10^{23}$ settings, which is more than 76 bits. The actual number to be checked is greater than 76 bits and less than 77 bits: 1.07×10^{23} settings means 2×17 billion years. The rotor settings are also rounded down to 29 bits: 712,882,560. Divide this by $100,000 \times 60$ settings/sec. $\times 60$ minutes/hour $= 1.98$ hours. Ray Miller, *The Cryptographic Mathematics of Enigma* (Fort Meade, MD: Center for Cryptologic History, 2019), https://www.nsa.gov/portals/75/documents/about/cryptologic-heritage /historical-figures-publications/publications/wwii/CryptoMathEnigma_Miller.pdf.

83. Compare https://wrens.org.uk/second-world-war-codebreaker and https://bombe .org.uk/historical-background/.

84. Magnus Exhale, "The Turing Bombe and US Navy Bombe Simulator," https:// www.lysator.liu.se/~koma/turingbombe/, updated 2019 with a simulation of the US Navy Bombe.

85. Paul Edwards, *A Vast Machine. Computer Models, Climate Data, and the Politics of Global Warming* (Cambridge, MA: MIT Press, 2010); Dourish adds that "the primary alternative for designing and assessing new nuclear weapon designs is digital simulation." Paul Dourish, *The Stuff of Bits* (Cambridge, MA: MIT Press, 2022), 5.

86. Paul Edwards, *The Closed World* (Cambridge, MA: MIT Press, 1997); Alexandre Koyré, *From the Closed World to the Infinite Universe* (Baltimore: Johns Hopkins University Press, 1957).

87. Claus Pias, "Simulation," in *Nach der Revolution* (Berlin: Tempus, 2017), 99.

88. Hugh Gusterson, "The Virtual Nuclear Weapons Laboratory in the New World Order," *American Ethnologist* 28, no. 2 (May 2001): 417–437.

89. Rob Kling and Walt Scacchi, "The Web of Computing," *Advances in Computers* 21 (1982), https://www.ics.uci.edu/~wscacchi/Papers/Vintage/WebOfComputing-Kling&Scacchi1982.pdf.

90. Oliver Slattery et al., "Stability Comparison of Recordable Optical Discs—A Study of Error Rates in Harsh Conditions," *Journal of Research of the National Institute of Standards and Technology* 109, no. 5 (2004): 517–524.

91. Peter Krapp, "Of Games and Gestures: Machinima and the Suspension of Animation," in *The Machinima Reader*, ed. Henry Lowood and Michael Nitsche (Cambridge, MA: MIT Press, 2011), 159–174.

92. Peter Benfell, "An Integrated Approach to Managing Electronic Records," *Records Management Journal* 12, no. 3 (2002): 94–97.

93. Margaret Hedstrom, "Digital Preservation: A Time Bomb for Digital Libraries," *Computers and the Humanities* 31, no. 3 (1997): 189–202.

94. British Computer Conservation Society, a joint venture of the Chartered Institute for IT, the Science Museum of London, and the Museum of Science and Industry in Manchester: https://www.computerconservationsociety.org.

95. Adrienne Muir, "Copyright and Licensing Issues for Digital Preservation and Possible Solutions," in *Proceedings of th⁴ 7th ICCC/IFIP International Conference on Electronic Publishing*, Minho, Portugal, 2003, 89–94.

96. Sally McInnes, "Electronic Records: The New Archival Frontier?" *Journal of the Society of Archivists* 19, no. 2 (1998): 211–220.

97. Jeff Rothenberg, "Ensuring the Longevity of Digital Documents," *Scientific American* 272, no. 1 (January 1995): 42–47; Jeff Rothenberg, *Using Emulation to Preserve Digital Documents* (The Hague: Koninklijke Bibliotheek, 2000).

98. Eric Oltmans and Nanda Kol, "A Comparison between Migration and Emulation in Terms of Costs," *RLG DigiNews* 9, no. 2 (2005), https://worldcat.org/arcviewer/1

/OCC/2007/08/08/0000070511/viewer/file1876.html#article0; Margaret Hedstrom and Clifford Lampe, "Emulation vs. Migration: Do Users Care?" *RLG DigiNews* 5, no. 6 (2001), http://worldcat.org/arcviewer/1/OCC/2007/08/08/0000070511/viewer /file2448.html#feature1.

99. Wolfgang Coy, *Perspektiven der Langzeitarchivierung multimedialer Objekte* (Berlin: Nestor Materialien, 2006), 5, http://files.d-nb.de/nestor/materialien/nestor_mat_05 .pdf.

100. Dourish, *The Stuff of Bits*, 80.

101. Dourish, *The Stuff of Bits*, 71.

102. Stuart Tucker, "Emulation of Large Systems," *Communications of the ACM* 8, no. 12 (1965): 753–761, here: 753.

103. Bob Supnik, "Simulators: Virtual Machines of the Past (and Future)," *ACM Queue* 2, no. 5 (July/August 2004): 56.

104. James Currall, Michael Moss, and Susan Stuart, "Authenticity: A Red Herring?" *Journal of Applied Logic* 6, no. 4 (December 2008), 534–544.

105. https://www.innovations-report.com/information-technology/report-14905/. A better site used to be at http://www.si.umich.edu/CAMILEON, but is no longer active.

106. See Jens-Martin Loebel, *Lost in Translation* (Glückstadt: Verlag Werner Hülsbusch, 2014).

107. Jeffrey van der Hoeven, Bram Lohman, and Remco Vedegem, "Emulation for Digital Preservation in Practice," *International Journal of Digital Curation* 2, no. 2 (2007): 123–132, https://doi.org/10.2218/ijdc.v2i2.35; Stewart Granger, "Emulation as a Digital Preservation Strategy," *D-LibMagazine* 6 (October 2000), http://www.dlib .org/dlib/october00/granger/10granger.html.

108. Raymond Lorie, *Long-Term Archiving of Digital Information* (Yorktown Heights, NY: IBM, 2001), Research Report RJ 10185 (95059).

109. Mark Guttenbrunner, Christoph Becker, and Andreas Rauber, "Keeping the Game Alive: Evaluating Strategies for the Preservation of Console Video Games," *International Journal of Digital Curation* 1, no. 5 (2010): 64–90.

110. Ian Bogost, "A Television Simulator," http://www.bogost.com/games/a_televi sion_simulator.shtml.

111. http://inform-fiction.org/zmachine/standards.

112. Lorenzo Franceschi-Bicchierai, "Forensic Analysts Accuse Billy Mitchell of Cheating for Donkey Kong Record," *VICE*, September 9, 2022, https://www.vice .com/en/article/wxngbn/forensic-analysts-accuse-billy-mitchell-of-cheating-for

-donkey-kong-record; compare the detailed analysis by Tanner Fokkens, posted at https://perfectpacman.com/2022/09/06/new-technical-analysis/.

113. Jerome McDonough et al., *Preserving Virtual Worlds: Final Report* (Urbana: University of Illinois Press, 2010), 63, https://archive.org/details/pvw.-final-report/page /63/mode/1up.

114. Henry Lowood, "The Future of Virtual Worlds," in *Online Worlds: The Convergence of the Real and the Virtual*, ed. Henry Bainbridge (London: Springer, 2010), 289–302.

115. Adam Farquhar and Helen Hockx-Yu, "PLANETS: Integrated Services for Digital Preservation," *International Journal for Digital Curation* 21, no. 2 (July 2008): 140–145, https://doi.org/10.2218/ijdc.v2i2.31; related projects include CASPAR (Cultural, Artistic and Scientific knowledge for Preservation, Access and Retrieval), coordinated by the UK Science and Technology Facilities Council, and DPE (Digital Preservation Europe), coordinated by the Humanities Advanced Technology and Information Institute (HATII) at the University of Glasgow.

116. "In archives or museums, preservation of emulators, restored machines, and software objects alone will not take us very far." Henry Lowood, "Playing History with Games: Steps towards Historical Archives of Computer Gaming," paper presented at the Electronic Media Group, Annual Meeting of the American Institute for Conservation of Historic and Artistic Works, Portland, OR, June 14, 2004; here cited after Raiford Guins, *Game After: A Cultural Study of Video Game Afterlife* (Cambridge, MA: MIT Press, 2014), 33.

117. Jane Hunter and Sharmin Choudhury, "Implementing Preservation Strategies for Complex Multimedia Objects," in *Research and Advanced Technology for Digital Libraries*, vol. 2769, ed. Traugott Koch and Ingeborg Sølvberg (Heidelberg: Springer, 2003), 473–486, https://link.springer.com/chapter/10.1007/978-3-540-45175-4_43.

118. Andreas Lange, "Save Game," in *Kultur und Informatik: Serious Games*, ed. Jürgen Sieck and Michael A. Herzog (Boizenburg, Germany: Verlag Werner Hülsbusch, 2009), 189–200; Keeping Emulation Environments Portable (KEEP), https://joinup .ec.europa.eu/collection/egovernment/document/keeping-emulation-environments -portable-keep; McDonough et al., *Preserving Virtual Worlds*, https://www.ideals .illinois.edu/items/17178.

119. Friedrich Kittler, "Museums on the Digital Frontier," in *The End(s) of the Museum*, ed. John Hanhardt and Thomas Keenan (Barcelona: Fundació Antoni Tapies, 1996), 67–80. Compare Friedrich Kittler, "Museen an der digitalen Grenze," in *Bild/Geschichte: Festschrift für Horst Bredekamp* (Berlin: De Gruyter, 2007), 109–118.

Chapter 2

1. Geof Bowker, *Memory Practices in the Sciences* (Cambridge, MA: MIT Press, 2005), 36.

2. Hans Dieter Hellige, "From SAGE via ARPANET to ETHERNET: Stages in Computer Communications Concepts between 1950 and 1980," *History and Technology* 11 (1994): 49–75; Michael Mahoney, "The History of Computing in the History of Technology," *Annals of the History of Computing* 10, no. 2 (1988), 113–125.

3. Roy Rosenzweig, "Wizards, Bureaucrats, Warriors and Hackers: Writing the History of the Internet," *American Historical Review* 103 (1998): 1530–1552; Thomas Haigh, Andrew Russell, and William Dutton, "Histories of the Internet," *Information & Culture* 50, no. 2 (2015): 143–159.

4. John Bell and Jon Ippolito, "Diffused Museums: Networked, Augmented, and Self-Organized Collections," in *International Handbook of Museum Studies*, vol. 3, ed. Michelle Henning (Hoboken, NJ: Wiley Blackwell, 2015), 473–498; Charlie Gere, "New Media Art and the Gallery in the Digital Age," in *New Media in the White Cube and Beyond: Curatorial Models for Digital Art*, ed. Christiane Paul (Berkeley: University of California Press, 2008), 13–25.

5. John Gillis, *Commemorations* (Princeton, NJ: Princeton University Press, 1994), 14.

6. Finn Brunton, "Notes from /dev/null," *Internet Histories* 1, no. 1–2 (2017): 138–145.

7. Tim Berners-Lee, "Statement from Sir Tim Berners-Lee on the 25th Anniversary of the Web," *Pew Research Internet Project*, March 11, 2014, http://www.pewinternet. org/2014/03/11/statement-from-sir-tim-berners-lee-on-the-25th-anniversaryof-the-web; Tim Berners-Lee, *Weaving the Web* (London: Orion, 2000).

8. Jane Winters, "Coda: Web Archives for Humanities Research—Some Reflections," in *The Web as History*, ed. Niels Brügger and Ralph Schröder (London: UCL Press, 2017), 238–248.

9. Charlie Gere, "Museums, Contact Zones and the Internet," in *Museum Interactive Multimedia: Cultural Heritage Systems Design and Interface*, ed. David Bearman and Jennifer Trant (Pittsburgh: Archives & Museum Informatics, 1997), 59–68, https:// www.archimuse.com/publishing/ichim97/gere.pdf; Katherine Jones-Garmil, ed., *The Wired Museum: Emerging Technology and Changing Paradigms* (Washington, DC: American Association of Museums, 1997).

10. Early Soviet computer networks implemented a multinational X.25 protocol from the start; see V. P. Shirikov, "Scientific Computer Networks in the Soviet Union," in *History of Computer Devices in Russia*, ed. Alexander Nitussov, Georg Trogemann, and Wolfgang Ernst (Wiesbaden: Vieweg, 2001) 168–176; compare Benjamin Peters, *How Not to Network a Nation: The Uneasy History of the Soviet Internet* (Cambridge, MA: MIT Press, 2016)

11. Cathleen Berger, "Virtual Tours of the Museum of the Fossilized Internet," https://blog.mozilla.org/mozilla/virtual-tours-of-the-museum-of-the-fossilized

-internet; for a part of Mozilla's sustainability project, see https://wiki.mozilla.org /Projects/Sustainability/Museum.

12. Andrew Stawowczyk Long, "Long-Term Preservation of Web Archives— Experimenting with Emulation and Migration Methodologies," *International Internet Preservation Consortium* 54 (2009), https://www.ltu.se/cms_fs/1.67312!/file/Longterm PresOfWebArchivesOsv.pdf; Bruce Sterling, "Digital Decay," in *Permanence through Change: The Variable Media Approach*, ed. Alain Depocas, Jon Ippolito, and Caitlin Jones (Montréal: Daniel Langlois Foundation for Art, Science, and Technology/ Solomon R. Guggenheim Museum, 2003), 11–22.

13. David Bearman, *Collecting Software: A New Challenge for Archives and Museums* (Toronto: Archives & Museum Informatics, 1985), https://www.archimuse.com /publishing/bearman_col_soft.html; Jeff Rothenberg, *Avoiding Technological Quicksand: Finding a Viable Technical Foundation for Digital Preservation* (Alexandria, VA: Council on Library and Information Resources, 1999), https://www.clir.org/pubs /reports/rothenberg.

14. Jill Lepore, "The Cobweb," *New Yorker*, January 19, 2015, https://www.newyorker .com/magazine/2015/01/26/cobweb; Brewster Kahle, "Archiving the Internet," *Scientific American*, March 1997, https://web.archive.org/web/19971011050140/http://www .archive.org/sciam_article.html.

15. Ted Nelson, *Project Xanadu*, https://xanadu.com; Belinda Barnet, "Hypertext Before the Web—or, What the Web Could Have Been," in *The SAGE Handbook of Web History*, ed. Niels Brügger and Ian Milligan (London: SAGE Publishing, 2019), 215–226.

16. https://www.museumofmediahistory.com/xanadu; Mike Thelwall and Liwen Vaughan, "A Fair History of the Web? Examining Country Balance in the Internet Archive," *Library & Information Science Research* 26, no. 2 (Spring 2004), 162–176; Richard Rogers, "Doing Web History with the Internet Archive," *Internet Histories* 1, nos. 1–2 (2017): 160–172.

17. Martin Campbell-Kelly and Daniel Garcia-Swartz, "The History of the Internet: The Missing Narratives," *Journal of Information Technology* 28, no. 1 (2013): 18–33; Merav Katz-Kimchi, "Popular Histories of the Internet as Mythopoetic Literature," *Information & Culture* 50, no. 2 (2015): 160–180.

18. Kevin Driscoll and Camille Paloque-Berges, "Searching for Missing Net Histories," *Internet Histories* 1, nos. 1–2 (2017): 47–59.

19. Charles Tilly, "Computers in Historical Analysis," *Computers and the Humanities* 7, no. 6 (1973): 323–336; Louis Ridenour, "Computer Memories," *Scientific American* 192 (June 1955): 92–100; Pierre Levy, "Building a Universal Digital Memory," in *Museums in a Digital Age*, ed. Ross Parry (London: Routledge, 2009), 107–115.

20. Vilem Flusser, "Gedächtnis," in *Philosophien der neuen Technologie* (Berlin: Merve, 1989), 41–55.

21. Pierre Nora, *Realms of Memory* (New York: Columbia University Press, 1996), 1–20.

22. J. Hillis Miller, "The Ethics of Hypertext," *diacritics* (Fall 1995): 31.

23. David Silver, "Internet/Cyberculture/Digital Culture/New Media/Fill-in-the-Blank Studies," *New Media & Society* 6, no. 1 (2004): 55–64; Barry Wellman, "The Three Ages of Internet Studies," *New Media & Society* 6, no. 1 (2004): 123–129.

24. International Council of Museums: ICOM Statutes, https://icom.museum/wp-content/uploads/2018/07/2017_ICOM_Statutes_EN.pdf.

25. Beth Lord, "Foucault's Museum," *Museum and Society* 4, no. 1 (March 2006), 6; Eilean Hooper-Greenhill, "The Museum in the Disciplinary Society," *Museum Studies in Material Culture*, ed. S. Pearce (London: Leicester University Press, 1989), 61–72.

26. Tony Bennett, "The Exhibitionary Complex," in *Grasping the World: The Idea of the Museum*, ed. Donald Preziosi (London: Routledge, 2019): 416.

27. Erkki Huhtamo, "On the Origins of the Virtual Museum," in *Museums in a Digital Age*, ed. Ross Parry (London: Routledge, 2009), 121–135.

28. Michael Temple, "Big Rhythm and the Power of Metamorphosis," in *The Cinema Alone: Essays on the Work of Jean-Luc Godard, 1985–2000*, ed. Michael Temple and James S. Williams (Amsterdam: Amsterdam University Press, 2000), 77–96.

29. Derek Allan, "Has André Malraux's Imaginary Museum Come into Its Own?" *Apollo International Art Magazine*, April 2, 2020, https://www.apollo-magazine.com/andre-malraux-museum-without-walls.

30. Walter Grasskamp, *The Book on the Floor: André Malraux and the Imaginary Museum* (Los Angeles: Getty Publications, 2016)

31. Martha Hollander, "The Imaginary Museum: Teaching Art History with Mobile Digital Technology," *Digital Humanities Quarterly* 12, no. 2 (2018), https://dhq-static.digitalhumanities.org/pdf/000390.pdf; Hubertus Kohle, "The Museum Goes Collaborative: On the Digital Escapades of an Analogue Medium," in *Images of the Art Museum: Connecting Gaze and Discourse in the History of Museology*, ed. Melania Savino and Eva-Maria Troelenberg (Boston: De Gruyter, 2015), 317–332.

32. Tony Bennett, *Museums, Power, Knowledge* (New York: Routledge, 2018), 181.

33. Paula Findlen, "The Museum: Its Classical Etymology and Renaissance Genealogy," *Journal of the History of Collections* 1, no. 1 (1989): 59–78.

34. Wolfgang Ernst, *Stirrings in the Archives* (Lanham, MD: Rowman & Littlefield, 2015), 84.

35. For example, https://museums.fandom.com/wiki/VMoC, https://web.archive.org/web/20141010105238/, http://archives.icom.museum/vlmp/computing.html, or http://curation.cs.manchester.ac.uk/computer50/www.computer50.org/kgill/index.html.

36. https://enter.ch, https://www.theasys.io/viewer/XRocuF2xmMWmEUizfYcPi6Y9vUKpNd.

37. https://www.f05.uni-stuttgart.de/informatik/fachbereich/computermuseum.

38. Geoff Berry, Judy Sheard, and Marian Quartly, "A Virtual Museum of Computing History: An Educational Resource Bringing the Relationship between People and Computers to Life," *A'E '11: Proceedings of the Thirteenth Australasian Computing Education Conference*, January 2011, 79–86.

39. Marc Weber, "Exhibiting the Online World," in *Making the History of Computing Relevant*, ed. Arthur Tatnall (New York: Springer, 2013), 3.

40. https://computerhistory.org/profile/marc-weber/.

41. Weber, "Exhibiting the Online World," 15; Andrew Blum, *Tubes: A Journey to the Center of the Internet* (New York: HarperCollins, 2012); Matthew Lyon and Katie Hafner, *Where Wizards Stay Up Late: The Origins of the Internet* (New York: Simon & Schuster, 1996).

42. Bradley Fider and Morgan Currie, "Infrastructure, Representation, and Historiography in BBN's Arpanet Maps," *IEEE Annals of Computing* 38, no. 3 (2016): 44–57; Andrew Russell, James Pelkey, and Loring Robbins, "The Business of Internetworking: Standards, Startups, and Network Effects," *Business History Review* 96, no. 1 (2022): 109–144.

43. Leslie Bedford, "Storytelling: The Real Work of Museums," *Curator* 44, no. 1 (2001): 27–34.

44. Janet Abbate, *Inventing the Internet* (Cambridge, MA: MIT Press, 1999); Christos Moschovitis, *History of the Internet: A Chronology 1843 to Present* (Santa Barbara, CA: ABC-CLIO, 1999); Lee Rainie and Barry Wellman, *Networked: The New Social Operating System* (Cambridge, MA: MIT Press, 2012).

45. In response to the groundbreaking IBM exhibit curated by Charles and Ray Eames, *A Computer Perspective* (Cambridge, MA: Harvard University Press, 1973).

46. Tilly Blyth, "Narratives in the History of Computing: Constructing the Information Age Gallery at the Science Museum," in *Making the History of Computing Relevant*, ed. Arthur Tatnall (New York: Springer, 2013), 25–34; Tilly Blyth, "Information Age? The Challenges of Displaying Information and Communication Technologies," *Science Museum Group Journal* (Spring 2015), http://dx.doi.org/10.15180/150303.

47. William Aspray, Len Shustek, and Norbert Ryska, "Great Computing Museums of the World, Part One," *Communications of the ACM* 53, no. 1 (January 2010): 43–46,

https://doi.org/10.1145/1629175.1629193; William Aspray et al., "Great Computing Museums of the World, Part Two," *Communications of the ACM* 53, no. 5 (May 2010): 45–49, https://doi.org/10.1145/1735223.1735239.

48. Jon Agar, "What Difference Did Computers Make?" *Social Studies of Science* 36, no. 6 (2006): 869–907.

49. https://cse.umn.edu and https://archives.lib.umn.edu/repositories/3/resources /41; David Allison, "Preserving Software in History Museums: A Material Culture Approach," in *History of Computing: Software Issues*, ed. Ulf Hashagen, Reinhard Keil-Slawik, and Arthur Norberg (Berlin: Springer, 2002), 263–272; a recent initiative in software preservation is https://www.softwareheritage.org/news/events/swhap_days _2022/.

50. The brochure was based on "Scientific Source Materials: A Note on Their Preservation," a publication of the American Institute of Physics' Center for History of Physics; see "Preserving Computer-Related Source Materials." *IEEE Annals of the History of Computing* 2, no. 1 (January–March 1980): 4–6, https://dl.acm.org/doi/abs/10 .1109/MAHC.1980.10010.

51. George MacDonald, "Change and Challenge: Museums in the Information Society," in *Museums and Communities*, ed. Christine Mullen Kreamer et al. (New York: Random House, 1993), 158–182.

52. Wilhelm Dilthey, "Archive der Literatur in ihrer Bedeutung für das Studium der Geschichte der Philosophie," in *Gesammelte Schriften*, vol. 4 (Stuttgart: Teubner, 1959), 574.

53. James Cortada, *Archives of Data-Processing History: A Guide to Major US Collections* (Westport, CT: Greenwood, 1990); Len Shustek, "What Should We Collect to Preserve the History of Software?" *IEEE Annals of the History of Computing* 28, no. 4 (October–December 2006): 112–111, doi: 10.1109/MAHC.2006.78; Henry Lowood, "The Lures of Software Preservation," in *Preserving.exe: Toward a National Strategy for Software Preservation* (Washington, DC: National Digital Information Infrastructure and Preservation Program, 2013), 4–11, http://www.digitalpreservation.gov /multimedia/documents/PreservingEXE_report_final101813.pdf.

54. Dave Hickey, "After the Prom," in *Perfect Wave: More Essays on Art and Democracy* (Chicago: University of Chicago Press, 2017), 95.

55. Assmann worries that "anyone who would equip an Internet museum a hundred years from now will run into difficulties, since the early stages are not archived anywhere." Aleida Assmann, "Zur Mediengeschichte des kulturellen Gedächtnisses," in *Medien des kollektiven Gedächtnisses*, ed. Astrid Erll and Ansgar Nünning (Berlin: De Gruyter, 2002), 55.

56. James Cortada, *The Digital Hand* (Oxford: Oxford University Press, 2003); Jon Agar, *The Government Machine* (Cambridge, MA: MIT Press, 2003).

57. Gordon Bell, "Out of a Closet: The Early Years of the Computer [X] Museum," Microsoft Research Silicon Valley Laboratory, April 4, 2011, https://www.microsoft .com/en-us/research/wp-content/uploads/2011/04/Bell_Origin_of_the_Computer _History_Museum_v2.pdf.

58. https://computerhistory.org/about/ and https://livingcomputers.org/About-LCML /Our-History.aspx.

59. https://www.digibarn.com/collections/index.html and https://museum.syssrc .com; another example is Larry Marcus's museum of dead technology, https://www .cnet.com/pictures/touring-a-vcs-personal-tech-museum-photos/.

60. https://acrmuseum.org, compare https://www.atlasobscura.com/places/american -computer-museum.

61. https://www.scart.be/?q=en/content/interview-gerard-alberts-uva.

62. A related publication, documenting the preparations for the exhibition Control-Alt-Collect in Bern, suggests that nostalgia led the first collectors of computers to include PCs; see Beatrice Uffer-Tobler, *Loading History* (Zurich: Chronos, 2001).

63. Michelle Henning, *Museums, Media, and Cultural Theory* (London: Open University Press, 2006), 130.

64. https://www.hnf.de/en/the-hnf/historical-background.html.

65. Norbert Ryska and Jochen Viehoff, "The Heinz Nixdorf Museum Forum, Central Venue for the History of Computing," in *Making the History of Computing Relevant*, ed. Arthur Tatnall (New York: Springer, 2013), 47–52.

66. https://www.hnf.de/en/permanent-exhibition/exhibition-areas/everything-goes -digital/the-world-at-your-fingertips-history-of-the-internet.html.

67. http://www.empcommission.org/.

68. https://kaffee.hnf.de/mjpg/video.mjpg.

69. https://www.deutsches-museum.de, https://technikmuseum.berlin/en.

70. Informatik: Die Geschichte der Rechenmaschinen, https://www.deutsches -museum.de/museumsinsel/ausstellung/informatik; this exhibit is closed until 2028, but see Friedrich L. Bauer, *Informatik: Führer durch die Ausstellung* (Munich: Deutsches Museum, 2004).

71. Robert Slater, "Konrad Zuse," in *Portraits in Silicon* (Cambridge, MA: MIT Press, 1987), 40–50; Konrad Zuse, *The Computer—My Life* (New York: Springer, 1987), 33–53.

72. Justine Czerniak, Eva Kudrass, and Bernd Lüke, "Das Netz. Menschen, Kabel, Datenströme: Die neue Dauerausstellung in der Ladestraße des Deutschen Technik-museums," *Deutsches Technikmuseum Berlin* 32, no. 2 (2016): 12–15.

73. Katy Beale, *Museums at Play: Games, Interaction and Learning* (Edinburgh: MuseumsEtc, 2011)

74. Wolfgang Ernst, *Digital Memory and the Archive* (Minneapolis: University of Minnesota Press, 2012), 84; compare Belinda Barnet, *Memory Machines: The Evolution of Hypertext* (London: Anthem Press, 2014).

75. Michael Stevenson and Anne Helmond, "Legacy Systems: Internet Histories of the Abandoned, Discontinued and Forgotten," *Internet Histories* 4, no. 1 (2020): 1–5.

76. Marc Weber, "Browsers and Browser Wars," in *The SAGE Handbook of Web History*, ed. Niels Brügger and Ian Milligan (London: SAGE Publishing, 2019), 270–296.

77. Wendy Chun, *Updating to Remain the Same* (Cambridge, MA: MIT Press, 2017).

78. Richard Wiggins, "Al Gore and the Creation of the Internet," *First Monday* 5, no. 10 (October 2000), https://doi.org/10.5210/fm.v5i10.799.

79. Lewis Mumford, *The Myth of the Machine* (New York: Harcourt Brace Jovanovich, 1964), 202; Reinhart Kosellek, *Futures Past: On the Semantics of Historical Time* (New York: Columbia University Press, 2004).

80. Paul Virilio, *Speed and Politics* (New York: Semiotext(e), 1986); Michael Cusumano and David Yoffie, *Competing on Internet Time* (New York: Free Press, 1998).

81. Friedrich Kittler, "Museen an der digitalen Grenze," in *Bild/Geschichte: Festschrift für Horst Bredekamp* (Berlin: De Gruyter, 2007), 109–118.

82. Manuel Castells, "Museums in the Information Era," in *Museums in a Digital Age*, ed. Ross Parry (London: Routledge, 2009), 431.

83. Michael Crawford, "Commemoration—When Remembering and Forgetting Meet," in *Time and Memory*, ed. Jo Alyson Parker, Paul André Harris, and Michael Crawford (Leiden: Brill, 2007), 223–228.

84. Roger Silverstone, Eric Hirsch, and David Morley, "Information and Communication Technologies and the Moral Economy of the Household," in *Consuming Technologies* (New York: Routledge, 1992), 9–17.

85. Nick Merriman, "Museum Visiting as a Cultural Phenomenon," in *The New Museology*, ed. Peter Vergo (London: Reaktion Books, 1989), 149–171.

86. Joseph Corn, *User Unfriendly: Consumer Struggles with Personal Technologies, from Clocks and Sewing Machines to Cars and Computers* (Baltimore: Johns Hopkins University Press, 2011).

87. Doron Swade, "Virtual Objects: Threat or Salvation?" in *Museums of Modern Science*, ed. Svante Lindqvist, Marika Hedin, and Ulf Larsson (Canton, OH: Nobel, 2000), 146.

88. Gordon Bell, "Bell's Law for the Birth and Death of Computer Classes," *Communications of the ACM* 51, no. 1 (January 2008): 86–94.

89. Theodor Adorno, "Valery Proust Museum," in *Prisms* (London: Neville Spearman, 1967), 175.

90. Didier Maleuvre, *Museum Memories: History, Technology, Art* (Stanford, CA: Stanford University Press, 1999), 17.

91. Some associate cyclical time with Athenian Greece, focusing on how daily, annual, and other cycles restart even after cataclysms, while associating linear time with Hebraic Jerusalem, telling stories that lead from creation to the end of history in the advent of the Messiah: Mircea Eliade, *The Myth of the Eternal Return*, trans. William R. Trask (Princeton, NJ: Princeton University Press, 2005 [1949]), Karl Löwith, *Meaning in History* (Chicago: University of Chicago Press, 1949). This tradition historicized history and made it seem like a secondary development taking off with writing and literacy, but separate from pre-nation-state, pre-writing, and pre-monotheistic humanity.

92. On the internet one finds Sigmund Freud's brief note "Vergänglichkeit" from 1915, https://www.textlog.de/freud-psychoanalyse-vergaenglichkeit-psychologie.html, translated as "On Transience"; see http://www.freuds-requiem.com/transience.html.

93. Peter Krapp, "The Error at the End of the Internet," in *Miscommunications: Errors, Mistakes and the Media*, ed. Maria Korolkova and Tim Barker (London: Bloomsbury, 2020), 251–264.

94. Ronda Hauben, *Netizens: On the History and Impact of Usenet and the Internet* (New York: Wiley, 1997).

95. Anne Helmond, "A Historiography of the Hyperlink: Periodizing the Web through the Changing Role of the Hyperlink," in *The SAGE Handbook of Web History*, ed. Niels Brügger and Ian Milligan (London: SAGE Publishing, 2019), 227–241.

96. http://theorderoftime.com/politics/cemetery; see also https://sophiewashere.wordpress.com/2015/02/04/the-order-of-time-and-the-internet-cemetery/.

97. https://patents.google.com/patent/KR20000049542A/en.

98. https://muda.co/closing/.

99. http://www.computermuseum.ru and http://www.icfcst.kiev.ua/museum; see Victor Kasyanov, "An Open Adaptive Virtual Museum of Informatics History in Siberia," in *History of Computing and Education 3*, ed. Arthur Tatnall and Bill Davey (Boston: Springer, 2008), 129–146.

100. Eduard Proydakov, "A Virtual Computer Museum," *Third International Conference on Computer Technology in Russia and in the Former Soviet Union*, 2014, 150–150; Vladimir Kitov and Alexander Nitusov, "Russian Virtual Museum of the IT History," *International Conference on Engineering Technologies and Computer Science*, 2018, 41–46.

101. Dani Polak, Joep Drummen, and Joeri Bakker, http://www.thebiginternetmuseum .com or https://symbolics.com/museum.

102. http://computerarchiv-muenchen.de/Computermuseum.html.

103. Martin Elton and John Carey, "The Prehistory of the Internet and Its Traces in the Present," *The Oxford Handbook of Internet Studies*, ed. William H. Dutton (Oxford: Oxford University Press, 2013); Niels Brügger, "When the Present Web Is Later the Past: Web Historiography, Digital History and Internet Studies," *Historical Social Research* 37, no. 4 (2012): 102–117.

104. Friedrich Kittler, "Museums on the Digital Frontier," in *The End(s) of the Museum*, ed. John Hanhardt and Thomas Keenan (Barcelona: Fundació Antoni Tapies, 1996), 73. See Kittler, "Museen an der digitalen Grenze," 114.

105. Geoffrey Tweedale, "The National Archive for the History of Computing," *Journal of the Society of Archivists* 10, no. 1 (January 1989): 1–8; Margaret Hedstrom and David Bearman, "Preservation of Microcomputer Software: A Symposium," *Archives and Museum Informatics* 4, no. 1 (Spring 1990): 10.

106. Geof Bowker, *Memory Practices in the Sciences* (Cambridge, MA: MIT Press, 2005), 12.

107. Dublin Core Metadata, http://dublincore.org/index.shtml; Dave Piscitello, "Metadata Collection and Controversy," *ICANN Blogs*, June 27, 2016, https://www .icann.org/en/blogs/details/metadata-collection-and-controversy-27-6-2016-en; Charles Zange, "Community Makers, Major Museums, and the Keet S'aaxw: Learning about the Role of Museums in Interpreting Cultural Objects," *MW2015: Museums and the Web*, April 8–11, 2015, https://mw2015.museumsandtheweb.com/index .html.

108. https://datatracker.ietf.org/doc/rfc8141/.

109. Simon Pockley, "Metadata and the Arts," in *International Yearbook of Library and Information Management 2003/2004* (Lanham, MD: Scarecrow Press, 2004). Pockley is collections manager for the Australian Centre for the Moving Image (ACMI).

110. Wolfgang Ernst, "Archi(ve)textures of Museology," in *Museums and Memory*, ed. Susan Crane (Stanford, CA: Stanford University Press, 2000), 29.

111. James Pelkey, Andrew Russell, and Loring Robbins, *Circuits, Packets, and Protocols: Entrepreneurs and Computer Communications 1968–1988* (New York: ACM, 2022), 124.

112. https://acms.org.au/about-us/ and https://www.maas.museum/; see https://www .smh.com.au/national/crash-goes-that-computer-museum-20040623-gdj6s6.html and https://www.news.com.au/technology/retro-technology-faces-the-tip/news-story/c9df 811bf0e26a80e4f1f5ccc4300a48.

113. https://www.monash.edu/it/about-us/museum-of-computing-history.

114. Bell, "Out of a Closet."

115. Interestingly, the museum organized field trips, including at least one to the Northbay AN/FSQ-7 SAGE site in Canada. Gordon Bell, "The Computer Museum Members' First Field Trip," *Communications of the ACM* 26, no. 2 (February 1983): 118–119.

116. Gordon Bell, "Digging for Computer Gold," *IEEE Spectrum* 22, no. 12 (December 1985): 56–62.

117. Dag Spicer, "Gordon Bell," *IEEE Annals of the History of Computing* 37, no. 1 (January–March 2015): 4–11, doi: 10.1109/MAHC.2015.9.

118. John Cassidy, *Dot.com: The Real Story of Why the Internet Bubble Burst* (London: Penguin, 2003).

119. https://www.tnmoc.org and https://bletchleypark.org.uk/our-story.

120. Claire Marston and James Wolfer, "Projecting Computing History: A Hybrid Live-Virtual Visit to the National Museum of Computing," *IEEE Global Engineering Education Conference*, April 25–28, 2017, 1438–1442, doi: 10.1109/EDUCON.2017.7943037.

121. Dag Spicer, "Museums, Computer," in *Encyclopedia of Computer Science*, ed. Anthony Ralston and Edwin D. Reilly (London: Wiley, 2003), 1211–1215.

122. Wolfgang Ernst, *Chronopoetics. The Temporal Being and Operativity of Technological Media* (Lanham, MD: Rowman & Littlefield, 2016), 80.

123. http://museums-online.org.

124. Michael Jones, "From Catalogues to Contextual Networks: Reconfiguring Collection Documentation in Museums," *Archives and Records* 39, no. 1 (2018), 4–20.

125. https://www.scienceandindustrymuseum.org.uk/objects-and-stories.

126. Hannover exhibits functional replicas of calculating machines Leibniz had constructed. https://www.uni-hannover.de/en/universitaet/profil/leibniz/leibnizausstellung/.

127. https://www.computermuseumofamerica.org/about/.

128. Catherine Liu, "Art Escapes Criticism, or Adorno's Museum," *Cultural Critique* 60 (Spring 2005): 217–244.

129. Adorno, "Valery Proust Museum," 185.

130. https://americanhistory.si.edu/collections/subjects/computers-business-machines.

131. https://americanhistory.si.edu/press/releases/internet-society.

132. Abigail De Kosnik, *Rogue Archives: Digital Cultural Memory and Media Fandom* (Cambridge, MA: MIT Press, 2016), 21.

133. Amy Bruckman, "The Day after Net Day: Approaches to Educational Use of the Internet," *Convergence: The International Journal of Research into New Media Technologies* 5, no. 1 (1999): 24–46; Gottfried Korff, "Die Popularisierung des Musealen und die Musealisierung der Populären," in *Museum als soziales Gedächtnis*, ed. Gottfried Fliedl (Klagenfurt: Kärntner Verlag, 1988), 9–23.

134. Igor Bonifacic, "Internet Archive Violated Publisher Copyrights by Lending eBooks, Court Rules," *Engadget*, August 13, 2023, https://www.engadget.com /internet-archive-violated-publisher-copyrights-by-lending-ebooks-court-rules -164629790.html; Blake Brittain, "Music Labels Sue Internet Archive over Digitized Record Collection," *Reuters*, August 12, 2023, https://www.reuters.com/legal/music -labels-sue-internet-archive-over-digitized-record-collection-2023-08-12.

135. Stephen Greenblatt, "Resonance and Wonder," in *Exhibition Cultures: The Poetics and Politics of Museum Display*, ed. Ivan Karp and Stephen Lavine (Washington, DC: Smithsonian Books, 1991), 42–56.

136. David Demand, "Why the Real Thing is Essential for Telling Our Stories," in *History of Computing: Learning from the Past*, ed. Arthur Tatnall (New York: Springer, 2010), 13–15; David Huffaker, "Spinning Yarns around the Digital Fire," *First Monday* 9, no. 1 (January 2004), https://firstmonday.org/ojs/index.php/fm/article/view /1110.

137. Michael Pannier, Eva Hornecker, and Sven Bertel, "Can't Touch This: The Design Case Study of a Museum Installation," in *Mensch und Computer* (Aachen: Gesellschaft für Informatik, 2016), reminiscent of Marcel Broodthaers drawing the foundation of a museum (*Musée d'Art Moderne, Département des Aigles*) in the sand on the beach of Le Coq in Belgium, wearing a "museum" hard hat and placing signs around the sand stating that touching the objects is absolutely forbidden: "a sand castle of avant-gardism vainly attempting to protect its only real content, the cultural status quo." Jon Ippolito and Richard Rinehart, *Re-Collection: Art, New Media, and Social Memory* (Cambridge, MA: MIT Press, 2014), 19.

138. https://zkm.de/en/artwork/zuse-z22; compare Peter-Michael Ziegler, "Die Zuse läuft wieder," *heise online*, March 9, 2005, http://www.heise.de/newsticker/meldung /Die-Zuse-laeuft-wieder-142122.html.

139. https://www.technikum29.de/en/, https://livingcomputers.org/.

140. Paul Wilson, "Evaluation of Touchable 3D-Printed Replicas in Museums," *Curator* 60, no. 4 (2017): 445–465; Marshall McLuhan asserts that "it is well known that even museum curators often prefer colored pictures to the originals of various objects," in *Understanding Media* (Cambridge, MA: MIT Press, 1995), 198.

141. Doron Swade, "Collecting Software: Preserving Information in an Object-Centered Culture," *History and Computing* 4, no. 3 (1992): 206–210.

142. Ben Fino-Radin, "Digital Preservation Practices and the Rhizome Artbase," https://media.rhizome.org/artbase/documents/Digital-Preservation-Practices-and -the-Rhizome-ArtBase.pdf.

143. https://www.scart.be/?q=en/content/interview-gerard-alberts-uva.

144. Ernst, *Chronopoetics*, 239.

145. https://livingcomputers.org/Online-Resources/Online-Systems.aspx; David Anderson, Janet Delve, and Vaughan Powell, "The Changing Face of the History of Computing: The Role of Emulation in Protecting Our Digital Heritage," in *Reflections on the History of Computing: Preserving Memories and Sharing Stories*, ed. John Dean and Arthur Tatnall (New York: Springer, 2012), 362–384; Stewart Granger, "Emulation as a Digital Preservation Strategy," *D-Lib Magazine* 6, no. 10 (October 2000), http:// www.dlib.org/dlib/october00/granger/10granger.html.

146. Ryska and Viehoff, "The Heinz Nixdorf Museum Forum," 47–52.

147. https://cacm.acm.org/blogs/blog-cacm/234005-more-replicas-of-historical -calculating-machines-found/fulltext; Silvio Hénin and Simona Casonato, "Fake but True: Model Maker Roberto Guatelli, Science Museums and Replicated Artifacts of Computing History," *IEEE Annals of the History of Computing* 42, no. 2 (April– June 2020): 20–32, doi: 10.1109/MAHC.2020.2990452.

148. Ernst, *Chronopoetics*.

149. Cornelia Weber et al., *Objekte wissenschaftlicher Sammlungen in der universitären Lehre* (Berlin: Hermann von Helmholtz-Zentrum für Kulturtechnik, Humboldt-Universität zu Berlin, 2016).

150. Swade, "Virtual Objects."

151. https://zuse-computer-museum.com.

152. Daniela Zetti and David Gugerli, "Computer History: The Pitfalls of Past Futures," *Zur Kulturgeschichte der Technik* 33 (December 2019): 1–23.

153. David Gugerli, *Wie die Welt in den Computer kam: Zur Entstehung digitaler Wirklichkeit* (Frankfurt: Fischer Verlag, 2018).

154. Ursula Winter, "Industriekultur: Fragen der Ästhetik im Technik- und Indus-triemuseum," in *Zeitphänomen Musealisierung: Das Verschwinden der Gegenwart und die Konstruktion der Erinnerung*, ed. Wolfgang Zacharias (Essen: Klartext Verlag, 1990), 246–260.

155. Lewis Mumford, "The Marriage of Museums," *Scientific Monthly* 7, no. 3 (September 1918): 252–260; John Thomas, "Coping with the Past: Patrick Geddes, Lewis Mumford and the Regional Museum," *Environment and History* 3, no. 1 (February 1997): 97–116.

156. Marie Malaro, "Deaccessioning: The American Perspective," *Management and Curatorship* 10, no. 3 (1991): 273–279; Pierre Bourdieu, *The Love of Art* (Stanford, CA: Stanford University Press, 1990): 85–99.

157. Thomas Elsaesser, "Introduction: Harun Farocki," *Senses of Cinema* 21 (2002), http://www.sensesofcinema.com/2002/21/farocki_intro; Elsaesser here echoes Deleuze, who inserted in a lecture version of his "Postscript on Control Societies" that the regrouping of people around arrangements of ubiquitous control can be done online: "It can be done through Minitel after all. Everything that you want—what's astounding would be the forms of control." Gilles Deleuze, "Having an Idea in Cinema," in *Deleuze and Guattari: New Mappings in Politics, Philosophy and Culture*, ed. Eleanor Kaufman and Kevin Heller (Minneapolis: University of Minnesota Press, 1998), 18; Gilles Deleuze, "Qu'est-ce sue de création?" https://www.webdeleuze.com/textes/134.

158. Anwesha Chakraborty and Federico Nanni, "The Changing Digital Faces of Science Museums: A Diachronic Analysis of Museum Websites," in *Web 25: Histories from 25 Years of the World Wide Web*, ed. Niels Brügger (New York: Peter Lang, 2017), 157–172; R. J. Wilson, "Behind the Scenes of the Museum Website," *Museum Management and Curatorship* 26, no. 4 (2011): 373–389.

159. Paul Marty, "Museum Informatics and Information Infrastructures: Supporting Collaboration across Intra-Museum Boundaries," *Archives and Museum Informatics* 13, no. 2 (1999): 169–179.

160. Eileen Hooper-Greenhill, "Measuring Learning Outcomes in Museums, Archives and Libraries," *International Journal of Heritage Studies* 10, no. 2 (2004): 157.

161. Cody Sandifer, "Technological Novelty and Open-Endedness: Two Characteristics of Interactive Exhibits That Contribute to the Holding of Visitor Attention in a Science Museum," *Journal of Research in Science Education* 40, no. 2 (2003): 121–137.

162. Paul Marty, "Museum Informatics: Sociotechnical Infrastructures in Museums," *Bulletin of the American Society for Information Science* 26, no. 3 (2000): 22–24.

163. Didier Maleuvre, *Museum Memories: History, Technology, Art* (Stanford, CA: Stanford University Press, 1999), 100.

164. Maurice Blanchot, "Museum Sickness," in *Friendship* (Stanford, CA: Stanford University Press, 1997), 41–49; Stephen Bitgood, "When Is Museum Fatigue Not Fatigue?" *Curator* 52, no. 2 (2009): 193–202, with reference to Benjamin Gilman, "Museum Fatigue," *Scientific Monthly* 2, no. 1 (1916): 62–74.

165. David Mason and Conal McCarthy, "Museums and the Culture of New Media," *Museum Management and Curatorship* 23, no. 1 (2008): 63–80.

166. Pew Research Center Internet and American Life Project, *Museums and Digital Communication*, https://www.pewresearch.org/internet/2013/05/17/museums-and-digital -communication/.

167. Geof Bowker, *Memory Practices in the Sciences* (Cambridge, MA: MIT Press, 2005), 23, 113.

168. Paul Edwards, "Making History: New Directions in Computer Historiography," *IEEE Annals of the History of Computing* 23, no. 1 (February 2001): 78–87.

169. Marc Weber, "A Common Language," *Internet Histories* 1, nos. 1–2 (2017): 26–38; Valerie Schafer and Benjamin Thierry, "From the Minitel to the Internet," in *The Routledge Companion to Global Internet Histories*, ed. Gerard Goggin and Mark McLelland (London: Routledge, 2017), 77–89.

170. Andrew Russell, "Hagiography, Revisionism and Blasphemy in Internet Histories," *Internet Histories* 1, nos. 1–2 (2017): 15–25.

171. http://expositions.mundaneum.org; Delphine Jenart, "The Internet: A Belgian Story? The Mundaneum," in *Making the History of Computing Relevant*, ed. Arthur Tatnall, Tilly Blyth, and Roger Johnson (New York: Springer, 2013), 79–85.

172. https://www.otlet.net; Paul Otlet, *Traité de Documentation* (Brussels: Editiones Mundaneum, 1934).

173. Alex Wright, *Cataloging the World: Paul Otlet and the Birth of the Information Age* (Oxford: Oxford University Press, 2014).

174. W. Boyd Rayward, "Visions of Xanadu: Paul Otlet (1868–1944) and Hypertext," *Journal of the American Society for Information Science* 45, no. 4 (1994): 235–250; W. Boyd Rayward, "The Case of Paul Otlet, Pioneer of Information Science, Internationalist, Visionary: Reflections on Biography," *Journal of Librarianship and Information Science* 23, no. 3 (1991): 135–145; Michael Buckland and Niels Lund, "Boyd Rayward, Documentation, Information Science," *Library Trends* 62 (Fall 2013): 302–310.

175. Vannevar Bush, "As We May Think," *Atlantic Monthly* 176, no. 1 (July 1945): 101–108; James Nyce and Paul Kahn, *From Memex to Hypertext—Vannevar Bush and the Mind's Machine* (New York: Academic Press, 1991).

176. Michelle Henning, *Museums, Media, and Cultural Theory* (London: Open University Press, 2006), 136; Gere, "Museums, Contact Zones and the Internet," 59–68.

177. Jon Ippolito, "Ten Myths of Internet Art," *Leonardo* 35, no. 5 (2002): 485–498; Rachel Wolff, "Keeping New Media New: Conserving High-Tech Art," *ARTNews*, October 2013, https://www.artnews.com/art-news/news/keeping-new-media-new-2312/.

178. Eva Grubinger, "C@C: Computer Aided Curating (1993–1995) Revisited," lecture at Tate Modern, June 4, 2005, http://evagrubinger.com/texts/eva-grubinger.

179. Domenico Quaranta, Collect the WWWorld: The Artist as Archivist in the Internet Age, Spazio Contemporanea (Brescia), September 24–October 15, 2011; House

for Electronic Arts (Basel), March 9–May 20, 2012; 319 Scholes (New York), October 18–November 4, 2012.

180. Noah Wardrip-Fruin et al., "The Impermanence Agent: Project and Context," 1998, http://www.impermanenceagent.org/agent/essay2; Mark Napier, "Digital Landfill," http://www.potatoland.org/landfill; Garrett Lynch, *Things to Forget*, 2002, http://www.asquare.org/things-to-forget; William Pope.L., "The Black Factory," 2009, http://www.theblackfactory.com.

181. Dieter Daniels and Gunther Reisinger, *Netpioneers 1.0: Contextualizing Early Net-Based Art* (Berlin: Sternberg Press, 2009); Ernst, *Digital Memory and the Archive*, 82.

182. https://artbase.rhizome.org/wiki/About.

183. Reese Greenberg, Bruce Ferguson, and Sandy Nairne, *Thinking about Exhibitions* (London: Routledge, 1996), 2.

184. Mumford pointed out that "until the eighteenth-century metropolis invented the museum as its special form, the city itself served as museum." Lewis Mumford, *The City in History* (New York: Harcourt Brace Jovanovich, 1961), 236.

185. Niklas Luhmann, "The Work of Art and the Self-Reproduction of Art," *Thesis Eleven* 12, no. 1 (1985): 4–27.

186. David Balzer, "An Internet Museum Sounds Like a Great Idea," *Globe and Mail*, August 28, 2021, https://www.theglobeandmail.com/opinion/article-an-internet -museum-sounds-like-a-great-idea-but-heres-why-it-shouldnt/.

187. Lewis Mumford, *The Culture of Cities* (New York: Harcourt Brace Jovanovich, 1966), 263.

Chapter 3

1. James Newman, "The Music of Microswitches: Preserving Videogame Sound," *Computer Games Journal* 7 (2018): 261–278.

2. Chiptune competitions featured at Synchrony in New York and Montreal in early 2020: https://synchrony.nyc; see the premature obituary by Daniel Oberhaus, "Who Killed the American Demoscene?" *Vice*, May 14, 2019, https://www.vice.com/en_ca /article/j5wgp7/who-killed-the-american-demoscene-synchrony-demoparty.

3. http://www.8bitpeoples.com/products/520241-bit-shifter-information-chase; https://8bitweapon.bandcamp.com/album/meantime-ep; https://dubmood.bandcamp .com/album/best-of-2001–2003.

4. Liz Ohanesian, "What, Exactly, Is 8-Bit Music?" *LA Weekly*, August 9, 2011, https:// web.archive.org/web/20121031235114/http://blogs.laweekly.com/westcoastsound

/2011/08/obsolete_chip_music.php; Culture Desk, "Bleep Bloop: The Charms of Chiptune," *New Yorker*, May 21, 2013, https://www.newyorker.com/culture/culture-desk/bleep-bloop-the-charms-of-chiptune.

5. Anders Carlsson, "Chip Music: Low-Tech Data Music Sharing," in *From Pac-Man to Pop Music*, ed. Karen Collins (Farnham: Ashgate Press 2008), 153–162; Kevin Driscoll and Joshua Diaz, "Endless Loop: A Brief History of Chiptunes," *Transformative Works & Cultures* 2 (2009), https://doi.org/10.3983/twc.2009.096.

6. "The computer was sorting numbers and the radio was going ZZZIIIPP! ZZZIIIPP! ZZZIIIPP! Well whaddaya know! My first peripheral device!!! The radio was picking up the switching noise of the 8800! I tried some other programs to see what they sounded like, and after about 8 hours of messing around I had myself a program that could produce musical tones and actually make music of a sort." Steve Dompier, "Altair Music of a Sort," *People's Computer Company Newsletter*, May 1975, 8

7. http://www.retrogramer.net; https://www.csw-verlag.com/RETRO-Magazin

8. Svetlana Boym, *The Future of Nostalgia* (New York: Basic Books, 2002), xiv.

9. David Lowenthal, "Nostalgia Tells It Like It Wasn't," in *The Imagined Past. History and Nostalgia*, ed. Christopher Shaw and Malcolm Chase (Manchester: Manchester University Press, 1989), 18–32.

10. Fredric Jameson, *Postmodernism, or the Cultural Logic of Late Capitalism* (Durham, NC: Duke University Press, 1991), 19.

11. https://www.museumofplay.org; https://www.computerspielemuseum.de; https://nvmusa.org.

12. https://media.ccc.de/b/conferences/vcfb.

13. Sean Fenty, "Why Old School Is Cool. A Brief Analysis of Classic Video Game Nostalgia," in *Playing the Past. History and Nostalgia in Video Games*, ed. Zach Whalen and Laurie Taylor (Nashville: Vanderbilt University Press, 2008), 19–31, here: 23.

14. Jaakko Suominen, "The Past as Future? Nostalgia and Retrogaming in Digital Culture," *Fibreculture* 11 (2008), http://eleven.fibreculturejournal.org/fcj-075-the-past-as-the-future-nostalgia-and-retrogaming-in-digital-culture/.

15. Martin Zeilinger, "Chiptuning Intellectual Property: Digital Culture between Creative Commons and Moral Economy," *Journal of the International Association for the Study of Popular Music* 3, no. 1 (2013), https://iaspmjournal.net/index.php/IASPM_Journal/article/view/599; Peter Kirn, "Chiptune Music Theft Continues," *Create Digital Music*, May 5, 2008, https://cdm.link/2008/05/chiptune-music-theft-continues-crystal-castles-abuses-creative-commons-license/.

16. Abigail de Kosnik, *Rogue Archives: Digital Cultural Memory and Media Fandom* (Cambridge, MA: MIT Press, 2016); Abigail de Kosnik, "Piracy is the Future of

Culture: Speculating about Media Preservation after Collapse," *Third Text* 34, no. 1 (2020): 62–70.

17. Stefan Höltgen, "Play That Pokey Music: Computer Archeological Gaming with Vintage Sound Chips," *Computer Games Journal* 7 (2018): 213.

18. https://earthkeptwarm.bandcamp.com/album/the-imitation-archive.

19. https://everything.explained.today/Pixelh8/.

20. Shintaro Miyazaki, *Algorhythmisiert: Eine Medienarchäologie digitaler Signale und unerhörter Zeiteffekte* (Berlin: Kadmos, 2013).

21. Stefan Höltgen, "Über den Sinn der Begriffe Nostalgie, Revival, und Retro," *Return* 28 (2016): 76–78; Stefan Höltgen, "Sounds Like a Melody," *Der Freitag* (July 27, 2013), https://www.freitag.de/autoren/stefan-hoeltgen/sounds-like-a-melody.

22. Karen Collins, *Game Sound. An Introduction to the History, Theory, and Practice of Videogame Music and Sound Design* (Cambridge, MA: MIT Press, 2008), 8; https://www.bbc.co.uk/programmes/m000dhs5.

23. Steven L. Kent, *The Ultimate History of Video Games: The Story behind the Craze That Touched Our Lives and Changed the World* (New York: Three Rivers Press, 2001), 41–2; Melanie Fritsch, "History of Video Game Music," *Music and Game: Perspectives on a Popular Alliance*, ed. Peter Moormann (Wiesbaden: Springer, 2013), 24–25.

24. Claus Pias, "The Game Player's Duty," in *Media Archaeology: Approaches, Applications, and Implications*, ed. Erkki Huhtamo and Jussi Parikka (Berkeley: University of California Press, 2011), 164–183.

25. Alexander Brandon, "Shooting from the Hip: An Interview with Hip Tanaka," *Gamasutra*, http://www.gamasutra.com/features/20020925/brandon_01.html; Alexander Brandon, *Audio for Games: Planning, Process and Production* (Berkeley, CA: New Riders, 2005).

26. https://computeher.com; https://8bitweapon.com.

27. Neil Lerner, "The Origins of Musical Style in Video Games, 1977–1983," in *The Oxford Handbook of Film Music Studies*, ed. David Neumeyer (Oxford: Oxford University Press, 2013), 319–347; Pater Maria, "Chipmusik ohne Soundchip," in *SHIFT-RESTORE-ESCAPE: Retrocomputing und Computerarchäologie*, ed. Stefan Höltgen (Winnenden: CSW, 2013), 81–96; Tim Summers, *Understanding Video Game Music* (Cambridge: Cambridge University Press, 2016).

28. Nick Montfort and Ian Bogost, *Racing the Beam: The Atari Video Computer System* (Cambridge, MA: MIT Press, 2009), 130–133; Nikita Braguinski, *RANDOM: Die Archäologie elektronischer Spielzeugklänge* (Bochum: Projekt, 2018), 183–221; see Henri Lefebvre's statement that "rhythms appear as regulated time, governed by rational rules, but in contact with what is least rational in human beings: the lived,

the carnal, the body." *Rhythmanalysis: Time Space, and Everyday Life* (London: Continuum, 2004), 9.

29. Contrast interviews with game composers Marty O'Donnell, Winifred Phillips, Inon Zur, Cris Velasco, Jesper Kyd, and Jason Graves in Tom Hoover, *Keeping Score: Interviews with Today's Top Film, Television, and Game Music Composers* (New York: Cengage Learning, 2009), 153–188, with the richly documented chiptune scene in the documentary and book *Beep: Documenting the History of Game Sound* by Karen Collins and Chris Greening (Waterloo: Ehtonal, 2016), and Leonard Paul's soundtrack for it, https://leonardjpaul.bandcamp.com/releases.

30. George Sanger, *The Fat Man on Game Audio* (Indianapolis: New Riders Publishing, 2004), 23. Sanger's claims to fame include the first General MIDI soundtrack for a game, the first direct-to-MIDI live recording of musicians, the first redbook soundtrack included with a game as a separate disk, the first score for a game considered a work of art, and the first soundtrack considered a selling point; Andrew Boyd, "When Worlds Collide: Sound and Music in Film and Games," *Gamasutra*, February 4, 2003, https://www.gamasutra.com/view/feature/131310/when_worlds_collide_sound_and_.php.

31. Thomas Gersic, "Toward a New Sound for Games," in *Playing the Past. History and Nostalgia in Video Games*, ed. Zach Whalen and Laurie Taylor (Nashville: Vanderbilt University Press, 2008), 145; Karen Collins, *Playing with Sound: A Theory of Interacting with Sound and Music in Video Games* (Cambridge, MA: MIT Press, 2013).

32. Simon Wood, "High Score: Making Sense of Music and Video Games," in *Sound and Music in Film and Visual Media: A Critical Overview*, ed. Graeme Harper (London: Bloomsbury, 2009), 129–148.

33. https://archive.org/details/hc152_too_bleep_to_blop_by_8_bit_betty.

34. Werner Meyer-Eppler, "Über die Anwendung elektronischer Klangmittel im Rundfunk," *Technische Hausmitteilungen des NWDR* 7–8 (1952): 130; Elena Ungeheuer, *Wie die elektronische Musik erfunden wurde* (Mainz: Schott, 1992), 136.

35. Ernest Cline, *Ready Player One* (New York: Random House, 2011); Austin Grossman, *You* (New York: Mulholland Books, 2013).

36. Nicolas Nova, *8-Bit Reggae: Collision and Creolization* (Paris: Editions Volumiques, 2014).

37. Donald Davies, "Very Early Computer Music," *Computer Resurrection: Bulletin of the Computer Conservation Society* 10 (Summer 1994): 19–21; Paul Doornbusch, "Computer Sound Synthesis in 1951—the Music of CSIRAC," *Computer Music Journal* 28, no. 1 (2004): 10–25.

38. Alex Yabsley, *The Sound of Playing. A Study into the Music and Culture of Chiptunes* (Brisbane: Griffith University Press, 2007); Douglas Kahn, "Between a Bach and a

Bard Place: Productive Constraint in Early Computer Arts," in *MediaArtsHistories*, ed. Oliver Grau (Cambridge, MA: MIT Press, 2007), 423–451; Tristan Perich's circuit board record albums *Noise Patterns* (2014) and *1 Bit Symphony* (2010) are among my favorite examples.

39. Jack Copeland and Jason Long, "Alan Turing: How His Universal Machine Became a Musical Instrument," *IEEE Spectrum* (2017), https://spectrum.ieee.org /tech-history/silicon-revolution/alan-turing-how-his-universal-machine-became -a-musical-instrument; Jonathan Fildes, "'Oldest' Computer Music Unveiled," *BBC News Online*, June 17, 2008, http://news.bbc.co.uk/go/pr/fr/-/2/hi/technology /7458479.stm; Heinz von Foerster and James W. Beauchamp, eds., *Music by Computers* (New York: Wiley, 1969). Historical pride of place also belongs to the Australian pioneer Geoff Hill and his sonic experiments with the CSIRAC at the University of Sydney in early 1951, and the British programmer Christopher Strachey, who worked with Turing in Manchester: Paul Dornbusch, *The Music of CSIRAC, Australia's First Computer Music* (Melbourne: Common Ground, 2005).

40. Andrew Hodges, *Alan Turing: The Enigma* (London: Vintage, 1992), 251.

41. Wolfgang Ernst, "Im Reich von Δt—Medienprozesse als Spielfeld sonischer Zeit," in *Sound Studies: Traditionen—Methoden—Desiderate*, ed. Holger Schulze (Bielefeld: transcript, 2008), 125–142; Wolfgang Ernst, "Elektroakustik ohne Musik? Das medienarchäologische Gehör," in *Elektroakustische Musik—Technologie, Ästhetik und Theorie als Herausforderung an die Musikwissenschaft*, ed. Tajana Böhme-Mehner (Essen: Die Blaue Eule, 2008), 58–68.

42. "Whether conceiving a general-purpose simulator, designing a digital control computer, or compressing signals into transmission channels, by the end of World War II engineers had begun to describe the world with the language of signals, noise, and information," David Mindell, *Between Human and Machine: Feedback, Control, and Computing before Cybernetics* (Baltimore: Johns Hopkins University Press, 2002), 321.

43. *Music from Mathematics*: Played by IBM 7090 Computer and Digital to Sound Transducer. DECCA 1961.

44. Wendy Carlos, "The ELTRO and the Voice of HAL," www.wendycarlos.com.

45. Severo Ornstein, *Computing in the Middle Ages: A View from the Trenches 1955–1983* (New York: Authorhouse, 2002), 25.

46. Ornstein, *Computing in the Middle Ages*, 63–67.

47. Ornstein, *Computing in the Middle Ages*, 231–235.

48. Peter Krapp, *Noise Channels: Glitch and Error in Digital Culture* (Minneapolis: University of Minnesota Press, 2011).

49. https://archive.org/details/CDK037.

50. Mark Katz, *Capturing Sound: How Technology Has Changed Music* (Berkeley: University of California Press, 2004).

51. Similar new technologies have not been adapted in cinema; Dolby Stereo dates back to *Star Wars* in 1976 and Dolby Digital to *Batman Returns* in 1992, though DTS, available since *Jurassic Park* in 1993, sounds better.

52. Eckhard Stolberg, "VCS Workshop," http://home.arcor.de/estolberg/texts/freqform.txt.

53. Paul Slocum, "Atari 2600 Music and Sound Programming Guide," http://qotile.net/files/2600_music_guide.txt.

54. Manfred Peschke and Virginia Peschke, "BYTE's Audio Cassette Standard Symposium," *BYTE* 6 (1976): 72–73, https://archive.org/stream/byte-magazine-1976-02/1976_02_BYTE_00-06_Color_Graphics#page/n73/mode/1up.

55. Nick Dittbrenner, *Soundchip Musik. Computer- und Videospielmusik von 1977–1994* (Osnabrück: epOs, 2005); Shigeru Miyazaki, *Algorhythmisiert: Eine Medienarchäologie digitaler Signale und unerhörter Zeiteffekte* (Berlin: Kadmos, 2013).

56. Remix.Kwed.Org is the biggest C64 remix file repository, AmigaRemix.com the biggest Amiga remix file repository, and HVSC (The High Voltage SID Collection) lets you download and play virtually every tune ever written for the Commodore 64.

57. Melanie Swalwell, "The Remembering and Forgetting of Early Digital Games: From Novelty to Detritus and Back Again," *Journal of Visual Culture* 6, no. 2 (2007), 255–273; Sebastian Felzmann, "Playing Yesterday: Mediennostalgie und Videospiele," in *Techniknostalgie und Retrotechnologie*, ed. Andreas Böhn and Kurt Möser (Karlsruhe: KIT, 2010), 197–215; Matthew T. Payne, "Playing the Deja-New," in *Playing the Past. History and Nostalgia in Video Games*, ed. Zach Whalen and Laurie Taylor (Nashville: Vanderbilt University Press, 2008), 51–68.

58. Game artist Cory Arcangel found Amiga floppy disks with images generated by Andy Warhol in 1985: Jamie Condliffe, "Andy Warhol's Lost Amiga Computer Art Rediscovered 30 Years On," *Gizmodo*, April 24, 2014, http://gizmodo.com/andy-warhols-lost-amiga-computer-art-rediscovered-30-ye-1566990245; https://www.warhol.org/exhibition/warhol-and-the-amiga; http://www.coryarcangel.com/news/2014/04/warhols-amiga. As Dourish points out, this discovery pivots on emulation: "the only Amiga that could load Warhol's art was a virtual one." Paul Dourish, *The Stuff of Bits* (Cambridge, MA: MIT Press, 2022), 61.

59. Kenneth McAlpine, *Bits and Pieces: A History of Chiptunes* (Oxford: Oxford University Press, 2019), 23

60. Karen Collins, "In the Loop: Creativity and Constraint in 8-Bit Video Game Audio," *Twentieth-Century Music* 4 (2008): 209–227.

61. http://visual6502.org/images/C012294_Pokey/pokey.pdf; http://krap.pl/mirrorz /atari/homepage.ntlworld.com/kryten_droid/Atari/800XL/atari_hw/pokey.htm.

62. https://hackaday.com/tag/atari-pokey/.

63. ASME (the Atari SAP Music Archive, offering emulation and plugins for POKEY playback) is at http://asma.atari.org/ and HVSC (the High Voltage SID Collection, a freeware project for Commodore 64 music, also known as SID music) at https://www .hvsc.c64.org/.

64. McAlpine, *Bits and Pieces*, 40.

65. McAlpine, *Bits and Pieces*, 64.

66. McAlpine, *Bits and Pieces*, 81.

67. Sites devoted to chiptunes include micromusic.net, chipmusic.org, noisechan-nel.org, and µCollective.org: Markku Reunanen and Antti Silvast, "Demoscene Platforms: A Case Study on the Adoption of Home Computers," in *History of Nordic Computing 2*, ed. John Impagliazzo, Timo Järvi, and Petri Paju (Berlin: Springer, 2009), 289–301.

68. Written by Karsten Obarski and released in 1987 by EAS Computer Technik for the Commodore Amiga.

69. Carlsson, "Chip Music," 153–162.

70. Marilou Polymeropoulou, "Chipmusic, Fakebit and the Discourse of Authenticity in the Chipscene," *Wider Screen* 1–2 (2014), http://widerscreen.fi/assets/polymeropoulou -wider-1-2-2014.pdf.

71. http://demoscene-the-art-of-coding.net/2021/03/20/demoscene-accepted-as -unesco-cultural-heritage-in-germany/.

72. Sebastian Tomczak, "Authenticity and Emulation—Chiptune in the Early Twenty-First Century," *International Computer Music Conference*, 2008, http://little-scale.blogspot .com/2008/09/authenticity-and-emulation-chiptune-in.html.

73. McAlpine, *Bits and Pieces*, 148.

74. Anders Carlsson, "The Forgotten Pioneers of Creative Hacking and Social Networking—Introducing the Demoscene," in *Re:live: Media Art Histories 2009 Conference Proceedings*, ed. Sean Cubitt and Paul Thomas (Melbourne: University of Melbourne & Victorian College of the Arts and Music, 2009), 16–20.

75. Matthias Pasdzierny, "Geeks on Stage? Investigations in the World of (Live) Chipmusic," in *Music and Game: Perspectives on a Popular Alliance*, ed. Peter Moormann (Wiesbaden: Springer, 2012), 180.

76. McAlpine, *Bits and Pieces*, 224

77. Japanese chiptune artist Toriena released an album called *FakeBit* (2020) without controversy.

78. Martin Zeilinger, "Chipmusic, Out of Tune: Crystal Castles and the Misappropriation of Licensed Sound," in *Dynamic Fair Dealing: Creating Canadian Culture Online*, ed. Rosemary Coombe, Darren Wershler, and Martin Zeilinger (Toronto: University of Toronto Press, 2013).

79. Dourish, *The Stuff of Bits*, 66.

80. https://github.com/utz82/bintracker; https://spectrumcomputing.co.uk/forums /viewtopic.php?t=78; earlier chiptunes relied on editors like Nanoloop or Little Sound DJ (a tracker for the Gameboy, http://www.littlesounddj.com/lsd/).

81. David Gunkel, *Of Remixology: Ethics and Aesthetics After Remix* (Cambridge, MA: MIT Press, 2016); Eduardo Navas, Owen Gallagher, and xtine burrough, eds., *The Routledge Companion to Remix Studies* (New York: Routledge, 2015); Margie Borschke, *This Is Not a Remix: Piracy, Authenticity, Popular Music* (London: Bloomsbury, 2017).

82. The 3DO console failed because consumers considered it too expensive in 1993, and it did not launch with quality titles; by 1997 it was gone.

83. Kenneth Gaburo, "The Deterioration of an Ideal, Ideally Deteriorized: Reflections on Pietro Grossi's Paganini Al Computer," *Computer Music Journal* 9, no. 1 (Spring 1985): 39–44; Francesco Giomi, "The Work of Italian Artist Pietro Grossi: From Early Electronic Music to Computer Art," *Leonardo* 28, no. 1 (1995): 35–39.

84. Eliot Bates, "Glitches, Bugs, and Hisses: The Degeneration of Musical Recordings and the Contemporary Music Work," in *Bad Music: The Music We Love to Hate*, ed. C. J. Washburne and M. Derno (London: Routledge, 2004), 275–293; Paul Théberge, *Any Sound You Can Imagine: Making Music/Consuming Technology* (Middletown, CT: Wesleyan University Press, 1997). Pickering notes, "it is ironic that Eno came to cybernetics via Beer; he should have read Pask. The musical insights Eno squeezed out of Beer's writings on management are explicit in Pask's writings on aesthetics." Andrew Pickering, *The Cybernetic Brain* (Chicago: University of Chicago Press, 2010), 308.

85. Sebastian Tomczak, "Authenticity and Emulation: Chiptune in the early 21st Century," *International Computer Music Conference*, 2008, http://milkcrate.com .au/_other/downloads/writing_stuff/tomczak.icmc2008.pdf; Brett Camper, "Fake Bit: Imitation and Limitation," *Proceedings of the 9th Digital Arts and Culture Conference*, December 12–15, 2009, https://escholarship.org/uc/item/3s67474h.

86. Stefan Höltgen, "Game Circuits: Platform Studies und Medienarchäologie als Methoden zur Erforschung von Computerspielen," in *Playing with Virtuality. Theories and Methods of Computer Game Studies*, ed. Benjamin Bigl and Sebastian Stoppe (Frankfurt: Peter Lang, 2013), 83–100.

87. "It must be noticed that noise is in no intrinsic way distinguishable from any other form of variety." W. Ross Ashby, *An Introduction to Cybernetics* (London: Chapman & Hall, 1956), 186.

Chapter 4

1. Jennifer Whitson and Bart Simon, "Game Studies Meets Surveillance Studies at the Edge of Digital Culture," *Surveillance and Culture* 12, no. 3 (2014): 311; Tal Zarsky, "Privacy and Data Collection in Virtual Worlds," in *The State of Play: Law, Games, and Virtual Worlds*, ed. Jack Balkin and Bethany Noveck (New York: New York University Press, 2006), 217–223.

2. Shoshana Zuboff, *The Age of Surveillance Capitalism* (New York: Public Affairs, 2019), 466; Jeff Yan and Hyun-Jin Choi, "Security Issues in Online Games," *Electronic Library* 20, no. 2 (2002): 125–133.

3. "3D Cyberspace Spillover: Where Virtual Worlds Get Real," redacted ODNI report posted by the Federation of American Scientists, http://fas.org/irp/eprint/virtual .pdf. One participant was Lt. Charles Cohen, Indiana State Police (see https://www .linkedin.com/in/ctcllc and http://issworldtraining.com/ISS_SocialNetworking/index .htm); other members were ethnographers who were later pressed to reconsider their involvement. Roberto Gonzalez, "Anthropology and the Covert: Methodological Notes on Researching Military and Intelligence Programs," *Anthropology Today* 28, no. 2 (April 2012): 21–25; David Price, *Cold War Anthropology: The CIA, the Pentagon, and the Growth of Dual Use Anthropology* (Durham, NC: Duke University Press, 2016).

4. Mark Mazzetti and Justin Elliott, "Spies Infiltrate a Fantasy Realm of Online Games," *New York Times*, December 9, 2013, http://www.nytimes.com/2013/12/10 /world/spies-dragnet-reaches-a-playing-field-of-elves-and-trolls.html; Tim Stevens, "Who's Watching the Warlocks and Why? Security and Surveillance in Virtual Worlds," *International Political Sociology* 9, no. 3 (September 2015), http://www .researchgate.net/publication/279448282_Who%27s_Watching_the_Warlocks_and _Why_Security_and_Surveillance_in_Virtual_Worlds.

5. Vernor Vinge, *True Names* (New York: Dell, 1981); Timothy Melley, *The Covert Sphere: Secrecy, Fiction, and the National Security State* (Ithaca, NY: Cornell University Press, 2012).

6. Vernor Vinge, "Introduction," in *True Names and the Opening of the Cyberspace Frontier*, ed. James Frenkel (New York: Tor, 2001), xv–xiii.

7. Nathaniel Popper, "Timothy May, Early Advocate of Internet Privacy, Dies at 66," *New York Times*, December 21, 2018, https://www.nytimes.com/2018/12/21 /obituaries/timothy-c-may-dead.html.

8. Vernor Vinge, "True Names," in *True Names and the Opening of the Cyberspace Frontier*, ed. James Frenkel (New York: Tor, 2001), 231.

9. Friedrich Kittler, "No Such Agency," *Fragmente. Schriftenreihe zur Psychoanalyse* 32/33 (1990): 287–292.

10. In 2009, the FAS together with the SRI issued a Request for Letters of Intent regarding research proposals on "Harnessing Virtual Worlds for Arts and Humanities Research," funded by the Mellon Foundation.

11. Richard Bartle, "MMO Morality," in *Computer Games and New Media Cultures: A Handbook of Digital Game Studies*, ed. Johannes Fromme and Alexander Unger (New York: Springer, 2012), 194.

12. Johan Huizinga, *Homo Ludens: A Study of the Play Element in Culture* (Boston: Beacon Press, 1955); Erving Goffman, *Frame Analysis: An Essay on the Organization of Experience* (San Francisco: Harper & Row, 1974); Miguel Sicart, *The Ethics of Computer Games* (Cambridge, MA: MIT Press, 2009).

13. Gregory Bateson, *Steps Towards an Ecology of Mind* (San Francisco: Chandler, 1972), 143.

14. Ulrike Schultze and Wanda Orlikowski, "Virtual Worlds: A Performative Perspective on Globally Distributed, Immersive Work," *Information Systems Research* 21, no. 4 (December 2010): 810; Carolyn Elefant and Nicole Black, *Social Media for Lawyers: The Next Frontier* (Chicago: American Bar Association, 2010).

15. William Gibson, *Count Zero* (New York: Gollancz, 1986).

16. Russell Brandon, "A Reporting Error Linked the PlayStation 4 to Paris Attacks," *The Verge*, November 16, 2015, https://www.theverge.com/2015/11/16/9745216 /playstation-4-paris-attacks-reporting-error; Jason Schreier, "Reporting Error Leads to Speculation That Terrorists Used PS4s to Plan Paris Attacks," *Kotaku*, November 16, 2015, https://kotaku.com/reporting-error-leads-to-speculation-that-terrorists -us-1742791584.

17. Shadia Nasralla, "Teenager in Austrian PlayStation Terrorism Case Gets Two Years," *Reuters*, May 26, 2015, https://www.reuters.com/article/us-mideast-crisis -austria/teenager-in-austrian-playstation-terrorism-case-gets-two-years-idUSKBN0OB 0LK20150526#A6v5BP0v3OF4jjDF.97.

18. The series *Occupied* (notable as the most expensive TV production in Norway's history) echoes the 1988 British television miniseries *A Very British Coup* (based on a 1982 novel with the same title by Labour politician Chris Mullin), in which a left-wing government is overthrown by security services because of its contrarian energy policy and withdrawal from international agreements; there is also a 2012 remake of the TV series under the title *Secret State* featuring Gabriel Byrne.

19. James Wolcott, "The Norwegian Thriller That Predicts the Disaster of Trump's Geopolitical Outlook," *Vanity Fair*, July 27, 2016, https://www.vanityfair.com /hollywood/2016/07/occupied-norwegian-thriller-netflix-donald-trump.

20. ODNI Summer Hard Problem Program, 2008, Call for Applications, http://www
.theiacp.org/Portals/0/pdfs/WhatsNew/Sharp2008.pdf.

21. http://us.battle.net/wow/en/forum/topic/9245745569?page=1.

22. Nicholas Carr, *Does IT Matter? Information Technology and the Corrosion of Competitive Advantage* (Cambridge, MA: Harvard Business School, 2004).

23. Robert O'Harrow, "Spies' Battleground Turns Virtual," *Washington Post*, February 6, 2008, D1, https://www.washingtonpost.com/wp-dyn/content/article/2008/02
/05/AR2008020503144.html.

24. http://www.theiacp.org/Portals/0/pdfs/WhatsNew/Sharp2008.pdf.

25. Charles Allen, "Terrorism in the Twenty-First Century: Implications for Homeland Security," Washington Institute for Near East Policy, 2008, http://www.washington
institute.org/policy-analysis/view/terrorism-in-the-twenty-first-century-implications
-for-homeland-security.

26. Gabrielle Pickard, "Will Terror Groups Use Virtual Worlds to Recruit New Members?" http://www.topsecretwriters.com/2014/04/will-terror-groups-use-virtual
-worlds-to-recruit-new-members/.

27. Clay Wilson, "Avatars, Virtual Reality Technology, and the US Military: Emerging Policy Issues," *Congressional Research Service*, April 9, 2008, https://www.fas.org/sgp/crs
/natsec/RS22857.pdf. Compare O'Harrow, "Spies' Battleground Turns Virtual."

28. Chris Vallance, "US Seeks Terrorists in Web Worlds," *BBC*, March 3, 2008, http://
news.bbc.co.uk/2/hi/technology/7274377.stm.

29. Intelligence Advanced Research Projects Activity (IARPA), "Reynard Program Summary," November 2013, https://www.propublica.org/documents/item/837419
-iarpa-reynard-summary-nov2013 or https://assets.documentcloud.org/documents
/837419/iarpa-reynard-summary-nov2013.pdf.

30. ODNI, "Data Mining Report," February 15, 2008, http://virtuallyblind.com/files
/dni_datamining_report_2008.pdf.

31. Science Applications International Corp., "Games: A Look at Emerging Trends, Uses, Threats and Opportunities in Influence Activities," https://www.propublica.org
/documents/item/889134-games or https://www.eff.org/files/2013/12/09/20131209
-nyt-nsa_games.pdf.

32. Compare Alice Lipowicz, "Trailblazer Loses Its Way: NSA Modernization Effort Suffers Cost Overruns, Delays," *Washington Technology*, September 10, 2005, http://
washingtontechnology.com/articles/2005/09/10/trailblazer-loses-its-way.aspx;
Donald L. Bartless and James B. Steele, "Washington's $8 Billion Shadow," *Vanity Fair*,
March 2007, http://www.vanityfair.com/news/2007/03/spyagency200703?printable
=true&currentPage=all.

33. Justin Elliot and Mark Mazzetti, "World of Spycraft: NSA and CIA Spied in Online Games," *New York Times*, December 9, 2013, https://www.propublica.org /article/world-of-spycraft-intelligence-agencies-spied-in-online-games; James Ball, "Xbox Live among Game Services Targeted by US and UK Spy Agencies," *The Guardian*, December 9, 2013, http://www.theguardian.com/world/2013/dec/09/nsa-spies -online-games-world-warcraft-second-life; James Vincent, "NSA and GCHQ Agents Spied on Online Gamers Using World of Warcraft and Second Life," *The Independent*, December 9, 2013, http://www.independent.co.uk/life-style/gadgets-and-tech/nsa -and-gchq-agents-spied-on-online-gamers-using-world-of-warcraft-and-second-life -8993432.html.

34. Noah Shachtman, "Pentagon Researcher Conjures Warcraft Terror Plot," *Wired*, September 15, 2008, http://www.wired.com/2008/09/world-of-warcra/.

35. Jon Dovey and Helen Kennedy, *Game Cultures: Computer Games as New Media* (London: Open University Press, 2006), 108.

36. Former naval officer Cory Ondrejka, chief technology officer for Linden Labs, in 2007 visited the NSA in Fort Meade and gave a presentation; he left Linden Labs in 2008. After working for Facebook from 2011 through 2014, he recently left Facebook, where he served as vice president of mobile strategy. See https://venturebeat .com/2014/12/16/facebook-engineering-vp-cory-ondrejka-departs-after-overseeing -oculus-acquisition/.

37. David Kravets, "US Intel: Osama bin Laden Avatar Could Recruit Terrorists Online for Centuries," *Wired*, January 8, 2014ar/.

38. Katherine Hayles, "Simulating Narratives," *Critical Inquiry* 26, no. 1 (Autumn 1999): 16.

39. Samuel Weber, "The Sideshow," *MLN* 88, no. 6 (1973): 1102–1133; Samuel Weber, "Uncanny Thinking," in *The Legend of Freud* (Stanford: Stanford University Press, 2000), 1–34; John Phillips, "Secrecy and Transparency," *Theory, Culture & Society* 28, nos. 7–8 (2011): 158–172.

40. Heidegger's Bremen lectures of 1949 (*Gesamtausgabe* #79, Frankfurt: Klostermann, 2005, 24–77) tackle the uncanny; Derrida observed that "between thinking and technics, as between thinking and science, there is the abyss." Jacques Derrida and Bernard Stiegler, *Echographies of Television* (London: Polity Press, 2002), 134.

41. Angela Tinwell, *The Uncanny Valley in Games and Animation* (New York: CRC Press, 2015).

42. Jacques Derrida, *Dissemination* (Chicago: Chicago University Press, 1981), 268.

43. Weber, "The Sideshow," 1132.

44. John le Carré, *Tinker Tailor Soldier Spy* (London: Knopf, 1974), 342.

45. Josh Lyons and Steven Nutt, "The Dangers of Web 2.0 Technology," *UWAC*, August 25, 2008, https://info.publicintelligence.net/How%20a%20Boy%20Becomes %20a%20Martyr%20-%20The%20Dangers%20of%20Web%202.0%20Technology .pdf; Shawn Musgrave, "Report Warned of MySpace and SecondLife as Jihadist Recruitment Tools," *MuckRock*, July 13, 2015, https://www.muckrock.com/news/archives /2015/jul/13/2008-report-warned-myspace-and-secondlife-jihadist. The Urban Warfare Analysis Center is a defunct part of the US Army Research Laboratory that was run by a military contractor.

46. Emily Siegel, "Social Media Can Stop ISIS," *The Hill*, May 5, 2015, http://thehill .com/blogs/congress-blog/technology/241032-social-media-can-stop-isis.

47. Jeremy Crampton, "Collect It All: National Security, Big Data and Governance," *GeoJournal* 80 (October 2014): 519–531, doi 10.1007/s10708-014-9598-y. SSRN: https:// ssrn.com/abstract=2500221 or http://dx.doi.org/10.2139/ssrn.2500221.

48. Ben Bain, "Taking Intelligence Analysis to the Virtual World," *Federal Computer Week*, September 4, 2008, http://fcw.com/Articles/2008/09/04/Taking-intelligence -analysis-to-the-virtual-world.aspx; see slides at http://www.slideshare.net/jmorriso /ASpaceX-Industry-Day-Briefing-7JUL08-JGM-r4; Noah Shachtman, "Spies Want a Second Life of Their Own," *Wired*, July 3, 2008, http://www.wired.com/2008/07 /spies-want-a-se/.

49. Susan Stucky, Ben Shaw, and Wendy Ark, "Virtual Environments Overview," April 2009, http://oai.dtic.mil/oai/oai?verb=getRecord&metadataPrefix=html&identi fier=ADA496980.

50. Josh Lauer, "Surveillance History and the History of New Media: An Evidential Paradigm," *New Media & Society* 14, no. 4 (June 2012): 566–582.

51. "Data Mining Report," ODNI Report to Congress, February 15, 2008, https://fas .org/blogs/secrecy/2008/02/dni_report_details_data_mining/; Kim Taipale, "Whispering Wires and Warrantless Wiretaps: Data Mining and Foreign Intelligence Surveillance," *NYU Review of Law and Security* no. 7, Supplemental Bulletin on Law and Security: *The NSA and the War on Terror*, Spring 2006, http://whisperingwires.info/ or http://ssrn.com/abstract=889120.

52. Katherine Wong, "The NSA Terrorist Surveillance Program," *Harvard Journal on Legislation* 43, no. 2 (2006): 517–534; Elizabeth B. Bazan and Jennifer K. Elsea, "Presidential Authority to Conduct Warrantless Electronic Surveillance to Gather Foreign Intelligence Information," *Congressional Research Service*, January 5, 2006, http://www.fas.org/sgp/crs/intel/m010506.pdf.

53. Taipale, "Whispering Wires and Warrantless Wiretaps."

54. Claire Birchall, "There's Been Too Much Secrecy in This City: The False Choice between Secrecy and Transparency in US Politics," *Cultural Politics* 7, no. 1 (2011):

133–156; Eva Horn, "Logics of Political Secrecy," *Theory, Culture & Society* 28, nos. 7–8 (2011): 103–122.

55. Priscilla Regan, *Legislating Privacy* (Chapel Hill: University of North Carolina Press, 1995), 221.

56. Helen Nissenbaum, *Privacy in Context: Technology, Policy and the Integrity of Social Life* (Stanford, CA: Stanford University Press, 2010), 127.

57. Nissenbaum, *Privacy in Context*, 243.

58. Nissenbaum, *Privacy in Context*, 66.

59. Peter Galison, "Removing Knowledge," *Critical Inquiry* 31, no. 1 (2004): 229–243.

60. "80% of Active Internet Users Will Have a Second Life in the Virtual World by the End of 2011," April 24, 2007, http://www.gartner.com/it/page.jsp?id=503861.

61. Glenn Greenwald, *No Place to Hide* (New York: Metropolitan Books, 2014), points to the idea that Snowden's moral compass was derived from playing games; Andrea Peterson, "How Videogames Prepared Edward Snowden to Leak NSA Secrets," *Washington Post*, May 14, 2014, https://www.washingtonpost.com/news/the-switch/wp/2014/05/14/how-video-games-prepared-edward-snowden-to-leak-nsa-secrets; Eddie Makuch, "Edward Snowden Was Inspired by Video Games to Expose Government Surveillance," *GameSpot*, May 14, 2014, https://www.gamespot.com/articles/edward-snowden-was-inspired-by-video-games-to-expose-government-surveillance/1100-6419636/.

62. Edward Snowden, *Permanent Record* (New York: Metropolitan Books, 2019), 25, is worth citing in detail: "It was the NES—the janky but genius 8-bit Nintendo Entertainment System—that was my real education. From *The Legend of Zelda*, I learned that the world exists to be explored; from *Mega Man*, 1 learned that my enemies have much to teach; and from *Duck Hunt*, well, *Duck Hunt* taught me that even if someone laughs at your failures, it doesn't mean you get to shoot them in the face. Ultimately, though, it was *Super Mario Bros* that taught me what remains perhaps the most important lesson of my life. I am being perfectly sincere. I am asking you to consider this seriously. *Super Mario Bros*, the 1.0 edition, is perhaps the all-time masterpiece of side-scrolling games." Compare the sentiment that "life only scrolls in one direction" to the related argument in Anna Poletti, "Intimate Economies: *PostSecret* and the Affect of Confession," *Biography* 34, no. 1 (Winter 2011): 25–36.

63. Alasdair Roberts, "Wikileaks: The Illusion of Transparency," *International Review of Administrative Sciences* 78, no. 1 (2012): 116–133; Peter Galison, "Secrecy in Three Acts," *Social Research* 77, no. 3 (2010): 941–974.

64. Peter Swire, "The Declining Half-Life of Secrecy and the Future of Signals Intelligence," *New America Cybersecurity Fellows Paper Series* 1 (July 2015), https://static.newamerica.org/attachments/4425-the-declining-half-life-of-secrets/Swire

_DecliningHalf-LifeOfSecrets.f8ba7c96a6c049108dfa85b5f79024d8.pdf; Richard Clark et al., "Liberty and Security in a Changing World," *Report and Recommendations of the President's Review Group on Intelligence and Communications Technologies*, December 12, 2013, http://www.whitehouse.gov/sites/default/files/docs/2013-12-12_rg_final _report.pdf.

65. Shoshana Zuboff, "Big Other: Surveillance Capitalism and the Prospects of an Information Civilization," *Journal of Information Technology* 30, no. 1 (2015): 75–89.

66. "International Strategy for Cyberspace: Prosperity, Security, and Openness in a Networked World," May 2011, http://www.au.af.mil/au/awc/awcgate/whitehouse /international_strategy_for_cyberspace.pdf.

67. "National Strategy for Trusted Identities in Cyberspace: Enhancing Online Choice, Efficiency, Security, and Privacy," http://www.au.af.mil/au/awc/awcgate /whitehouse/strat_for_trusted_id_in_cyber_2011.pdf; "National Strategy for Information Sharing and Safeguarding," December 2012, http://www.au.af.mil/au/awc /awcgate/whitehouse/nat_strat_info_share_oct2007.pdf.

68. Roman Yampolsky, Brendan Klare, and Anil Jain, "Face Recognition in the Virtual Worlds: Recognizing Avatar Faces," *11th International Conference on Machine Learning and Applications*, 2012, http://www.cse.msu.edu/biometrics/Publications /Face/YampolskiyKlareJain_FRVirtualWorld_RecognizingAvatarFaces.pdf.

69. Charles Stross, "Spy Kids," *Foreign Policy*, August 29, 2013, http://foreignpolicy .com/2013/08/29/spy-kids; Bruce Schneier, "The Spooks Need New Ways to Keep Their Secrets Safe," *Financial Times*, September 5, 2013, http://www.ft.com/cms/s /420a9a64-163c-11e3-a57d-00144feabdc0.

70. Office of the Director of National Intelligence (ODNI), "2014 Report on Security Clearance Determinations," April 2015, http://www.dni.gov.

71. Walt Scacchi, ed., *The Future of Research in Computer Games and Virtual Worlds: Workshop Report*, Institute for Software Research, July 2012, http://www.isr.uci.edu /tech_reports/UCI-ISR-12-8.pdf.

72. Walt Scacchi, Craig Brown, and Kari Nies, "Exploring the Potential of Virtual Worlds for Decentralized Command and Control," *Proceedings of the 17th International Command and Control Research and Technology Symposium*, Washington, DC, June 2012; R. Granlund, K. Smith, and H. Granlund, "C3 Conflict: A Simulation Environment for Studying Teamwork in Command and Control," *Proceedings of the 16th International Command and Control Research and Technology Symposium*, 2011; K. Hudson and M. Nissen, "Command and Control in Virtual Environments: Designing a Virtual Environment for Experimentation," *Proceedings of the 15th International Command and Control Research and Technology Symposium*, 2010.

73. Universal Declaration of Human Rights, http://www.un.org/en/documents/udhr /index.shtml#a12; United Nations Office of the High Commissioner for Human

Rights, International Covenant on Civil and Political Rights, http://www.ohchr.org /en/professionalinterest/pages/ccpr.aspx; Alfred Kobsa, "Personalized Hypermedia and International Privacy," *Communications of the ACM* 45, no. 5 (May 2002): 64–67.

74. Tal Zarsky, "Privacy and Data Collection in Virtual Worlds," in *State of Play: Law, Games, and Virtual Worlds*, ed. Jack Balkin and Beth Simone Noveck (New York: New York University Press, 2006), 217–223; Lori Andrews, "Privacy and Data Collection in the Gameful World," in *The Gameful World: Approaches, Issues, Applications*, ed. Stephen Waltz and Sebastian Deterding (Cambridge, MA: MIT Press, 2015), 359–369.

75. Dan Geer (chief information security officer for In-Q-Tel), "Trade-Offs in Cybersecurity," October 9, 2013, http://geer.tinho.net/geer.uncc.9x13.txt. Reed's Law as cited by Geer was first formulated in David P. Reed, "The Law of the Pack," *Harvard Business Review* (February 2001); 23–24; see Mark Granovetter, "The Strength of Weak Ties—Revisited," *Sociological Theory* (1983): 201–233; David Rosenblum, "What Anyone Can Know: The Privacy Risks of Social Networking Sites," *IEEE Security & Privacy* 5, no. 3 (May/June 2007): 40–49.

76. Aric Toler, "From Discord to 4chan: The Improbable Journey of a US Intelligence Leak," *bellingcat*, April 6, 2023, https://www.bellingcat.com/news/2023/04/09/from -discord-to-4chan-the-improbable-journey-of-a-us-defence-leak; Alex Hern, "Pentagon Leak Traced to Video Game Chat Group Users Arguing over War in Ukraine," *The Guardian*, April 11, 2023, https://www.theguardian.com/world/2023/apr/11 /pentagon-leak-traced-to-video-game-chat-group-users-arguing-over-war-in-ukraine.

77. danah boyd, "Whistleblowing Is the New Civil Disobedience: Why Edward Snowden Matters," http://www.zephoria.org/thoughts/archives/2013/07/19/edward -snowden-whistleblower.html; Bruce Schneier, "Government Secrecy and the Generation Gap," *Schneier on Security*, September 9, 2013, http://www.schneier.com/blog /archives/2013/09/government_secr_1.html; Lloyd C. Gardner, *The War on Leakers: National Security and American Democracy, from Eugene V. Debs to Edward Snowden* (New York: New Press, 2016).

78. https://www.moma.org/collection/works/199053?locale=en, http://www.simon dennysecretpower.com.

79. *Secret Power* is also the title of a 1996 book by Nicky Hager revealing New Zealand's international intelligence collaborations under the Five Eyes agreement: https://www .nickyhager.info/Secret_Power.pdf; international press about Simon Denny is at https://mch.govt.nz/news-events/news/secret-power-exhibition-attracts-international -attention and https://www.digiart21.org/art/modded-server-rack-display-with-some -interpretations-of-david-darchicourt-designs-for-nsa-defense-intelligence.

80. https://www.nsa.gov/news-features/press-room/Article/1629538/introducing -the-cybertwins-nsas-newest-cryptokids. The Venice Biennale installation also featured

work by Darchicourt for a board game called *Positive Press* about the rewards of spin control and disinformation. Chris Kraus, "Here Begins the Dark Sea," in *Simon Denny: Secret Power*, ed. Robert Leonard and Simon Denny (Cologne: Walther König, 2015), 19–25; Anthony Byrt, *This Model World: Travels to the Edge of Contemporary Art* (Auckland: Auckland University Press, 2016).

81. Ian Duncan, "Former NSA Illustrator Finds His Work the Focus of a Major International Art Show," *Baltimore Sun*, May 5, 2015, http://www.baltimoresun.com /business/federal-workplace/bal-former-nsa-illustrator-finds-his-work-the-focus-of-a -major-international-art-show-20150505-story.html; see Hans Ulrich Obrist's 2016 interview with Simon Denny in *CURA21*, https://curamagazine.com/a-transcribed -conversation-between-simon-denny-and-hans-ulrich-obrist/.

82. Ryan Gallagher, "Inside the Secret World of NSA Art," *The Intercept*, June 11, 2015, https://theintercept.com/2015/06/11/secret-power-nsa-darchicourt-art-denny/.

83. Charlotte Higgins, "The Artist Who Did Reverse Espionage on the NSA," *The Guardian*, May 5, 2015, https://www.theguardian.com/artanddesign/2015/may/05 /edward-snowden-nsa-art-venice-biennale-reverse-espionage.

84. Interview with Simon Denny (dated September 14, 2015) in *Electronic Beats*, https://www.electronicbeats.net/why-the-graphics-in-nsa-leaks-are-21st-century -masterpieces; Robert Leonard and Simon Denny, eds., *Simon Denny: Secret Power* (Cologne: Walther König, 2015).

85. Jon Agar, "Putting the Spooks Back In: The UK Secret State and the History of Computing," *Information & Culture* 51, no. 1 (2016): 102–124.

Chapter 5

1. Sandra Braman, "New Information Technologies and the Restructuring of Higher Education," in *Digital Academe: The New Media and Institutions of Higher Education and Learning*, ed. Brian Loader and William Dutton (New York: Routledge, 2002), 268–289.

2. Ian Bogost, *Unit Operations. An Approach to Videogame Criticism* (Cambridge, MA: MIT Press, 2006), 179.

3. W. Westera et al., "Serious Games for Higher Education: A Framework for Reducing Design Complexity," *Journal of Computer Assisted Learning* 24, no. 5 (2008): 420–432.

4. David Gugerli, "Kybernetisierung der Hochschule: Zur Genese des universitären Managements," in *Die Transformation des Humanen: Beiträge zur Kulturgeschichte der Kybernetik*, ed. Michael Hagner and Erich Hörl (Frankfurt: Suhrkamp, 2008), 414–439. See Walter Krieg, *Kybernetische Grundlagen der Unternehmensgestaltung* (Stuttgart: Haupt, 1971).

5. By 1957, Gehlen saw in cybernetics the last technical step toward the objectivization of mind, and in 1966, Heidegger announced that philosophy would be

inherited by cybernetics: "Nur ein Gott kann uns retten: Martin Heidegger im Inter-view mit Rudolf Augstein," *Der Spiegel* 23 (1966): 136ff; Arnold Gehlen, *Die Seele im Technischen Zeitalter* (Hamburg: Rowohlt, 1957), 14–22.

6. Chris Newfield, *Unmaking the Public University: The Forty Year Assault on the Middle Class* (Cambridge, MA: Harvard University Press, 2008); Benjamin Ginsberg, *The Fall of the Faculty: The Rise of the All-Administrative University and Why It Matters* (Oxford: Oxford University Press, 2011; Chris Newfield, *The Great Mistake: How We Wrecked Public Universities and How We Can Fix Them* (Baltimore: Johns Hopkins University Press, 2016).

7. Peter Strohschneider, "Zu einigen aktuellen Entwicklungslinien des deutschen Wissenschaftssystems," in *Gebrochene Wissenschaftskulturen: Universität und Politik im 20. Jahrhundert*, ed. Michael Grüttner (Göttingen: Vandenhoek und Ruprecht, 2010), 367–377.

8. Sylvia Paletschek, "Die Erfindung der Humboldtschen Universität: Die Konstruk-tion der deutschen Universitätsidee in der ersten Hälfte des 20. Jahrhunderts," *Histo-rische Anthropologie* 10 (2002): 183–205; Rainer Christoph Schwinges, ed., *Humboldt International: Der Export des deutschen Universitätsmodells im 19. und 20. Jahrhundert* (Basel: Schwabe, 2001).

9. Beth Baker, "Gentrifying the University and Disempowering the Professoriate: Professionalizing Academic Administration for Neoliberal Governance," *AAUP Jour-nal of Academic Freedom* 11 (2020): 1–9.

10. James Cortada, *The Digital Hand: How Computers Changed the Work of American Manufacturing, Transportation, and Retail Industries* (Oxford: Oxford University Press, 2006); Martin Campbell-Kelly, *From Airline Reservations to Sonic the Hedgehog: A His-tory of the Software Industry* (Cambridge, MA: MIT Press, 2003).

11. Stephen Johnson, "Three Approaches to Big Technology: Operations Research, Systems Engineering, and Project Management," *Technology and Culture—The Interna-tional Quarterly of the Society for the History of Technology* 39 (1997): 891–919; M. Fortun and S. Schweber, "Scientists and the Legacy of World War II: The Case of Operations Research," *Social Studies of Science* 23 (1993): 595–642; Arne Kaijser and Joar Til-berg, "From Operations Research to Futures Studies: The Establishment, Diffusion, and Transformation of the Systems Approach in Sweden, 1945–1980," in *Systems, Experts, and Computers: The Systems Approach in Management and Engineering, World War II and After*, ed. Agatha Hughes and Thomas Parke (Cambridge, MA: MIT Press, 2000), 385–412.

12. Thomas Haigh, "A Veritable Bucket of Facts: Origins of the Data Base Manage-ment System," *SIGMOD Record* 35 (2006): 35–49.

13. Simon Critchley, "What Is the Institutional Form of Thinking?" *The Undecidable Unconscious* 1 (2014): 119–133.

14. James Rhyne Killian, *Sputnik, Scientists, and Eisenhower: A Memoir of the First Special Assistant to the President for Science and Technology* (Cambridge, MA: MIT Press, 1977); Daniel Speich, "Sputnik-Schock und Bildungsoffensive: Wissenschaftspolitische Dynamik in the 1960er Jahren," in *ETHistory 1855–2005: Sightseeing durch 150 Jahre ETH Zürich*, ed. Monika Burri and Andrea Westermann (Baden: hier+jetzt, 2005), 45–47.

15. Michael Gibbons et al., *The New Production of Knowledge: The Dynamics of Science and Research in Contemporary Societies* (London: SAGE, 1994); Luc Weber and James Duderstadt, eds., *Reinventing the Research University* (London: Economica, 2004).

16. Ian Bogost, *Persuasive Games* (Cambridge, MA: MIT Press, 2007), 1.

17. William Rouse and Kenneth Roff, "Organizational Simulation: From Modeling and Simulation to Games and Entertainment," in *Organizational Simulation* (New York: Wiley, 2005), 1.

18. The Knowledge Navigator concept was described by Apple Computer CEO John Sculley in his book *Odyssey: Pepsi to Apple—A Journey of Adventure, Ideas, and the Future* (New York: HarperCollins, 1987) as a device accessing a networked database of hypertext information, using software agents for search. The Starfire demo by Sun Microsystems was a promotional video inspired by the Apple demo and filmed in 1994, demonstrating ideas for a computer user interface.

19. Jesse Ausubel et al., "Simulating the Academy: Toward Understanding Colleges and Universities as Dynamic Systems," in *What Higher Education Is Doing Right*, ed. W. Massy and J. W. Meyerson (Princeton, NJ: Princeton University Press, 1997), 107–120; Manuel London, *Achieving Performance Excellence in University Administration: A Team Approach to Organizational Change and Employee Development* (Westport, CT: Praeger, 1995).

20. Ben Sawyer, *Serious Games: Improving Public Policy through Game-Based Learning and Simulation* (Washington, DC: Woodrow Wilson International Center for Scholars, 2002).

21. *Virtual U* is extant on disc (it was at www.virtual-u.org but the domain seems to have expired). It ran on Windows 2000/XP/9X/ME; see http://serious.gameclassification.com/EN/games/1289-Virtual-U/index.html.

22. Tanya Schevitz, "Video Game Simulates University Administration," *San Francisco Chronicle*, January 14, 2000, https://phe.rockefeller.edu/VU_sfgate14Jan2000/. *Virtual U* was funded with $1 million by the Alfred P. Sloan Foundation (where Ausubel then worked), and by Massy's consulting company, the Jackson Hole Group.

23. NCHEMS (National Center for Higher Education Management Systems) established an Information Exchange Program; foundations and think tanks tinker with how higher education is funded, structured, and studied.

24. David Hopkins and William Massy, *Planning Models for Colleges and Universities* (Stanford, CA: Stanford University Press, 1981); Ausubel et al., "Simulating the Academy," 107–120.

25. Hopkins and Massy, *Planning Models for Colleges and Universities*, 1; Massy had been trying to develop quantitative models for higher education for years, as documented in this tome's voluminous bibliography.

26. Martin Greenberger, Matthew Crenson, and Brian Crissey, eds., *Models in the Policy Process* (New York: Russell Sage Foundation, 1976).

27. Ausubel et al., "Simulating the Academy."

28. Robert Birnbaum, *How Colleges Work: The Cybernetics of Academic Organization and Leadership* (San Francisco: Jossey-Bass, 1988), 201.

29. Hopkins and Massy, *Planning Models for Colleges and Universities*, 9.

30. See also E. L. Boyer, *Scholarship Reconsidered: Priorities of the Professoriate* (Princeton, NJ: Carnegie Foundation for the Advancement of Teaching, 1991).

31. Economist Howard Bowen warned in 1977 that "the idea that sound, hard-headed, rational business management procedures will resolve the financial problems of higher education surely exaggerates the potential returns from any conceivable managerial technique." Compare Hopkins and Massy, *Planning Models for Colleges and Universities*, 13, and Howard Bowen, "Systems Theory, Excellence, and Values: Will They Mix?" *NACUBO Professional File* 9, no. 2 (February 1977): 1–6, https://ia903009 .us.archive.org/23/items/ERIC_ED136637/ ERIC_ED136637.pdf.

32. Hopkins and Massy, *Planning Models for Colleges and Universities*, cite a presentation given by Paul Gray in 1976, "College and University Planning Models," at the Conference on Academic Planning for the Eighties and Nineties, University of Southern California, January 22–23, 1976.

33. Archived by the Stanford Digital Repository is a *Virtual U* tutorial, https://purl .stanford.edu/ns109jh1009.

34. Paul Starr, "Policy as a Simulation Game," *American Prospect* 5, no. 17 (March 21, 1994), http://www.prospect.org/print/V5/17/starr-p.html.

35. William Massy, "Virtual U: The University Simulation Game," *EduCause*, 1999, https://www.educause.edu/ir/library/html/edu9937/edu9937.html.

36. Allison Littlejohn and Niall Sclater, "The Virtual University as a Conceptual Model for Faculty Change and Innovation," *Interactive Learning Environments* 7, nos. 2–3 (1999): 209–225.

37. Littlejohn and Sclater, "The Virtual University as a Conceptual Model."

38. For research leading to the development of *Virtual U*, see William Massy and R. Zemsky, "Faculty Discretionary Time: Departments and the Academic Ratchet,"

Journal of Higher Education 65, no. 1 (January–February 1994): 1–22; William Massy and R. Zemsky, "A Utility Model for Teaching Load Decisions in Academic Departments," *Economics of Education Review* 16, no. 4 (1997): 349–365.

39. Terese Rainwater et al., "Virtual U 1.0 Strategy Guide," Stanford Digital Repository, https://purl.stanford.edu/hs380qp5652.

40. Email from Ben Sawyer, cofounder of the consulting firm Digitalmill, November 27, 2019. Compare the suggestion that "Presidents should cultivate the emergence of leadership within the various subunits of the institution" in Birnbaum, *How Colleges Work*, 206.

41. This *Virtual U* should not be confused with another higher education simulation game of the same name: Linda Harasim, "A Framework for Online Learning: The Virtual-U," *Computer* 32, no. 9 (September 1999): 44–49, doi: 10.1109/2.789750.

42. URLWire, May 27, 2003, http://www.urlwire.com/new/052703.html.

43. Clark Kerr, *The Uses of the University* (Cambridge, MA: Harvard University Press, 2001), 192

44. Seymour Papert, "Does Easy Do It? Children, Games, and Learning," *Game Developer* (June 1998): 88, http://www.papert.org/articles/Doeseasydoit.html; David Shaffer, "Epistemic Games," *Innovate: Journal of Online Education* 1, no. 6 (August/ September 2005), https://nsuworks.nova.edu/innovate/vol1/iss6/2.

45. Kerr, *The Uses of the University*, 195.

46. Kerr, *The Uses of the University*, 195.

47. Thomas Pfeffer, *Virtualization of Universities: Digital Media and the Organization of Higher Education Institutions* (New York: Springer, 2012); Stefan Rieger, "Virtual Humanities," in *Handbuch Virtualität*, ed. D. Kasprowicz and S. Rieger (New York: Springer, 2019), 1–21.

48. Fadi P. Deek, Maura A. Deek, and Robert S. Friedman, "The Virtual Classroom Experience: Viewpoints from Computing and Humanities," *Interactive Learning Environments* 7, nos. 2–3 (1999): 113–136; Sabine Payr, "The Virtual University's Faculty: An Overview of Educational Agents," *Applied Artificial Intelligence* 17, no. 1 (2003): 1–19.

49. See "Higher Ed Simulation and Learning Tool Launches VirtualU 2.0," http:// distance-educator.com/virtual-u-20-released-as-free-download/.

50. As Derrida asked at Stanford: "Where is to be found the communitary place and the social bond of a campus in the cyberspatial age of the computer, of tele-work, and of the World Wide Web?" Jacques Derrida, "The University without Condition," in *Without Alibi* (Stanford, CA: Stanford University Press, 2002), 210; Jacques Derrida, "The Future of the Profession or the University without Condition (Thanks to the Humanities, What Could Take Place Tomorrow)," in *Jacques Derrida and the*

Humanities: A Critical Reader, ed. Tom Cohen (Cambridge: Cambridge University Press, 2001), 24–57.

51. Kari Paul, "Students Voice Concerns as Colleges Plan to Reopen," *The Guardian*, August 17, 2020.

52. Ashley Smith, "California State Audit Criticizes Calbright College for Mismanagement," *Ed Source*, May 12, 2021.

53. Sara Weissman, "A Third Attempt to Close Calbright," *Inside Higher Ed*, March 29, 2022, https://www.insidehighered.com/news/2022/03/29/third-attempt -close-calbright-college.

54. Ian Bogost, *Unit Operations. An Approach to Videogame Criticism* (Cambridge, MA: MIT Press, 2006), 179.

55. As Massy admits, "if a player's institution is a liberal arts college pushing for grants, you wouldn't have nearly as much response as a research university, and if you do it from an English department or Classics, you are not going to have as much luck as will electrical engineering." Cited in Goldie Blumenstyk, "A Computer Game Lets You Manage the University," *Chronicle of Higher Education*, January 7, 2000, https://phe.rockefeller.edu/VU_chron7Jan2000.

56. Birnbaum speaks of the administered university, where "executives and faculty form separated and isolated conclaves in which they are likely to communicate only with people similar to themselves. The use of more sophisticated management techniques can make things even worse." Birnbaum, *How Colleges Work*, 7.

57. Rainwater et al., "VirtualU 1.0 Strategy Guide."

58. Ausubel et al., "Simulating the Academy."

59. Casey O'Donnell, "Getting Played: Gamification, Bullshit, and the Rise of Algorithmic Surveillance," *Surveillance & Society* 12, no. 3 (2014): 349–359; Mathias Fuchs, Sonia Fizek, and Paolo Ruffino, eds., *Rethinking Gamification* (Lüneburg: meson press, 2014).

60. Ted Friedman, "Semiotics of Sim City," *First Monday* 4, no. 4 (April 1999), https://doi.org/10.5210/fm.v4i4.660.

61. Hopkins and Massy, *Planning Models for Colleges and Universities*, 181.

62. Peter Krapp, "Realism: Civilization," in *How to Play Videogames*, ed. Nina Hunteman and Matthew Payne (New York: New York University Press, 2019), 44–51.

63. Hopkins and Massy, *Planning Models for Colleges and Universities*, 463

64. Hopkins and Massy, *Planning Models for Colleges and Universities*, 183.

65. Birnbaum, *How Colleges Work*, 7.

66. This information is taken from a fifty-page report I wrote for the UC Academic Senate headquarters in Oakland. It was presented to the Academic Council, to President Yudof and Provost Pitts, to the chancellors of the UC campuses, and to the UC Board of Regents in spring 2010, provoking the IR response discussed in this text. My report is archived at http://www.universityofcalifornia.edu/senate/ucpb.choices .pdf.

67. See the UCPB Report on Faculty Hiring, November 8, 2022, https://senate.univer sityofcalifornia.edu/_files/reports/sc-md-report-on-faculty-hiring.pdf for more detail.

68. Philip Mousavisadeh, "A Proliferation of Administrators," *Yale Daily News*, November 10, 2021, https://yaledailynews.com/blog/2021/11/10/reluctance-on-the -part-of-its-leadership-to-lead-yales-administration-increases-by-nearly-50-percent/.

69. Douglas Belkin and Scott Thurm, "Hiring Spree Fattens College Bureaucracy— and Tuition," *Wall Street Journal*, December 28, 2012, https://online.wsj.com/article /SB10001424127887323316804578161490716042814.html.

70. Andrea Fuller et al., "Breaking Down the Spending at One of America's Priciest Public Colleges," *Wall Street Journal*, December 28, 2023, https://www.wsj.com /us-news/education/breaking-down-spending-at-one-of-americas-priciest-public -colleges-2d74ec48.

71. Bill Readings, *The University in Ruins* (Cambridge, MA: Harvard University Press, 1997).

72. James Beniger, *The Control Revolution* (Cambridge, MA: Harvard University Press, 1986), 210.

73. Vance Fried, "Opportunities for Efficiency and Innovation: A Primer on How to Cut College Costs," in *Future of American Education Project*, American Enterprise Institute, 2010.

74. Helmut Schelsky, *Einsamkeit und Freiheit: Idee und Gestalt der deutschen Universität und ihrer Reformen* (Hamburg: Rowohlt, 1963).

75. Ian Bogost, *Unit Operations* (Cambridge, MA: MIT Press, 2006), 179.

76. Clayton M. Christensen and Henry Eyring, *The Innovative University: Changing the DNA of Higher Education from the Inside Out* (San Francisco: Jossey-Bass, 2011), 332– 336; William Massy, *Reengineering the University: How to Be Mission Centered, Market Smart, and Margin Conscious* (Baltimore: Johns Hopkins University Press, 2016).

77. Massy, *Reengineering the University*, 430.

78. Dennis Charsky, "From Edutainment to Serious Games: A Change in the Use of Game Characteristics," *Games and Culture* 2, no. 5 (February 11, 2010): 177–198, https://doi.org/10.1177/1555412009354727; Michael Zyda, "From Visual Simulation to Virtual Reality to Games," *Computer* 38, no. 9 (2005): 25–32.

79. Bogost, *Unit Operations*, 98.

80. James Paul Gee, "What Would a State of the Art Instructional Video Game Look Like?" *Innovate: Journal of Online Education* 1, no. 6 (August/September 2005), https://nsuworks.nova.edu/innovate/vol1/iss6/1; C. Girard, J. Ecalle, and A. Magnan, "Serious Games as New Educational Tools: How Effective Are They? A Meta-Analysis of Recent Studies," *Journal of Computer Assisted Learning* 29, no. 3 (2013): 207–219; Z. Merchant et al., "Effectiveness of Virtual Reality Based Instruction on Students' Learning Outcomes in K-12 and Higher Education: A Meta-Analysis," *Computers & Education* 70 (2014): 29–40.

81. "Pleasure cannot be regarded as the defining characteristic of play." L. S. Vygotsky, *Mind in Society* (Cambridge, MA: Harvard University Press, 1978), 92.

82. Bogost, *Unit Operations*, 120.

83. Dimitrios Vlachopoulos and Agoritsa Makri, "The Effect of Games and Simulations on Higher Education: A Systematic Literature Review," *International Journal of Educational Technology in Higher Education* 14, no. 22 (2017): 6; Shalini R. Tiwari, Lubna Nafees, and Omkumar Krishnan, "Simulation as a Pedagogical Tool: Measurement of Impact on Perceived Effective Learning," *International Journal of Management Education* 12, no. 3 (2014): 260–270; L. Nadolny and A. Halabi, "Student Participation and Achievement in a Large Lecture Course with Game-Based Learning," *Simulation & Gaming* 47, no. 1 (2015): 51–72.

84. M. E. W. Danckbaar et al., "An Experimental Study on the Effects of a Simulation Game on Students' Clinical Cognitive Skills and Motivation," *Advances in Health Sciences Education* 21, no. 3 (2016): 505–521; M. L. Angelini, "Integration of the Pedagogical Models 'Simulation' and 'Flipped Classroom' in Teacher Instruction," *SAGE Open* 6, no. 1 (2016); R. Cozar-Gutierrez and J. M. Saez-Lopez, "Game-Based Learning and Gamification in Initial Teacher Training in the Social Sciences: An Experiment in MinecraftEdu," *International Journal of Educational Technology in Higher Education* 13, no. 1 (2016).

85. Richard Blunt, "Do Serious Games Work? Results from Three Studies," *eLearn Magazine*, December 2009, https://elearn.acm.com/archive.cfm?aid=1661378; David W. Shaffer, "Thick Authenticity: New Media and Authentic Learning," *Journal of Interactive Learning Research* 10, no. 2 (1999): 195–215.

86. https://www.old-games.com/download.4986/virtual-u.

87. Blumenstyk, "A Computer Game Lets You Manage the University."

88. See Timothy Kaufman-Osborn, *The Autocratic Academy: Reenvisioning Rule within America's Universities* (Durham, NC: Duke University Press, 2023).

89. Theodore Roszak, "On Academic Delinquency," in *The Dissenting Academy* (New York: Vintage Books, 1969), 8; for the long and surprisingly stable tradition of this

type of accusation, see Ludwig Wachler, *Aphorismen über die Universitäten und über ihr Verhältnis zum Staat* (Marburg, 1801).

Conclusion

1. Harun Maye, "Was ist eine Kulturtechnik?" *Zeitschrift für Medien- und Kulturforschung* 1 (2010): 112–135; Bernhard Siegert, "Kulturtechnik," in *Einführung in die Kulturwissenschaft*, ed. Harun Maye and Leander Scholz (Munich: Fink, 2011), 95–118.

2. Walter Benjamin, "The Work of Art in the Age of Mechanical Reproduction," in *Illuminations* (New York: Schocken, 1968), 239.

3. Gregory Bateson, *Steps to an Ecology of Mind* (San Francisco: Chandler, 1972), 416.

4. Katherine Hayles, "The Power of Simulation," *Critical Inquiry* 26, no. 1 (1999): 1–26.

5. Jean-François Lyotard, *Libidinal Economy* (Bloomington: Indiana University Press, 1993), 215; David Hill, "Lyotard and the Inhumanity of Internet Surveillance," in *Internet and Surveillance: The Challenges of Web 2.0 and Social Media*, ed. Christian Fuchs et al. (New York: Routledge, 2012), 106–123.

6. Alexander Galloway, "The Cybernetic Hypothesis," *differences: A Journal of Feminist Cultural Studies* 25, no. 1 (2014): 107–131; Peter Galison, "Ontology of the Enemy: Norbert Wiener and Cybernetic Vision," *Critical Inquiry* 21, no. 1 (1994): 228–266; Geof Bowker, "How to Be Universal: Some Cybernetic Strategies," *Social Studies of Science* 23, no. 1 (1993): 107–127.

7. Regina Friess, "Symbolic Interaction in Digital Games," in *Computer Games and New Media Cultures: A Handbook of Digital Game Studies*, ed. Johannes Fromme and Alexander Unger (London: Springer, 2012), 250.

8. Jörg Pflüger, "Wo die Quantität in Qualität umschlägt," in *Hyperkult II: Zur Ortsbestimmung analoger und digitaler Medien*, ed. Martin Warnke, Wolfgang Coy, and Georg Christoph Tholen (Bielefeld: transcript, 2005), 27–94, points to Karl Marx, *Das Kapital*, vol. 1, in *Karl Marx/Friedrich Engels: Werke*, vol. 23 (Berlin: Karl Dietz Verlag, 2001), 327.

9. Peter Krapp, "Realism: Civilization," in *How to Play Videogames*, ed. N. Hunteman and M. Payne (New York: New York University Press, 2019), 44–51.

10. "The new Humanities would thus treat, in the same style but in the course of a formidable reflexive reversal, both critical and deconstructive, the history of the as if and especially the history of this precious distinction between performative acts and constative acts." Jacques Derrida, "The University without Condition," in *Without Alibi* (Stanford, CA: Stanford University Press, 2002), 233.

11. Olga Chernikova et al., "Simulation-Based Learning in Higher Education: A Meta-Analysis," *Review of Educational Research* 90, no. 4 (August 2020): 499–541.

12. Thomas Kuhn, *The Structure of Scientific Revolutions* (Chicago: University of Chicago Press, 1967), 166.

13. Sherry Turkle, *Simulation and Its Discontents* (Cambridge, MA: MIT Press, 2009), 88.

14. Trevor Owens, *The Theory and Craft of Digital Preservation* (Baltimore: Johns Hopkins University Press, 2018), 7.

15. Friedrich Kittler, "Museums on the Digital Frontier," *The End(s) of the Museum*, ed. John Hanhardt and Thomas Keenan (Barcelona: Fundació Antoni Tapies, 1996), 70.

16. Michelle Henning, "New Media," in *A Companion to Museum Studies*, ed. Sharon Macdonald (London: Blackwell, 2009), 305.

17. Maurice Blanchot, *Friendship* (Stanford, CA: Stanford University Press, 1997), 34.

18. Wendy Chun, *Programmed Visions* (Cambridge, MA: MIT Press, 2011), 137.

19. https://www.theguardian.com/uk-news/2014/jan/31/footage-released-guardian -editors-snowden-hard-drives-gchq; video at https://www.theguardian.com/world /video/2014/jan/31/snowden-files-computer-destroyed-guardian-gchq-basement -video.

20. https://www.sciencemuseum.org.uk/what-was-on/top-secret; http://www.vam .ac.uk/content/exhibitions/all-of-this-belongs-to-you; https://www.raytheon.co.uk /news/2021/04/30/top-secret-exhibition-goes-manchester-celebrating-100-years -communications; https://www.theguardian.com/media/2015/feb/27/guardians-des troyed-snowden-laptop-to-feature-in-major-va-show; https://www.bl.uk/events/ breaking-the-news; https://thelondonpress.uk/2022/04/22/smashed-guardian-hard -drives-feature-in-british-library-exhibition-media/.

21. https://needtoknowgame.com.

22. Ian Bogost, "The Rhetoric of Video Games," in *The Ecology of Games: Connecting Youth, Games, and Learning*, ed. Katie Salen (Cambridge, MA: MIT Press, 2008), 117–140, here: 136.

23. See Paul Weinstein, *How to Cut Administrative Bloat at US Colleges* (Washington, DC: PPI, 2023), https://www.progressivepolicy.org/pressrelease/new-report-how-to -cut-administrative-bloat-at-u-s-colleges/; compare American Council of Trustees and Alumni, *The Cost of Excess: Why Colleges Must Control Runaway Spending* (Washington DC: ACTA, 2021), https://www.goacta.org/resource/cost-of-excess/.

24. On taking humans out of the loop in higher education, see Philip Agre, "Infrastructure and Institutional Change in the Networked University," in *Digital Academe: The New Media and Institutions of Higher Education and Learning*, ed. Brian Loader and William Dutton (New York: Routledge, 2002), 152–166.

25. Clark Kerr, *The Uses of the University* (Cambridge, MA: Harvard University Press, 1982), 185.

26. Robert Birnbaum, *How Colleges Work: The Cybernetics of Academic Organization and Leadership* (San Francisco: Jossey-Bass, 1988), 202.

27. Theodor W. Adorno, "Culture and Administration," *Telos* 37 (1978): 93–111.

28. Raymond Williams, *Keywords: A Vocabulary of Culture and Society* (New York: Oxford University Press, 1987), 87.

29. Niklas Luhmann, *The Reality of the Mass Media* (Stanford, CA: Stanford University Press, 2000), 86.

30. Sybille Krämer, "Was haben Medien, der Computer und die Realität miteinander zu tun?" in *Medien—Computer—Realität. Wirklichkeitsvorstellungen und neue Medien* (Frankfurt: Suhrkamp, 1998), 255.

31. Sybille Krämer and Horst Bredekamp, "Culture, Technology, Cultural Techniques—Moving Beyond Text," *Theory, Culture & Society* 30, no. 6 (2013): 20–29.

32. Friedrich Kittler, "ex musica," in *ex machina: Beiträge zur Geschichte der Kulturtechniken*, ed. Tobias Nanz und Bernhard Siegert (Weimar: VDG, 2006), 141–162.

33. Sybille Krämer and Horst Bredekamp, "Kultur, Technik, Kulturtechnik," in *Bild, Schrift, Zahl* (Munich: Fink, 2003), 11–22.

34. Bruno Latour, *Pandora's Hope: Essays on the Reality of Science Studies* (Cambridge, MA: Harvard University Press, 2000), 70.

35. Jussi Parikka, "Afterword: Cultural Techniques and Media Studies," *Theory, Culture & Society* 30, no. 6 (2013): 149; Erhard Schüttpelz, "Body Techniques and the Nature of the Body: Re-Reading Marcel Mauss," *Limbus* 3 (2010): 177–194.

36. Thomas Macho, "Second-Order Animals: Cultural Techniques of Identity and Identification," *Theory, Culture and Society* 30, no. 6 (2013): 31; Erhard Schüttpelz, "Die medienanthropologische Kehre der Kulturtechniken," in *Kulturgeschichte als Mediengeschichte oder vice versa?* ed. Lorenz Engell, Bernhard Siegert, and Joseph Vogl (Weimar: Universitätsverlag, 2006), 87–110.

37. Bernhard Siegert, *Cultural Techniques* (New York: Fordham University Press, 2015), 3; Reinhold Martin, "Unfolded, Not Opened: On Bernhard Siegert's Cultural Techniques," *Grey Room* 62 (Winter 2016): 102–115.

38. Friedrich Kittler, "The World of the Symbolic Is the World of the Machine," in *Literature, Media, Information Systems*, ed. John Johnston (Amsterdam: GB Arts, 1997), 130–146; Sybille Krämer, "The Cultural Techniques of Time-Axis Manipulation," *Theory, Culture & Society* 23, nos. 7–8 (2006): 93–109.

39. Norbert Elias, *An Essay on Time* (Chicago: University of Chicago Press, 2007); Niklas Luhmann, "Sinn als Grundbegriff der Soziologie," in *Theorie der Gesellschaft oder Sozialtechnologie: Was leistet die Systemforschung?* ed. Jürgen Habermas and Niklas Luhmann (Frankfurt: Suhrkamp, 1971), 54.

40. Yuri Lotman and Boris Uspenskyi, "On the Semiotic Mechanism of Culture," *New Literary History* 9, no. 2 (Winter 1978), 211–232; Aleida and Jan Assmann, "Das Gestern im Heute. Medien und soziales Gedächtnis," in *Die Wirklichkeit der Medien,* ed. Klaus Merten, Siegfried Schmidt, and Siegfried Weischenberg (Opladen: West-deutscher Verlag, 1994), 114–140.

41. Wendy Chun, *Programmed Visions* (Cambridge, MA: MIT Press, 2011), 137.

42. Andrew Binstock, "Interview with Alan Kay," *Dr. Dobb's Journal,* July 10, 2012, http://www.drdobbs.com/article/print?articleId=240003442.

43. Donna Haraway, "A Manifesto for Cyborgs," *Socialist Review* 15 (1985): 81.

44. William Bogard, *The Simulation of Surveillance* (Cambridge, MA: Cambridge University Press, 1996), 182.

45. Lorenz Engell, *Das Gespenst der Simulation: Ein Beitrag zur Überwindung der "Medientheorie" durch Analyse ihrer Logik und Ästhetik* (Weimar: VDG, 1994).

46. Paul Bradley, "The History of Simulation in Medical Education and Possible Future Directions," *Medical Education* 40, no. 3 (2006): 254–262.

47. Marvin Minsky, ed., *Semantic Information Processing* (Cambridge, MA: MIT Press, 1968), 7; Allen Newell, "Intellectual Issues in the History of Artificial Intelligence," in *The Study of Information: Interdisciplinary Messages,* ed. Fritz Machlup and Una Mansfield (New York: Wiley, 1983), 187–227.

48. David Jacques, "The Academic Game: A Simulation of Policy-Making in a University," *SAGSET Journal* 6 (1976): 3–19; Mantz Yorke, David McCormick, and Tony Chapman, "Virtual Realities: Simulations as Catalysts for Policy Development in Higher Education," in *Simulations and Games for Emergency and Crisis Management,* ed. John Rolfe, Danny Saunders, and Tony Powell (London: Routledge, 2020), 63–74.

49. Ken Jones, "The Damage Caused by Simulation Games," *The International Simulation and Gaming Yearbook,* vol. 5 (London: Kogan Page, 1997), 11–21.

50. Part of that talk was first published in German as Peter Krapp, "Zwischen Wahn und Weisheit der Massen: Computerspiele und die Ökonomie der Zerstreuung," in *Soziale Medien—Neue Massen: Medienwissenschaftliche Symposien der DFG,* ed. I. Baxmann, T. Beyes, and C. Pias (Zurich: diaphanes, 2014), 63–88. Other parts of this research project were published online; see Peter Krapp, "Ranks and Files: On Metacritic and Gamerankings," *Flow,* December 2012, http://flowtv.org/2012/12/ranks

-and-files/; and "MMO Models: Crowd-Sourcing Economedia," *Flow*, March 2013, http://flowtv.org/2013/03/mmo-models/, though none of those online texts are reproduced here.

51. Part of a much earlier version of the chapter on game sounds was first published in German as Peter Krapp, "Let It Bleep, Keep It Sample: Wie klingt Retrogaming?" in *Retrogames und Retro-Gaming*, ed. Ann-Marie Letourneur, Michael Mosel, and Tim Raupach (Glückstadt: VWH, 2015), 231–244.

52. My Stanford talk is archived at http://mediax.stanford.edu/events/virtual-espio nage-gchq-and-nsa-take-on-mmos.

53. My senate report is archived at http://www.universityofcalifornia.edu/senate/ucpb .choices.pdf and may be worth revisiting.

Index